D1570413

THE LOGIC OF SUBCHAPTER K:

A CONCEPTUAL GUIDE TO THE TAXATION OF PARTNERSHIPS

Fourth Edition

By

Laura E. Cunningham

Professor of Law,
Benjamin N. Cardozo
School of Law

Noël B. Cunningham

Professor of Law,
New York University
School of Law

AMERICAN CASEBOOK SERIES®

WEST®

A Thomson Reuters business

Mat #40777923

American Casebook Series is a trademark registered in the U.S. Patent and Trademark Office.

COPYRIGHT © 1996 WEST PUBLISHING CO.
© West, a Thomson business, 2000, 2006
© 2011 Thomson Reuters
    610 Opperman Drive
    St. Paul, MN 55123
    1–800–313–9378
Printed in the United States of America

ISBN: 978–0–314–19985–0

To Paul R. McDaniel,
friend and mentor

Acknowledgement

Since the publication of the third edition of this book in 2006, there have been significant changes in the way partnerships are taxed. These changes include new regulations under section 706 dealing with varying interests in a partnership, the withdrawal of the proposed regulations under section 707 dealing with the disguised sale of partnership interests, the increasing importance of the allocation of partnership items under section 704(b) in accordance with the partners' interest in the partnership, and the increased flexibility of the allocation of excess nonrecourse liabilities under section 752. The fourth edition provides a thorough discussion of each of these changes.

We are grateful for the many constructive comments we received in response to the prior editions from colleagues and students alike. We have attempted to address them in this issue. We are also grateful for the research assistance of David Kunes and Caroline Waldner. And finally, as always, special thanks to our friend and colleague Len Schmolka who has been so helpful in the preparation of all four editions.

Financial support was graciously provided by the Filomen D'Agostino Faculty Research Fund and the Research Fund of the Benjamin N. Cardozo School of Law, Yeshiva University.

Summary of Contents

Table of Contents

TABLE OF CONTENTS

TABLE OF CONTENTS

TABLE OF CONTENTS

Table of Cases

The principal cases are in bold type. Cases cited or discussed in the text are in roman type. References are to pages. Cases cited in principal cases and within other quoted materials are not included.

Table of Code Sections

Table of Revenue Rulings

Table of Regulations

THE LOGIC OF SUBCHAPTER K:

A CONCEPTUAL GUIDE TO THE TAXATION OF PARTNERSHIPS

Fourth Edition

Chapter One

CHOICE OF ENTITY: WHAT IS A PARTNERSHIP FOR TAX PURPOSES?

Introduction

The taxation of partners and partnerships is governed by Subchapter K of the Internal Revenue Code (§§ 701–761), and the huge volume of regulations issued by the Treasury under that subchapter. Subchapter K creates a pass-through regime; that is, unlike entities subject to the corporate tax, entities taxed as partnerships do not pay tax on their income. The partnership acts as a conduit, through which its various items of income and loss flow to the individual partners, who must annually report their shares of those items on their own income tax returns. Subchapter K provides rules governing the character, timing and the amount of income or loss allocated to each partner, the tax consequences of moving property into and out of partnerships, and characterization of transactions between partners and their partnerships.

Subchapter K has a well-earned reputation as one of the most complex areas of the tax law; while a flow-through regime sounds simple enough in concept, implementing that regime is another matter. The principal purpose of this book is to guide the reader through the intricacies of partnership tax while keeping the conceptual goal of Subchapter K in focus. You will find as you proceed that each chapter is inextricably related to both the preceding and following chapters—that is the nature of the subject. Once you have completed the journey, you will understand why it was so difficult: Subchapter K is the proverbial seamless web.

This book has sixteen chapters that are designed to introduce the reader to the taxation of partnerships. The book is not intended to be read in isolation; rather it should be read in conjunction with

1

the Code and the regulations. These latter materials are complex and very often difficult to understand, and we hope that this book will make the task of mastering them more manageable and more enjoyable.

Our study of Subchapter K starts in earnest with *Chapter Two*. In this chapter we discuss three preliminary issues. First we explore the definition of a partnership for tax purposes: What business ventures are governed by Subchapter K? Since 1997 it has been much easier and simpler for non-corporate business entities to choose to be taxed as partnerships. Next we explore how and why a start-up business venture might elect to be taxed as a partnership rather than a corporation. Finally, we introduce the reader to the most pervasive conceptual problem in Subchapter K: Should a partnership be viewed as an aggregate of its members, or should it be viewed as an entity with an existence independent of its members?

Definition of Partnership

In contrast with the Uniform Partnership Act (UPA) definition of partnerships, which is "an association of two or more persons to carry on as co-owners a business for profit,"[1] the definition of a partnership for tax purposes is extremely broad in scope. Code § 761 defines a partnership as including "a syndicate, group, pool, joint venture, or other unincorporated organization through, or by means of which any business, financial operation, or venture is carried on and which is not within the meaning of this Title, a corporation or trust or estate."[2] The so-called "check-the-box" regulations,[3] which are discussed in more detail below, supplement the Code definition. Those regulations create a regime in which all "business entities" with two or more members are taxed either as partnerships or corporations.[4] It is necessary to determine if a "business entity" has been formed, because only then can Subchapter K apply. "Business entities" are defined as "any entity recognized for federal tax purposes,"[5] and the regulations state that "a joint venture or other contractual arrangement may create a separate entity for federal tax purposes if the participants carry on a trade, business, financial operation or venture and divide the profits therefrom." This definition goes well beyond the local law definition of the UPA, and is broad enough to encompass many

---

1. UPA § 6.
2. § 761(a).
3. § 301.7701–1 et seq.
4. §§ 301.7701–2, 301.7701–3. Unincorporated entities, including local law partnerships, are taxed as corporations only if they are publicly traded, or if the

elect that tax treatment. Incorporated entities are taxed as corporations.

5. Trusts and other entities specially treated under the Code are excluded from the "business entity" definition. § 301.7701–2(a).

common economic relationships, such as that of lessor to lessee, employer to employee, or lender to borrower, which are not within the traditional definition of a partnership.[6] While the instances in which those relationships give rise to a partnership for tax purposes are relatively rare, the issue frequently arises when taxpayers jointly own and operate property.

ex. *Biz entities*

The regulations provide some guidance in determining when a joint venture or other contractual arrangement will create an independent entity for tax purposes.[7] Undertakings solely to share expenses do not create a separate entity. The regulations contrast "mere co-owners" who maintain and lease their jointly owned property with the co-owners of an apartment building who not only lease the property, but provide services as well, either directly or through an agent. It appears that the two features which distinguish an entity from mere co-ownership are *business activity* and the *sharing of profits*. To illustrate, if two persons jointly purchase a taxicab for each to use 12 hours a day for their own individual profit, a partnership would not exist because of the lack of joint profit motive. However, if they leased the cab to a third party, sharing the rental payments, a partnership might exist as they would have the requisite joint profit motive. The principal inquiry would be whether their activities with respect to the cab rose to the level of the conduct of a business. This would depend on whether the co-owners were responsible for, and shared the various expenses of keeping up the cab, as opposed to simply sharing rental payments from a net lease.

X

2 important features

Entity characterization has numerous consequences to the co-owners. Once characterized as an entity, the enterprise will be taxed as a partnership unless it elects to be taxed as a corporation (as discussed below), and it will be subject to the reporting and filing requirements imposed by Subchapter K. If the co-owners are unaware that they have created a partnership for tax purposes, they may inadvertently trigger adverse tax consequences. For example, suppose A and B each own 50% of Blackacre, rental real estate that has appreciated in value. If A and B are mere co-owners, A may, independently of B, exchange her undivided interest in Blackacre for Whiteacre without the recognition of gain under § 1031. If A and B are partners, however, an exchange by A would be characterized as an exchange of her partnership interest (property not eligible for nonrecognition under § 1031) for Whiteacre, and A would recognize gain. Alternatively, suppose Blackacre is destroyed by fire and A and B receive the insurance proceeds,

if (entity) then --- taxed as part. unless specified as corp

---

6. See McKee, Nelson & Whitmire, *Federal Taxation of Partnerships and Partners (3rd Ed.)*, ¶ 3.03 for a detailed discussion of these issues (hereinafter McKee et al.).

7. § 301.7701–1(a)(2).

which they reinvest in real estate. Under § 1033, if A and B are partners, their *partnership* must elect nonrecognition under § 1033 and make the necessary reinvestment. If they are unaware of the existence of the partnership, and elect individually, they both would have to recognize their gains.[8]

Section 761 authorizes an "election-out" procedure for certain might-be partnerships. If an unincorporated organization is used for investment purposes, and not for the active conduct of a business, and the income of the individual members can be determined without the need to compute the organization's taxable income, then at the election of all members, the organization will not be taxed under Subchapter K. Because the election out procedure is available only to co-owners who probably would not be classified as partnerships in the first place (because of the lack of business activity), it is at best an insurance policy for those investors who want to be sure to preserve the right to make individual tax elections with respect to their property.

Choice of Form of Doing Business

When two or more persons start a business, they must choose the form in which they will operate. Both tax and non-tax considerations will guide the choice. Historically, the choice was primarily between the corporate form of doing business, and the partnership form (either general or limited partnership). For the last twenty years a third alternative has become available in most states, the limited liability company (or "LLC"). For reasons which are discussed below, the LLC has become an increasingly popular choice.

The non-tax considerations that will influence the choice of form of doing business include the owners' desire to limit their personal liability for the business' debts, the ability to easily transfer ownership interests in the business, and the ability of the managers of the business to contract on behalf of the company without consulting each and every owner. Each of these characteristics are present in the corporate form of doing business. Limited partnerships have some of these advantages, though not all: there must be at least one general partner who is liable for the business' debts and although limited partners are not liable for the partnership's debt, they will lose this protection if they participate in management. LLCs represented a major innovation, because they have all of these favorable corporate characteristics without one major disadvantage of the corporate form: they are taxed as partnerships (i.e., under the rules of Subchapter K), and are not subject

8. See, e.g., *Demirjian v. Commissioner*, 54 T.C. 1691 (1970), *aff'd*, 457 F.2d 1 (3d Cir.1972).

to the corporate tax. Which brings us to the tax considerations that will influence the choice of business form: corporations are taxed very differently from partnerships and LLCs, and in most cases the tax considerations will dictate the choice.

The existence of the double tax on corporate income is the primary tax consideration that influences the choice of business entity. Another significant consideration is the fact that start-up corporations (particularly highly leveraged ones) are unable to utilize anticipated losses in the early years. Most corporations ("C Corporations")[9] are subject to two levels of tax on their income, one at the corporate level, and another at the shareholder level when earnings are distributed to shareholders as dividends. Historically, dividends received by individual shareholders were treated as ordinary income. Since 2001, however, dividends received from domestic corporations are treated as net capital gain and subject to a maximum tax rate of 15%.[10] If the corporation loses money, its losses accumulate as "net operating losses" ("NOLs"), which will offset future income. In contrast with C Corporations, the income of partnerships and LLCs is subject to a single tax; the income and losses of the venture pass through the entity and are included or deducted directly by the owners of the business. Some corporations can avoid the corporate level tax and pass through *some* of their losses to their shareholders by electing to be taxed under Subchapter S of the Code ("S Corporations"). Because of the substantial restrictions on that election, and since the rules under Subchapter S are generally less favorable than those under Subchapter K,[11] most business entities should prefer partnership status to that of Subchapter S.[12]

9. The name derives from the fact that Subchapter C of the Code contains the rules that govern these corporations.

10. At the time of this writing, the Bush Tax cuts are to expire at the end of 2010. At this time it is unclear what the maximum rate on capital gains will be, and whether dividends will be eligible for this rate. The Obama administration's current proposal is for the maximum rate on traditional capital gains and dividends to go up to 20%.

11. While S Corporations are taxed under rules similar to those which apply to partnerships, there are various distinctions that cause the tax law to favor the choice of a partnership over an S Corporation. Subchapter S imposes restrictions on the number and identity of S Corporation shareholders. Unlike partnerships, which have enormous flexibility in allocating income among their partners, S Corporation income must be

shared proportionately. Also significant is the extent to which losses of an S Corporation will flow through to its shareholders. Unlike partners, S Corporation shareholders cannot take into account their share of the entity's liabilities in determining their basis, and hence their share of S Corporation losses. §§ 1366(d)(1) and 1367. There are other advantages of operating in partnership form rather than as an S Corporation, such as the ability to distribute appreciated property without recognition of gain. § 731.

12. For certain enterprises, there is at least one significant advantage of operating as an S Corporation rather than as a partnership. This advantage stems from the fact that a shareholder of an S Corporation can be an employee, while a partner of a partnership cannot. For this reason, a general partner's entire dis-

Despite the existence of the double tax on C Corporations, until the early 1980's the corporate form was a popular choice for start-up businesses. It had the non-tax advantages described above, and offered some opportunity for tax savings. The rate of tax on corporate income was substantially lower than that on individuals.[13] Because the second level of tax does not apply until earnings are distributed, earnings could be accumulated at the corporate level at a lower tax cost than if they were taxed directly to the owners. Since 1981, however, the corporate rate has risen relative to the individual rate, so that this benefit is no longer available in any meaningful sense: Indeed, today the top marginal rate for both individuals and corporations is 35%. Corporate income, however, will eventually be subject to an additional tax when distributed.

Under current law, unless a start-up company wants to go public, there is very little reason to choose to operate as a C Corporation.[14] Most of the non-tax advantages of operating in corporate form are now available in most states in the form of the LLC, and the double tax creates a clear tax bias against the corporate form. An LLC offers all of its members limited liability without restrictions on their participation in the enterprise. Furthermore, ownership interests in an LLC can be freely transferable if its members so choose. For these reasons, given the ease with which a noncorporate entity can choose to be taxed as a partnership under the check-the-box regulations, it will be unusual for start-up companies to choose to be C Corporations.[15]

Electing Partnership Treatment: The "Check the Box" Regulations

As a technical matter, determining how a business entity will be characterized for tax purposes is rather straight-forward. As a threshold matter, if the ownership interests of the entity are publicly traded, the entity will be taxed as a C Corporation, even if it is a partnership or LLC for local law purposes.[16] If the entity is

---

tributive share of business profits is subject to self-employment taxes, both old-age, survivors and disability insurance (OASDI) as well as hospital insurance (HI). In 2010, OASDI is an amount equal to 12.4% of the first $106,800 of income, and HI is 2.9% on the entire distributive share. §§ 1401(a) & (b). Furthermore, partners are not eligible for various fringe benefits available to employees. See, e.g., §§ 79 and 132.

13. For example, in 1980 the highest marginal rate for individuals was 70%, compared to 46% for corporations.

14. There may be traditions in a given industry which would favor the corporate form in spite of the tax considerations arguing against it. See Joseph Bankman, *The Structure of Silicon Valley Start-ups*, 41 UCLA Law Review, 1737 (1994).

15. See, e.g., Kurtz, *The Limited Liability Company and the Future of Business Taxation: A Comment on Professor Berger's Plan*, 47 Tax L. Rev. 815 (1992).

16. § 7704.

organized as a corporation under local law, the entity will be taxed as a C Corporation unless it is eligible (and elects) to be an S Corporation. All other business entities with two or more members, including partnerships and LLCs, will be taxed as partnerships *unless* the entity makes an affirmative election to be taxed as a C Corporation.[17] For reasons discussed above, such an election will be extremely rare.

This rather cut and dried approach to entity classification has been available since 1997. Prior to that time, when Treasury issued the entity classification regulations[18] (often referred to as the "check-the-box" regulations), it was significantly more complicated to determine if limited partnerships and limited liability companies would be treated as partnerships or corporations for tax purposes. This determination was made by comparing the number of corporate characteristics of the entity to the number of non-corporate characteristics. Because limited partnerships and LLCs have some of the characteristics which make corporations attractive as a form of doing business, such as limited liability, centralized management and freely transferable ownership interests, the prior regulations presented a serious threat that if owners were not careful, their limited partnership or LLC would be characterized as "associations taxable as corporations". Thus, taxpayers forming limited partnerships and LLC's were often compelled to retain tax counsel to ensure that their business entity would be characterized as a partnership. Although the counsel's analysis was complicated (and expensive), it was very easy for partnership characterization to prevail, for the regulations and the Service demonstrated a pro-partnership bias. Because it became apparent that the old regulations created little more than an expensive elective regime, Treasury issued the check-the-box regulations to make the election explicit, and less cumbersome.

The Competing Concepts: Aggregate Versus Entity

Underlying Subchapter K are two historically competing concepts of how partnerships should be viewed (and treated) under our tax system, the aggregate and the entity concepts. Under a pure aggregate conception, partners would be viewed as co-owners, each with an undivided interest in the partnership's assets, and each partner would account separately for her share of all partnership transactions. Under a pure entity conception, the partnership

---

17. § 301.7701–3. A noncorporate business entity such as an LLC that has only one member is disregarded for Federal tax purposes. § 1.7701–2(a).

18. § 301.7701–1 through –3.

would be treated as a separate and distinct taxpayer, adopting a method of accounting and a taxable year and annually reporting its taxable income. The partners would each own an undivided interest in the partnership entity, and would be viewed very much like shareholders in a corporation.

When Subchapter K was enacted in 1954, Congress adopted a hybrid approach. For most purposes, a partnership is treated as an aggregate of its partners. A partnership is not a taxpayer, and its partners report their shares of partnership operations each year on their own tax returns. Nevertheless, as you will learn in *Chapter Three*, in some important ways a partnership is treated as an entity. A partnership must adopt a method of accounting, a taxable year and report its taxable income each year on an information return. The partnership has a basis in each of its assets, and the character of its income is determined at the partnership level. In computing its income, the partnership must make various elections, such as how to depreciate its assets, or whether to use the installment method. We will see that most of these entity attributes are necessary to avoid the administrative nightmare that would result if each partner had to calculate her own share of partnership income using her own accounting method, taxable year, method of depreciation, etc.

As you explore Subchapter K, you will find that usually these two conceptions of partnerships are not in conflict—they are just different ways to view the enterprise. There are many situations, however, where these conceptions directly compete, resulting in both complexity and uncertainty. As these situations arise, we will use these terms to help explain the origin of the problem.

Chapter Two

PARTNERSHIP FORMATION: THE BASICS

Introduction

Having identified in *Chapter One* the type of entity governed by Subchapter K, we will begin our study of the mechanics of partnership taxation with a discussion of the basic rules regarding formation and operation of partnerships.

As you embark on your study of partnership taxation, you may find it helpful to keep in mind Congress' overriding purpose in adopting Subchapter K: to provide flexible and simple rules for those choosing to do business in the partnership form. Thus, the rules applicable to formation (as well as dissolution) of partnerships are crafted to ensure nonrecognition of gain or loss wherever feasible, and matters concerning calculating each partner's share of an item of income and deduction are largely left to the agreement of the partners. The original simplicity of the partnership taxation scheme, however, has been largely undermined by one of the most complex regulatory structures in the income tax. This complexity is primarily a response (some would argue overreaction) to sophisticated taxpayer attempts to manipulate this relatively simple and flexible scheme to obtain tax benefits unintended by Congress.

Nevertheless, the basic provisions concerning formation and operations of partnerships reflect Congress' original goal of flexibility and simplicity. As we will learn in this chapter, the formation of a partnership rarely results in recognition of gain or loss. In *Chapter Three*, you will see that the role of the partnership entity for tax purposes is quite limited: to serve as an accounting entity to assist the partners (and the IRS) in calculating their shares of the venture's income and deductions.

Basic Statutory Scheme

Consistent with Congress' intent not to impose any tax barriers to prevent or impede parties from choosing the partnership form of doing business, the formation of a partnership is generally a nonrecognition transaction for both the contributing partners and the newly created firm. This treatment reflects Congress' view that the partners have not closed out their investment in the contributed property but have merely changed the form of that investment to a partnership interest.

The basic statutory provisions dealing with the formation of a partnership are fairly straightforward and easy to apply.

Section 721: Nonrecognition. Except in the case of certain investment partnerships,[1] § 721 protects both the partnership and its partners from recognizing any gain or loss on the transfer of property to a partnership in exchange for an interest in the partnership.

Section 722: Partners' "Outside Basis." Under § 722, each contributing partner takes as her basis in the partnership interest received an amount equal to the sum of the adjusted basis she had in any contributed property, plus any cash contributed.[2] The partner's basis in her interest is commonly referred to as her "outside basis," a term that we will use frequently throughout this book. This is in contrast to the partnership's basis in the contributed property, which is referred to as the "inside basis." On the theory that the partner has merely changed the form of her investment in the contributed property, she is permitted to "tack" the holding period she had in that property to the holding period of her partnership interest.[3]

Section 723: Partnership's "Inside Basis." Under § 723, the partnership takes a transferred basis in contributed property equal to that of the contributing partner.[4] The partnership is also entitled to tack the partners' holding periods to its own.[5]

---

1. See § 721(b). This exception was created to prevent taxpayers from diversifying their investment portfolios without recognition of gain, and generally applies only if more than 80% of the partnership's assets are held for investment and are readily marketable. See § 351(e) and § 1.351–1(c)(1)(ii).

2. As we will see below, under § 752(a) each partner's share of partnership liabilities is treated as a cash contribution by the partner, which further increases her outside basis.

3. § 1223(1). Some items contributed to a partnership, such as money, in-

ventory and services, do not have holding periods. Therefore when a partner receives her interest in the partnership in exchange for such items, her holding period in the partnership interest received begins upon formation of the partnership.

4. This is the amount described above as "inside basis". If the contributing partner recognized gain under § 721(b), the partnership would increase its inside basis in the property by that amount.

Common Issues on Formation

Although the basic statutory scheme is easy to master, there are a host of issues that can arise upon the formation of a partnership which require our attention. We touch on all those we consider significant here, while some are discussed in further detail in subsequent chapters.

Property vs. Services

It is not entirely clear what constitutes "property" for purposes of § 721. The term, however, has been broadly construed in this context and includes such things as money, installment obligations, goodwill, and even accounts receivable of a cash method taxpayer.[6] It does not, however, encompass services. If a person contributes her services in exchange for a capital interest in a partnership, this exchange is not protected by § 721 and is a taxable event. The treatment of a partner who receives a partnership interest in exchange for services is discussed more fully in *Chapter Nine*.

As a result of the disparate treatment of contributions of property and services, it is not surprising that the Courts have often had to determine whether what was contributed to a partnership constituted property or was merely services. An excellent example of this problem is found in *Stafford v. United States*.[7] In *Stafford*, the taxpayer, a real estate developer, successfully negotiated a very favorable letter of intent with an insurance company for the financing of a hotel. The government argued that the exchange of that letter for a partnership interest merely compensated the taxpayer for his services in negotiating the letter, while the taxpayer argued that the letter was property in its own right. The court held that, although probably not enforceable, the letter was of value and constituted property for purposes of § 721(a).[8]

Contributions of Appreciated (or Depreciated) Property

Generally § 704(a) gives partnerships enormous flexibility in allocating their income, loss and deductions among their partners.

---

5. § 1223(2).

6. Cases construing the term "property" for § 351 purposes have held that the term "property" for § 721 purposes is analogous. See, e.g., *Stafford v. United States*, 611 F.2d 990, 995–997 (5th Cir. 1980).

7. Id.

8. See also *United States v. Frazell*, 335 F.2d 487 (5th Cir.1964) (geological maps created by contributing partner were held to constitute property).

built-in gain or loss

This flexibility, however, does not extend to pre-contribution gain and loss. If a partner contributes property that has an inherent gain or loss at the time of contribution, this "built-in" gain or loss *must* be taken into account by the contributing partner.[9] The rules for accomplishing this are the subject of *Chapter Seven*. As we shall see in *Chapter Seven*, the regulations allow a built-in gain or loss to be taken into account using any "reasonable method," including what is known as the "traditional method."[10] As a preview, in its simplest form the traditional method for allocating built-in gain or loss from non-depreciable property defers recognition of the gain or loss until the partnership ultimately recognizes it, and then allocates the gain or loss to the contributing partner. To illustrate, consider the following:

> ***Example #1:*** A contributes stock with a value of $100 and a basis of $60 to the ABC partnership. Three years later, ABC sells the stock for $130, resulting in a $70 tax gain. Under the traditional method, ABC must first allocate $40 of this gain to A. Subject to the limitations of § 704(b) (discussed in *Chapter Five*), the partners may agree to allocate the remaining $30 of gain in any way they like.

Contribution of Depreciable Property

The contribution of depreciable property raises two issues, one for the contributing partner and one for the partnership. The issue for the contributing partner is whether the contribution will trigger recapture of depreciation under § 1245 or § 1250 in spite of the general nonrecognition rule of § 721. By their own terms, §§ 1245 and 1250 appear to trigger recognition of gain in what might otherwise be expected to be a nonrecognition transaction.[11] Yet both sections contain a list of internal exceptions, including transactions described in § 721.[12] Therefore, the contributing party is protected from the recognition of recapture on contribution. The contributed property remains subject to recapture upon a later disposition by the partnership, and the partnership's potential recapture gain includes the depreciation taken by the contributing partner.[13]

---

9. § 704(c)(1)(A).

10. § 1.704–3(a).

11. Both § 1245(a) and § 1250(a) have what is known as "strong-arm" language which states: "Such gain shall be recognized notwithstanding any other provision in this subtitle."

12. See § 1245(b)(3) and § 1250(d)(3). These exceptions limit the amount characterized as ordinary income under the applicable recapture rule to gain that is *otherwise* recognized in the exchange. As we shall see later in this Chapter, gain may be recognized in context of the formation of a partnership if a contributing partner sheds a sufficient amount of liabilities. See § 1.1245–4(c)(4)Ex. 3.

13. This is accomplished in § 1245 through the definition of "recomputed basis", which includes depreciation taken by the taxpayer "and any other taxpayer" on the property. Section 1250

The issue of concern to the partnership is how it should calculate its cost recovery deductions with respect to the contributed property. In general, the partnership simply steps into the shoes of the contributing partner; just as the partnership "inherits" the contributing partner's adjusted basis in the property, it succeeds as well as to that partner's method of cost recovery.[14] Thus, for example, if the contributing partner elected to depreciate the contributed property under the alternative depreciation system,[15] then the partnership must also use this system.

Characterization of Gains and Losses From the Disposition of Contributed Property

For purposes of characterizing gains and losses, § 702(b) treats a partnership as a distinct entity, separate and apart from its partners. Thus, property that is inventory or "dealer property" in the hands of a partner might become a capital asset upon contribution to a partnership engaged in a different trade or business. Consistent with the Code's pervasive concern with the possibility of converting ordinary income into capital gains (and capital losses into ordinary losses), § 724 establishes three special characterization rules for gain or loss recognized on contributed property.[16]

Unrealized receivables. If the contributed property is an "unrealized receivable" (as defined in § 751(c)) in the hands of the contributing partner, any gain or loss that is recognized by the partnership on the disposition of that property is characterized as ordinary, no matter how long it is held by the partnership.[17]

Inventory items. If the contributed property is an "inventory item" (as defined in § 751(d)) in the contributing partner's hands, then any gain or loss that is recognized on that property by the partnership *within 5 years of the contribution* shall be characterized as ordinary.[18]

Capital loss property. If a partner contributes property that is a capital asset in her hands and that has a built-in loss, then, to the extent of the amount of that built-in loss, any loss recognized

---

defines "depreciation adjustments" for recapture purposes similarly in § 1250(b)(3). Note that under § 704(c) recapture attributable to depreciation taken by the contributing partner would be allocated to her.

14. § 168(i)(7). For the year of contribution, the contributing partner and the partnership must share that year's cost recovery deduction.

15. See § 168(g).

16. Compare § 735 which contains a parallel set of characterization rules for property that is distributed by a partnership to a partner. See *Chapter Eleven.*

17. § 724(a).

18. § 724(b).

on that property by the partnership *within 5 years of the contribution* shall be characterized as capital.[19]

An Interim Example

To illustrate several of the above issues, consider the following example:

Example #2: A, B and C form an equal partnership in which each is entitled to one third of all income and loss from the partnership's operations. A contributes land with a value of $100 and a basis of $60. This land is a § 1231 asset in A's hands. B contributes machinery with a basis of $50 and a value of $75, and $25 cash. B purchased this machinery for $110 and has taken $60 in depreciation. C contributes stock, a capital asset in C's hands, with a value of $100 and a basis of $200. The tax consequences to the partners and the partnership on formation are as follows:

To the partners: The tax consequences to A and C are straightforward. Under § 721, neither A nor C has any gain or loss on the exchange. Under § 722, each takes an exchanged basis in her respective partnership interest equal to the adjusted basis she had in the contributed property; therefore, A's outside basis is $60 and C's is $200. They are both entitled to a tacked holding period. Under § 704(c), each partner will be responsible for the pre-contribution gain/loss in her property. Thus, when the partnership sells the land and the stock, the first $40 of gain on the land will be taxed to A, and the first $100 of loss on the stock must be allocated to C.

The tax consequences to B are also relatively straightforward. B is entitled to nonrecognition under §§ 721 and 1245(b)(3) and takes as her outside basis the sum of her adjusted basis in the machinery ($50) plus the cash contributed ($25), or $75. Since cash does not have a holding period, B takes a split holding period in her partnership interest. Three quarters of her interest will have a tacked holding period, and one quarter will have a new one.[20] Finally, B must also take into account the pre-contribution gain inherent in the machinery. As explained in *Chapter Seven*, this will be done as the partnership holds and depreciates the property.

To the partnership: The tax consequences to ABC are as follows: Under § 721, ABC has no gain or loss. Under § 723, ABC takes a transferred basis in each of the properties re-

19. § 724(c).

20. Under § 1.1223-3(b), the holding period of a partnership interest in a case such as this is determined based upon the relative fair market values of the property contributed. There is no tacking for that portion of the interest received for the cash.

ceived; therefore, ABC takes a basis of $60 in the land, $200 in the stock, and $50 in the machine. ABC must use the same method of depreciation that B was using. The pre-contribution depreciation taken by B is subject to recapture when ABC ultimately disposes of the machinery.

If ABC sells the stock within 5 years of its contribution, the first $100 of loss therefrom will be characterized as a capital loss under § 724(c), even if the partnership is a dealer in securities.

Liabilities—In General

As with all other areas of the tax law, the presence of liabilities significantly complicates Subchapter K. The partnership rules relating to liabilities are based upon the same general principles that govern the treatment of liabilities throughout the Code. Consistent with the aggregate theory of partnerships, § 752 (and the regulations thereunder) provide rules for dividing partnership liabilities among the partners, and each partner is treated as making a cash contribution to the partnership in an amount equal to her share. As a result, each partner is given credit in her outside basis for her share of partnership liabilities. In this way, investors are treated substantially alike, whether they invest as partners or in their individual capacities.[21]

As a general rule, when an individual borrows money to invest, even without personal liability, she is given basis for the borrowed funds but does not recognize income.[22] Under this rule, which is based upon the assumption that the borrowed funds will eventually be repaid, the taxpayer is currently given basis credit for future outlays. To illustrate, if an individual, T, purchases Blackacre for $1,000 by paying $100 cash and giving a $900 mortgage for the balance, T's basis in Blackacre is $1,000. Essentially, T is treated just as if she used her own funds for the investment and, thus, is entitled to cost recovery deductions based on her entire basis, including the mortgage. As the full mortgage has already been reflected in basis, payments of principal on the mortgage have no effect on basis. However, if all or any part of this liability is discharged or assumed by another party, then T must account for this discharge of indebtedness. For example, if T eventually sells Blackacre to X for $300 cash, with X assuming the $900 mortgage,[23]

---

21. You should compare this treatment with that of a shareholder in an S Corporation who is not given any credit in her outside basis for corporate liabilities. See § 1367.

22. The seminal case dealing with nonrecourse mortgages is *Crane v. Commissioner*, 331 U.S. 1 (1947).

23. It is not necessary for the buyer to assume personal liability for the

T's amount realized on the sale would be $1,200—the cash *plus* the principal amount of the mortgage at the time of sale.[24]

The partnership rules relating to liabilities are based upon these general principles. Like T, a partnership's basis in its assets ("inside basis") includes partnership liabilities. Yet, because it is the partners who will ultimately deduct depreciation on the partnership's assets, and because a partner can deduct losses only up to the amount of her basis in the partnership ("outside basis"), partnership liabilities must also be reflected in the partners' outside bases. This is the role of § 752.

Under § 752(a), each partner is treated as contributing cash to the partnership in an amount equal to any partnership liabilities that she assumes, and any increase in her share of partnership liabilities. This will necessarily include the partner's initial share of partnership liabilities upon formation of the partnership. In combination with § 722, this has the effect of increasing the partner's outside basis by the amount of such increase. Correspondingly, under § 752(b), a partner is treated as having received a distribution of cash from the partnership in an amount equal to the amount of any of her individual liabilities that are assumed by the partnership, and any decrease in her share of partnership liabilities. In combination with § 733, this has the effect of reducing the partner's outside basis (but not below zero) by the amount of the distribution. To the extent that the "cash" distribution exceeds the partner's outside basis, the partner must recognize gain.[25]

The regulations under § 752 provide the rules necessary to allocate liabilities among the partners. The rules differ for recourse and nonrecourse liabilities. Recourse liabilities are allocated to those partners who bear the "economic risk of loss" associated with those liabilities. The regulations determine who bears the risk of loss by identifying who would have the ultimate responsibility for the liability if all assets of the partnership became worthless and the liability became due. In general, recourse liabilities are shared in accordance with how the partners share losses.

Since no partner will ultimately be liable for any portion of a nonrecourse liability, nonrecourse liabilities are allocated differently. As a general rule, they are allocated among the partners in the same way the partners share profits.[26] The theory is that payments on the liability, if any, will come from profits from the venture; therefore, it is more appropriate to allocate nonrecourse liabilities

---

mortgage to be included in the seller's amount realized. See § 1.1001–2(a)(4).

24. *Commissioner v. Tufts,* 461 U.S. 300 (1983).

25. § 731(a)(1).

26. The rules for allocating nonrecourse liabilities are often far more complicated and are discussed fully in *Chapter Eight.*

in accordance with how the partners share profits rather than how they share losses.

These general principles sound deceptively simple. In fact commercial lending arrangements are so complex that the § 752 regulations require analysis of all agreements among the partners, and between the partners and the lender, to determine just how a specific liability should be shared. These rules are discussed in detail in *Chapter Eight*.

Contribution of Encumbered Property

When a partner contributes encumbered property to a partnership, the partnership replaces the partner as obligor on the loan.[27] Thus, the contributor is simultaneously relieved of her personal liability on the loan, and as a partner becomes responsible for a share of all of the partnership's liabilities, including the one encumbering the contributed property. This results in both a decrease in her personal liabilities and an increase in her share of partnership liabilities. Both of these adjustments are deemed to occur simultaneously and only the net change is taken into account.[28] Section 752 treats changes in a partner's share of liabilities as cash transactions: when there is a net increase in a partner's share of partnership liabilities, she is treated as having made a cash contribution in that amount; when there is a net decrease in her share of partnership liabilities, she is treated as having received a cash distribution. These rules have two important consequences: (i) a partner's outside basis reflects her share of partnership liabilities, and (ii) under some circumstances, the "deemed" cash distribution which occurs on the contribution of encumbered property may result in recognition of gain.

To illustrate, consider the following:

Example #3: A and B form an equal partnership, AB, in which they will share all income, gain and loss equally. A contributes land with a fair market value of $180 on which there is a recourse mortgage of $80, which AB assumes. At the time of contribution, A's basis in the land is $75. B contributes $100 cash. Assume that under § 752 the mortgage is allocated equally between A and B.

In this transaction, as a result of the assumption by the partnership of the $80 mortgage, B's share of partnership

---

27. For purposes of simplicity at this point, assume that the liability is recourse and the contributor is a general partner. In fact, the same basic rules apply whether the liability is recourse or not. The transferee of encumbered property is treated as if it assumed the liability to the extent the liability does not exceed the value of the property. § 1.752–1(e).

28. § 1.752–1(f).

liabilities increases from $0 to $40. This amount is treated as a
cash contribution. Therefore, B's outside basis is equal to $140
determined as follows:

$100 cash contributed
<u>+40</u> net increase in liabilities
$140

A, on the other hand, has a net decrease in partnership
liabilities of $40. Although the assumption by AB of the $80
mortgage is treated as a decrease of $80 in her individual
liabilities, A is also given credit for her share of that partnership liability of $40. A's outside basis is equal to $35, determined as follows:

$75 adjusted basis in land contributed
<u>−40</u> net decrease in liabilities
$35

If the contributing partner's net decrease in liabilities is greater than her total basis in all the assets she contributes, the
contribution will result in gain. For example, if A's basis in the land
had been only $30, the deemed cash distribution of $40 would have
exceeded her basis by $10, resulting in a $10 gain and a zero [0]
outside basis.[29]

Contributions of Accounts Receivable and Payable

When accounts receivable are contributed to a partnership by a
cash method taxpayer, the specter of the assignment of income
doctrine is raised. Under this doctrine, the income inherent in the
accounts receivable must be taxed to the contributing partner. This
is accomplished in Subchapter K by: (i) treating the accounts
receivable as property for purposes of § 721; (ii) assigning the
partnership a transferred (typically zero) basis in the receivables
under § 723; (iii) characterizing the income realized by the partnership upon collection of the receivables as ordinary under § 724: and
(iv) allocating the income to the contributing partner under
§ 704(c).

Accounts payable and other accrued but unpaid items that are
contributed (or assigned) to a partnership by a cash method taxpayer are treated under rules similar to those for contributed property.
That is, these payables are not considered partnership liabilities for

---

29. §§ 731(a) & 733. If the liability
encumbering the property is nonrecourse, the regulations contain a special
rule designed to avoid this result. See
§ 1.752–3 and *Chapter Eight*.

purposes of § 752[30] and under § 704(c)(3) the partnership must allocate to the contributor, or in this case the assignor, of the liabilities, the deduction for the payables when they are paid. This rule prevents two untoward results: (i) the recognition of gain on the contribution of certain ongoing businesses to partnerships, and (ii) the equivalent (or the reverse) of assigning income (i.e., assigning deductions).

To illustrate, suppose A and B form an equal partnership to which A, a cash method taxpayer, contributes zero basis accounts receivable with a fair market value of $100 and accounts payable of $40. B contributes $60 cash. In the absence of a special rule for accounts payable, A would have a net decrease in partnership liabilities of $20, resulting in a $20 gain. This result would clearly inhibit cash method proprietors from entering into partnerships. Section 704(c)(3) solves this problem: there is no gain upon formation. Instead, the partnership *must allocate to A* both the income from the accounts receivables when they are received, as well as the deductions from the payables when they are paid.

Organization and Syndication Expenses

When a partnership is formed, there invariably are a variety of organizational expenses[31] that are incurred. These include the legal and accounting fees incident to the creation of the partnership as well as various filing fees.[32] Very often there are also syndication expenses, that is, those expenses incurred in connection with selling the partnership interests. Syndication expenses are those connected with the issuing and marketing of the partnership interests, including legal, accounting and brokerage fees.[33] Under § 709(a) neither organization nor syndication expenses are deductible. Since both types of expenses are incurred in connection with creation of the partnership entity, they are properly chargeable to capital.

Because these rather harsh rules encouraged taxpayers to manipulate their expenses in attempts to characterize them as currently deductible, Congress provided some relief for partnership formation expenses, as it did in § 195 for business start-up expenses and in § 248 for corporation organizational expenses. Under

---

30. § 1.752–1(a)(4).

31. Organization expenses are defined in § 709(b)(2) as those expenditures which

(A) are incident to the creation of the partnership;

(B) are chargeable to capital account; and

(C) are of a character which, if expended in the creation of the partnership having an ascertainable life, would have been amortized over such life.

32. § 1.709–2(a).

33. § 1.709–2(b). See also Rev. Rul. 88–4, 1988–1 C.B. 264 (the cost of a tax opinion is a syndication expense).

§ 709(b) a partnership may elect to currently deduct the lesser of: (i) the amount of organization expenses (*not* syndication expenses) or (ii) $5,000, reduced by the amount by which its organization expenses exceed $50,000. Those organizational expenses that are not deducted currently may be amortized over 180 months (i.e., 15 years).[34] Syndication expenses continue to be nondeductible, nonamortizable capital expenditures.[35]

34. § 248 (allowing similar amortization for the organizational expenses incident to creating a corporation).

35. This relatively poor tax treatment of syndication fees is undoubtedly a reaction to the widespread use of syndicated partnerships by the tax shelter industry.

Chapter Three

PARTNERSHIP OPERATIONS: THE BASICS

Introduction

Just as the overriding theme in the rules governing the formation of partnerships is flexibility in moving to the partnership form of doing business, the overriding theme of the rules applicable to partnership operations is also flexibility: the rules are designed to ensure that the tax consequences track the economics of whatever deal the partners strike.

A partnership is not technically a taxpayer.[1] Its primary function for tax purposes is to facilitate the computation of each partner's share of the venture's profit or loss. This is primarily an accounting function: once income or loss from partnership operations is calculated, those amounts are passed through to the partners who are responsible for reporting their shares on their own tax returns. As a practical matter, however, to perform this function, it is necessary to treat a partnership as a taxpayer for certain purposes. The common thread is that a partnership is treated as an entity whenever doing so facilitates computation of the partners' shares of income and deduction.

Because it is the partnership, not the individual partners, that is carrying on the enterprise, it would be unduly cumbersome (let alone unrealistic) to require each of the partners to keep her own set of books for the enterprise's activities. This would require each partner to account for the enterprise's accounts receivables, cost-of-goods-sold, depreciation, etc. This could certainly become an accounting, as well as an auditing, nightmare, especially if the individual partners had different taxable years and accounting methods. For these reasons, a partnership must adopt a taxable year,

---

1. § 701.

choose a method of accounting, and make certain elections just as if it were a taxpayer. The partnership is also required to compute its taxable income (as defined in § 703(a)) and to file an informational return (Form 1065), that informs the IRS and the partners about the entity's operations. At the same time the partnership provides each partner with a statement (Form K–1) which informs them of their respective shares of the income and deductions incurred at the partnership level. This process enables the partners to report their shares of partnership income, and also allows the IRS to audit the operations of the enterprise as a whole.

Partnership Taxable Years

Under § 706(a), a partner must include her distributive share of partnership income "for any taxable year of the partnership ending within or with the taxable year of the partner." Under this rule, the key date is the last day of the partnership's taxable year: it is on that date that each partner is treated as receiving and paying (in the case of cash method partners) or accruing (for accrual method partners) her distributive share of the partnership's income and deductions for the partnership's taxable year which has just ended. Therefore, for example, a calendar year partner in a partnership with a June 30 fiscal year will include in her income for calendar year 2010 her share of the partnership's income and deductions for the period beginning July 1, 2009 and ending June 30, 2010.

Prior to 1986, there were few restrictions on a partnership's choice of taxable year. Often a partnership would choose a year for the sole purpose of deferring its partners' inclusion of partnership income. To illustrate, suppose A, B and C, all calendar year taxpayers, form an equal partnership which will have net income of $10,000 a month during all of 2010. If ABC elects a calendar year, then all income earned by the partnership during calendar year 2010 would be reported by its partners on their 2010 returns, and there would be no deferral. If, on the other hand, ABC were to elect a fiscal year ending on January 31, the $110,000 earned from February 1 through December 31 of 2010 would not be included in the partners' income for 2010. Because the last day of the partnership's year, January 31, 2011, ends within the partners' 2011 calendar year, it is on that year's return that they will report the income. Thus, the partners would defer reporting eleven months of the partnership's income for a full year,[2] which amounts to a one

---

2. To generalize, the number of months of deferral for a particular partner with respect to partnership income is always equal to the number of months from the beginning of the partnership's taxable year until the end of the partner's taxable year. Thus, in the above example, as there are 11 months from

year interest-free loan from the government equal to the tax due on that income. Yes, the "loan" is paid back when the partners ultimately report the income on their 2011 returns, but look what's happened in the meantime: the income for the period February 1, 2011 to December 31, 2011 is not reported on the 2011 return of the partners, but is also deferred to 2012. Because this deferral occurs year after year, the partners are indefinitely postponing paying tax on eleven months of income. The value of this postponement is economically equivalent to a series of one year interest-free loans from the government.

Congress amended § 706(b) in 1986 in reaction to the widespread use of this deferral technique. The amendments severely limit a partnership's choice of taxable year. Under the current rules, if the partnership is able to establish a valid business purpose for choosing a particular taxable year, a partnership may use that taxable year. However, in the absence of a business purpose, a partnership *must* adopt its "required taxable year" unless it makes an election under § 444.[3]

Establishing a valid business purpose for purposes of § 706(b) is a difficult task. The legislative history and subsequent administrative pronouncements establish guidelines for what will be considered a valid business purpose, and the rules are quite difficult to satisfy.[4] It is clear that administrative convenience to the partnership or its accountants is not sufficient to justify adoption of a non-required year. Nor, obviously, is the desire to maximize deferral for the partners. What will qualify as a business purpose is a year that conforms to the partnership's "natural business year." For example, a partnership that operates a ski resort, and whose business activities cease in April of each year, might succeed in applying for a fiscal year ending in April or May.

Section 706(b)(1)(B) establishes priority rules for determining a partnership's "required taxable year:"[5]

> *First tier*: if one or more partners with the same taxable year own in the aggregate more than a 50% interest in profits *and* capital, then the partnership must adopt that taxable year (referred to in the statute as the "majority interest taxable year"). Most partnerships, certainly those owned more than 50% by individuals, will fall within this rule. However, if the partnership has no majority interest taxable year then,

2/1 to 12/31, each calendar year partner would have 11 months of deferral. Cf. § 444(b)(4).

3. Discussed below.

4. See, e.g., Rev. Proc. 87–32, 1987–2 C.B. 396.

5. "Required taxable year" is the phrase used in § 444(e) to describe the year required under § 706(b) without taking into account business purpose.

Second tier: if all of the principal partners (those owning 5% or more of profits *or* capital) have the same taxable year, then the partnership must adopt that taxable year. If not, then,

Third tier: the regulations require the partnership to adopt that year which results in the "least aggregate deferral."

The third tier is by far the most complicated and deserves some further explanation. To determine which taxable year results in the least aggregate deferral, the regulations require one to "test" each of the partners' taxable years. The aggregate deferral for a particular year is equal to the sum of each partner's deferral for that year. The deferral for each partner is simply the product of the number of months of deferral times that partner's profits interest. The partnership's required taxable year is the year that yields the least aggregate deferral.[6]

To illustrate, consider the following: XYZ is a partnership which is comprised as follows:

Partner	Profits	Taxable Year
X Corp	30%	6/30
Y Corp	40%	8/30
Z (individual)	30%	Calendar

Assuming no business purpose for any particular year, XYZ's required taxable year is determined as follows:

Under § 706(b):

(1) There is no "majority interest taxable year," as no combination of partners holding more than 50% in profits and capital share the same taxable year.

(2) X, Y and Z are all principal partners, yet none shares the same taxable year.

(3) It therefore becomes necessary to determine which of the three taxable years of the partners (6/30, 8/31 or 12/31) would result in the least aggregate deferral.[7] This is done by testing each one of these years.

---

6. § 1.706–1T(a).

7. For reasons that might not be intuitive to all readers, the taxable year with the least aggregate deferral *must* be one of the taxable years of a partner.

Assuming the adoption of X Corp.'s 6/30 fiscal year:

Partner	Taxable Year	Profits Interests	Months of Deferral	Interest X Deferral
X Corp	6/30	30%	0	0
Y Corp	8/31	40%	2	.8
Z	12/31	30%	6	1.8
Aggregate Deferral				2.6

Assuming the adoption of Y Corp.'s 8/31 fiscal year:

Partner	Taxable Year	Profits Interests	Months of Deferral	Interest X Deferral
X Corp	6/30	30%	10	3.0
Y Corp	8/31	40%	0	0
Z	12/31	30%	4	1.2
Aggregate Deferral				4.2

Assuming the adoption of Z's calendar year:

Partner	Taxable Year	Profits Interests	Months of Deferral	Interest X Deferral
X Corp	6/30	30%	6	1.8
Y Corp	8/31	40%	8	3.2
Z	12/31	30%	0	0
Aggregate Deferral				5.0

Thus, because use of a 6/30 fiscal year results in the "least aggregate deferral," the partnership must adopt that year.[8]

An obvious problem arising with this method of determining a partnership's required taxable year is that the composition of a partnership is not static: the partnership may amend its agreement from time to time to vary the partners' interests in profits and capital, and to admit or retire partners. So it becomes necessary to identify the point in time when the determination of a permitted year is to be made. Thereafter, in a partnership with frequently changing interests, one must decide how often the partnership must change its taxable year to conform to the § 706(b) rules. The Code addresses this problem by, in general, requiring the partnership to "test" the validity of its taxable year on the first day of each year, and if the test shows the taxable year to be invalid then it must be changed. However, once the partnership is required to change its taxable year because of the "majority interest taxable

---

8. Note that the computation of deferral only relates to number of months of income deferred by each partner, and does not attempt to take into account their respective tax rates.

year" rule, the partnership will not be required to change its taxable year again for a minimum of 3 years.[9]

Section 444 Election. Even in the absence of a valid business purpose, under § 444, for a price, a partnership may elect to adopt a taxable year other than its required taxable year as long as the year chosen does not result in more than three months of deferral. For example, if a partnership's required taxable year is the calendar year, the partnership may elect to adopt a fiscal year ending in September, October or November. The price for making this election is that the partnership must make a "required payment" each year to offset the benefits of the deferral. This payment, which is redetermined each year, is essentially an interest free deposit in an amount intended to approximate the taxes that are deferred.[10]

Method of Accounting

A partnership, like any other taxpayer, must choose a method of accounting, but its choice is limited by the identity of its partners. Under § 448, just as C corporations are generally prohibited from using the cash method of accounting, so too are partnerships with C corporations as partners.[11] This prohibition was aimed primarily at large businesses and does not apply to partnerships (other than tax shelters) for any year unless average annual gross receipts of the partnership for the prior 3 years exceeds $5 million.[12]

In addition, if a partnership comes within the definition of a "tax shelter" in § 461(i)(3),[13] then it too must use the accrual method of accounting, no matter what its size.[14] This rule was part of the 1980's crackdown on the tax shelter industry, which relied in large part on cash method partnerships making substantial prepayments of expenses. The definition of tax shelters in § 461(i)(3) is broad enough to encompass not only traditional tax shelters, but also all publicly offered partnerships as well.

The Computation of A Partnership's Taxable Income

In General

Section 701 is the basic expression of Subchapter K's aggregate theory of partnerships: "A partnership as such shall not be subject

---

9. § 706(b)(4)(B).

10. § 7519.

11. § 448(a)(2). For this purpose, C corporations that are personal service corporations are treated as individuals. Thus, for example, a law partnership with one or more professional corpora-

tions as partners is not subject to this rule. § 448(b)(2).

12. § 448(b)(3) & (c).

13. § 448(d)(3).

14. Tax shelters are not eligible for the $5,000,000 gross receipts exception. § 448(a)(3).

to the income tax imposed by this chapter. Persons carrying on business as partners shall be liable for income tax only in their separate or individual capacities." Section 702 elaborates by requiring each partner to account separately for her share of (i) various items separately listed in § 702(a)(1)–(7), which include, for example, capital gains and losses and (ii) bottom line income or loss, computed without regard to the separately listed items.

The computation of a partnership's taxable income is prescribed in § 703(a). It is determined in the same way as the taxable income of an individual with certain modifications. The most important modification is that the items described in § 702(a) are separately stated. As discussed immediately below, the reason for separately stating these items is that they may have special significance to individual partners. Section 703(a) also denies two types of deductions that individuals are normally permitted. The first type consists of deductions that are considered inappropriate for partnerships, such as the deduction for personal exemptions[15] and the additional itemized deductions.[16] The second type consists of deductions the benefits of which are (or have been) directly passed through to the partners in their individual capacities. These are the deductions for certain foreign taxes, charitable contributions, net operating losses, and depletion of oil and gas wells.[17]

Separately Stated Items

It is worth pausing at this point to focus upon the separately stated items in § 702(a), for they highlight the interaction of the entity and aggregate notions of partnership taxation.

One inherent characteristic of the aggregate notion of taxing partnership income is that each partner has a different tax profile into which the partnership items must be incorporated. There are some items that will affect all partners the same way, without regard to their tax profiles, and which can safely be included in "bottom line" income or loss. But there are numerous other items

15. § 151 et seq.

16. See §§ 211–221.

17. The reasons for not permitting these deductions at the partnership level differ. Foreign taxes and charitable contributions are not permitted as a deduction, but must be separately stated under § 702(a)(4) and (a)(6). In the case of foreign taxes, this allows each partner to individually opt to take a deduction or a credit as permitted by § 901. In the case of charitable contributions, it was thought that it was more appropriate for each partner to run the gamut of all of the special rules and limitations of § 170 rather than the partnership. Similarly, the aggregate approach was also considered more appropriate in the case of depletion: Under § 613A(c)(7)(D) each partner must individually compute her own deduction for depletion. Finally, the reason that net operating losses are not currently permitted is that these losses will have already been taken into account by the partners in the year that the losses were incurred.

of partnership income and deduction that may affect each partner differently depending upon her tax profile. For example, consider partnership AB whose only tax item for the year is a $4,000 capital gain, which is allocated equally between its two partners, A and B. If A has no other capital gains or losses for the year, and B has a $3,000 capital loss for the year, the tax effect of the $2,000 partnership capital gain allocated to each will be dramatically different. A will report a $2,000 net capital gain, while B will report a net $1,000 capital loss. If this partnership gain was expressed merely as net $4,000 income for the year, without specifying its character as capital, the partners would not have the information necessary to adequately report their income for the year. Thus, the partnership's information return must separately state this capital gain, as well as any other "variable effect" items, i.e., items whose tax consequences will vary from partner to partner.

The Code specifically lists certain variable effect items in § 702(a)(1)-(6). These include both short and long term capital gains and losses (for the reason illustrated above), gains and losses from § 1231 property (which each partner must throw into her individual "hotchpot"), charitable contributions (which each partner will combine with her other contributions before applying the relevant limitations of § 170), dividends eligible for the dividends received deduction (available only to corporate partners) and those that constitute net capital gain under § 1(h)(11) (available only to noncorporate partners), and foreign taxes paid (which each partner will separately elect to deduct or take as a credit under the rules of § 901).

Recognizing that this list is not exhaustive, Congress authorized the Treasury to expand it in regulations, which Treasury did in § 1.702–1(a)(8)(i) by listing other specific items. But even more significant is the language of § 1.702–1(a)(8)(ii), which states "[e]ach partner must also take into account separately his distributive share of any partnership item which if separately taken into account by any partner would result in an income tax liability for that partner different from that which would result if that partner did not take the item into account separately...." This very broad language puts a tremendous burden on partnerships and partners to be on the watch for items that might have a "variable effect." Obviously, such items will change as Congress changes the Code; one obvious example that comes to mind is the ever-evolving alternative minimum tax (AMT).[18] As the law changes to include and exclude items from the AMT base, so too will change the list of items with variable effect.

---

18. See §§ 55–59.

Partnership Elections

As we noted at the outset, it is sometimes necessary for administrative and accounting reasons to treat the partnership as an entity, even though the income is ultimately taxed under the aggregate theory to each individual partner. One instance in which this is true is partnership elections. Consider, for example, a partnership that sells property under the installment method. Section 453 requires the partners to report the income from the installment sale under the installment method, i.e., as payments are received, unless an election to the contrary is made under § 453(d). Whose election? Can one partner utilize the installment method while another opts out? Such issues are resolved in § 703(b) in favor of elections at the *entity* level, with only three exceptions.[19] Thus, in our example, the sale will be treated as an installment sale for all partners, unless the partnership makes a § 453(d) election, in which case it will not be treated as an installment sale by anyone.

Adjustments to the Partners' Outside Basis

A partner's outside basis is a measure of her after-tax investment in the venture. Thus, in *Chapter Two* we saw that a partner's outside basis includes her contributions to the partnership (§ 722) and is reduced by distributions from the partnership (§ 733). In addition, a partner's outside basis must be adjusted to account for the operations of the partnership, in order to prevent over-or under-taxing a partner. These adjustments are described in § 705(a). Under § 705(a)(1) we are instructed to *increase* a partner's outside basis by the sum of the partner's distributive share of (i) taxable income and (ii) tax exempt income. Under § 705(a)(2), after reducing the partner's outside basis by distributions to her under § 733, we *decrease* a partner's outside basis by her distributive share of (i) partnership losses, and (ii) § 705(a)(2)(B) expenditures.[20]

To understand the need for these adjustments, consider for, example, partnership AB, which is formed on the first day of year one by A and B, each contributing $500 cash. Assume AB, A and B are all calendar year, cash method taxpayers. During the course of

---

19. The exceptions are the elections under §§ 108(b)(5), 617 and 901. In addition to the election under § 453(d), other examples of common elections which must be made by the partnership are those permitted by § 168 with respect to depreciation methods, that permitted by § 179 to expense the cost of certain depreciable property, and the § 709 election to amortize organizational expenses. For a more complete list see McKee et al. at ¶ 9.01[7].

20. There are also adjustments for depletion that will not be addressed in this book.

year one, AB earns $100, which is allocated equally between A and B, and each reports $50 on their respective tax returns; AB makes no distributions. On the first day of year two A sells her partnership interest to C for its fair market value of $550 (representing one-half of the value of the AB assets of $1100). If A's outside basis were $500, determined under § 722 and *unadjusted* for her share of year one income, A would report a gain of $50 on the sale of her partnership interest. A would be paying tax twice on the partnership's year one income, a result clearly not intended by Subchapter K. Therefore, A's outside basis must be increased by the income she reports to reflect the tax-paid investment in the partnership.[21]

A partner must also increase her outside basis by her share of the partnership's tax exempt income.[22] This is necessary in order to allow the partners the full benefit of the tax exemption. To illustrate, suppose the income earned by AB in the above example were tax exempt, and hence *not* included in A's year one income. If A did not increase her basis for her $50 share of that income, a sale of her partnership interest to C would result in a $50 gain, thereby resulting in eventual taxation of the tax exempt income.

There are also several events that require a partner's outside basis to be adjusted downward. These events are mirror images of those that require increases. First of all, basis must be decreased, but not below zero, by distributions made to the partners during the year.[23] These distributions have the effect of reducing a partner's tax-paid investment in the partnership. Next, § 705(a)(2)(A) requires a downward adjustment to outside basis for partnership losses. This adjustment is necessary to prevent partners from benefiting twice from the same loss. Consider if in the above example AB had a taxable loss of $100 in year one, which was allocated to, and deducted by, A and B on their year one tax returns. If A were to sell her interest in the partnership to C on the first day of year two for its fair market value of $450, unless A's basis had been reduced for the $50 loss reported by her in year one she would report an *additional* loss of $50 on the sale, a clearly wrong result. Finally, a downward adjustment is also required for certain non-deductible and non-capitalizable expenses of the partnership. Similar to the adjustment upward for tax exempt income, this adjustment is necessary to ensure that a non-deductible item is not eventually given the effect of a deduction on a later sale.

---

21. § 705(a)(1)(A).

22. § 705(a)(1)(B). Increases are also authorized for the excess of depletion deductions over the basis of the property subject to depletion, a case we will ignore for present purposes.

23. §§ 733 and 705(a)(2).

To illustrate these adjustments, consider the following:

Example: CD is an equal, calendar year partnership. C and D are calendar year taxpayers, and on January 1 of the current year each has an outside basis of $100. On December 1 of the current year the partnership distributes cash of $10 to C. In addition, C's distributive share of CD's items of income, loss and deduction for the current year are as follows:

Ordinary business income	$50
Tax exempt income	15
Capital loss	(20)
Charitable deduction	(10)

C's outside basis as of the end of the current year will be computed as follows:

Outside Basis (as of 1/1)	$100
§ 705(a)(1)(A) Ordinary business income	50
§ 705(a)(1)(B) Tax exempt income	15
§ 705(a)(2)	
December 1 distribution[24]	(10)
Capital loss	(20)
Charitable deduction	(10)
Outside basis (as of 12/31)	$125

---

24. Mid-year distributions that are essentially "draws" against current income are treated as if made on the last day of the partnership's year. § 1.731–1(a)(1)(ii).

Chapter Four

FINANCIAL ACCOUNTING
AND MAINTENANCE OF
CAPITAL ACCOUNTS

Introduction

Much to the dismay of many law students, the taxation of partnerships cannot be understood without a rudimentary understanding of a few basic financial accounting tools, especially balance sheets and capital accounts. It is possible for even "accounting phobics" to master these concepts with a little patience, and our goal in this chapter is to introduce them at a very basic level.

A partnership's financial accounts are commonly referred to as its "books." Knowledge of how these accounts are created and maintained is not only very helpful in conceptualizing many of the difficult issues of partnership taxation, but also is essential to understanding most of the Treasury regulations concerning partnerships issued in the last 25 years. Treasury promulgated its own rules for maintaining capital accounts under § 1.704–1(b)(2)(iv), and has made these rules the cornerstone for many of the most complex partnership regulations, including those governing special allocations under § 704(b), allocations of liabilities under § 752, and allocations of pre-contribution gain or loss under § 704(c). Therefore, while this chapter discusses basic principles of financial accounting, it necessarily incorporates the modifications to those principles contained in the Treasury's capital accounting rules.

It is important to keep in mind two things while studying this chapter. First, our concern here is with *financial* accounting, *not* computing taxable income and loss of the partnership. The purpose of financial accounting is to reflect the economic well-being of a firm and the relationship among its partners, and it is quite independent of determining tax liability of the partners. The tax law, however, uses the financial accounts of a partnership as a surrogate for economic reality and those accounts are therefore extremely important in evaluating all partnership transactions.

Second, the capital accounting rules described in this chapter are not governed by generally accepted accounting principles (GAAP), but by tax accounting principles. For example, capital accounts will be maintained on a cash basis if the partnership is a cash method taxpayer. Even if the partnership is an accrual method taxpayer, if a partnership receives a current payment for future services the payment will generally be included in income for tax purposes and be treated as current income under the capital accounting rules, even though it would not be income under GAAP until it is earned. Thus, students with an accounting background should approach these rules with caution, and an open mind.

Essential Elements of Financial Accounting

The two principal tools used by accountants to analyze the economic well being of a firm are the firm's income statement and its balance sheet. The income statement summarizes the economic activity of the firm over various periods of time, including the partnership's taxable year. It specifies the amount and nature of the firm's revenue, as well as its expenses. In contrast, the balance sheet represents a snapshot of the firm's financial situation at a particular point in time, often the end of the firm's year. A balance sheet is constructed based upon the following accounting identity:

Assets = Liabilities + Equity

As a matter of convention, assets appear on the left hand side of the sheet, and liabilities and equity appear on the right.

The values used for the assets on the balance sheet, referred to as "book values," are generally historical cost, adjusted for depreciation. Book value is not necessarily the same as fair market value, and may or may not be the same as tax basis. Accountants use historical cost because it is thought to be more reliable, and certainly less expensive than requiring periodic appraisals. Hence, book value does not normally reflect unrealized gains and losses.[1]

In the partnership context, the total partners' equity is expressed as the "capital accounts" of the partners. Each partner has a separate capital account, the balance of which represents her equity in the partnership, i.e., the amount that she would receive on liquidation if the partnership sold all of its assets for their book

---

1. One important exception to this general rule occurs when the partnership revalues its assets in connection with certain transactions. These rules are discussed below.

value, paid off its creditors, and distributed the net proceeds to the partners. In order to maintain the accounting identity of Assets = Liabilities + Equity, capital account balances must necessarily be adjusted to reflect increases or decreases in the partnership's assets that are not caused by increased or decreased liabilities. Thus, capital accounts are adjusted periodically to reflect any contributions to, or distributions from, the partnership's assets that may have occurred, as well as any increase in partnership assets caused by income or any decrease in assets caused by losses that the partnership may have experienced.[2]

Most of our discussion of financial accounting will focus upon capital accounts. At any point in time these accounts reflect the financial relationship among the partners and the adjustments to these accounts reflect the manner in which the partners have agreed to share the profits and losses from their venture. In a very real way, the capital accounts, if properly kept, reflect the current state of the economic deal among the partners.

Basic Capital Accounting Rules

The financial accounts of a partnership, including its capital accounts, are maintained using the partnership's normal method of accounting and must be adjusted periodically to take into account the partnership's operations for the year, as well as any contributions to, or distributions from, the partnership that may have occurred.[3] Each of these adjustments deserves some elaboration.

Contributions.[4] A partner's capital account is increased by the amount of money plus the fair market value of any property (net of liabilities) contributed by that partner. There are two aspects of this rule that should be emphasized: First, the contributing partner's tax basis in the property is not relevant for this purpose. The theory is that the partners will have struck their business deal on the basis of the contributed property's value, not its tax attributes. Second, since liabilities are separately stated on the balance sheet, the adjustment to the capital account is *net* of any liabilities on the property. This is also consistent with the notion that the balance of a capital account should represent the equity of the partner, after liabilities are deducted.

Operations. A partner's capital account is increased by her share of the partnership's income for the year, and is decreased by her share of the partnership's losses for the year. For this purpose,

---

2. Indeed, one might view the income statement of a partnership as a detailed explanation of the adjustments to the partners' capital accounts.

3. The basic capital accounting rules are found in § 1.704–(1)(b)(2)(iv)(b).

4. § 1.704–(1)(b)(2)(iv)(d).

the tax character of the income or loss does not matter: Tax exempt income is treated the same as ordinary income, and capital losses and passive activity losses are treated the same as ordinary business losses. Remember that the function of capital accounts is to reflect the partners' economic shares of the partnership's assets, thus the tax character of any receipt, and the deductibility of any expense, is irrelevant; if the book value of partnership assets increases or decreases for any reason other than increased or decreased liabilities, then a corresponding increase or decrease in capital *must* occur.

One important expense which will go into the computation of book income is depreciation: basic accounting principles require that the value of exhaustible assets be reduced to reflect exhaustion, wear and tear. Although the regulations require that it be computed consistently with tax depreciation, book depreciation is a concept quite independent of the cost recovery deductions to which the partners may be entitled. Each year, the amount of book depreciation reduces both the *book* value of the depreciable asset, as well as the balance in the partners' capital accounts.

Distributions.[5] A partner's capital account is decreased by the amount of money plus the fair market value of any property (net of liabilities) distributed to that partner. This is the mirror image of contributions and is treated consistently. Notice once again that the adjustment is based on *value*, not tax basis, and the adjustment is made net of liabilities. Distributions of property raise one additional complication: Any inherent gain or loss in the property distributed, even though not recognized for tax purposes, must be taken into account for book purposes. This is necessary to insure that the partners share the inherent gain or loss in the distributed property in accordance with their agreement.

To illustrate why this is necessary, suppose A and B are equal partners who each have a balance in their capital account of $500. AB plans to distribute $200 cash to A and $200 worth of stock to B, and the stock has a book value of $150. There has been $50 of appreciation in the stock that has never been reflected on the partnership's books. Nevertheless, as an economic matter, A and B are receiving equal distributions and the adjustments to their capital accounts should be the same. This is accomplished by requiring AB first to recognize and allocate between the partners the $50 of inherent gain in the stock for book purposes and then to reduce their respective capital accounts by the full amount of the distribution. In this case that would mean each partner's capital account first would be increased from $500 to $525 and then reduced by $200 to $325.

---

5. § 1.704–(1)(b)(2)(iv)(e).

Liabilities.[6] On a balance sheet, liabilities are separately stated and *not* reflected in capital accounts.[7] Therefore, no adjustments are made to capital accounts when a partnership borrows or repays a loan, and the adjustments to capital accounts for contributed and distributed property are made net of liabilities.

Illustration

The following illustration is intended to introduce you to the basic capital accounting rules. It is not intended to be comprehensive.

A and B form a partnership; each contributes $400. They will share all profits and losses equally. AB's initial balance sheet is as follows:

Assets		Liabilities & Capital	
	Book		
Cash	$800		
		Capital Accounts	
			Book
		A	$400
		B	400
			$800

Initial Transactions: The partnership immediately buys an apartment building for $1,000, paying $200 cash and giving a $800 mortgage for the balance. AB also invests some of its excess cash in stock ($150) and tax exempt bonds ($150). After these acquisitions, AB's balance sheet would look as follows:

Assets		Liabilities & Capital	
	Book		
Cash	$300		
Stock	150	Mortgage	$800
Bonds	150		
Bldg	1,000		
	$1,600	**Capital Accounts**	
			Book
		A	$400
		B	400
			$800

It should not be surprising that none of these acquisitions has any effect on the capital accounts of the partners; each partner's equity remains at $400. First, with respect to the stocks and bonds, the partnership has simply changed the composition of its assets.

---

6. § 1.704–(1)(b)(2)(iv)(c).

7. You should contrast this with the determination of outside basis, which *does* reflect each partner's share of partnership liabilities.

Second, and more importantly, note that although the gross value of AB's assets has increased by $800, this amount is precisely offset by the new mortgage.

Operations: AB depreciates the building over 20 years using the straight-line method (i.e., $50 per year). During its first year of operations, AB has dividend income of $10, tax exempt income of $15, and net rental income from the building of $35 (rents of $85 less depreciation of $50) for a total of $60 of income which A and B share equally. During the year, the stock went up in value to $200. There were no distributions. After reflecting all these transactions, AB's balance sheet would look as follows:

Assets		Liabilities & Capital	
	Book		
Cash [8]	$410		
Stock	150	Mortgage	$800
Bonds	150		
Bldg.	950		
	$1,660	**Capital Accounts**	
			Book
		A	$430
		B	430
			$860

You should note several things. First, each partner's capital account is increased by her share of income for the year, *including tax exempt income.*[9] Second, the book value of the building goes down by the amount of depreciation. Finally, even though the stock has increased in value to $200, its book value remains $150.

Year end transactions: Assume that AB engages in three additional transactions at year end. First it makes a $100 principal payment on the mortgage; second, it makes a charitable contribution of $10; and third, it distributes the stock to A and $200 cash to B.

The payment of the mortgage has no effect on the capital accounts, because it is a reduction in assets offset by a reduction in liabilities. The charitable contribution reduces the partnership's assets by $10 without a corresponding decrease in liabilities. In effect, the partnership has made a charitable contribution on behalf of the partners; it is economically equivalent to a distribution by the partnership to the partners, followed by a charitable contribu-

---

8. AB's cash increased by $110 during year one: $25 from the dividends and the tax exempt interest, and $85 from the building rents. Depreciation is a non-cash expense, so that it reduces in- come, but not cash. Depreciation is reflected on the balance sheet by reducing the book value of the building to $950.

9. § 1.704–(1)(b)(2)(iv)(b)(3).

tion by the partners themselves. Therefore the balances in A's and B's capital accounts must be reduced to reflect the expense.[10]

The distribution is more complicated. AB must first recognize the $50 of appreciation in the stock for *book* (not tax) purposes and allocate it equally between A and B.[11] Then AB must reduce the partners' capital accounts to reflect the distribution of the cash and stock. These adjustments will be made as follows:

	A	B
Opening Balance	$430	$430
Charitable contribution	(5)	(5)
Book gain on stock	25	25
Distribution	(200)	(200)
Closing Balance	$250	$250

After these transactions, AB's balance sheet would look as follows:

Assets		Liabilities & Capital	
	Book		
Cash	$100	Mortgage	$700
Bonds	150		
Bldg	950		
	$1,200	**Capital Accounts**	
			Book
		A	$250
		B	250
			$500

Introduction to Tax Capital Accounts: Contributions and Revaluations

Now that you feel comfortable with the basic partnership accounting rules, we must introduce a complication: tax capital. As discussed above, the partners' book capital accounts reflect the manner in which they share partnership equity, i.e., how much each would receive were the partnership to sell its assets at book value, pay off its creditors, and distribute the balance to the partners. Those accounts do not provide any information regarding the partners' shares of tax attributes of the partnership, specifically inside basis. Often the partners' shares of inside basis will be consistent with their shares of book capital. Yet there are two common circumstances in which this will not be true. The first occurs when property is contributed to a partnership and is reflected on the partnership's books at a value that differs from its

---

10. § 1.704–1(b)(2)(iv)(b)(6). This adjustment is necessary for the same reasons discussed in *Chapter Three* for

requiring a basis adjustment for the payment.

11. § 1.704–1(b)(2)(iv)(e)(1).

basis. The second occurs when the partnership revalues its assets from historical cost to current fair market value; again the book values of the assets will differ from their tax bases. For reasons that will be discussed briefly below and in detail in *Chapter Seven*, in these circumstances it is important to be able to identify how the partners share inside basis. Tax capital accounts provide that information.

Contributions

We have already discussed the capital accounting rules for contributions of property, which require contributed property to be reflected at its fair market value at the time of contribution, regardless of its basis. Therefore, if C and D form an equal partnership to which C contributes land with a value of $150 and a basis of $100, and D contributes cash of $150, the partnership's opening balance sheet is as follows:

Assets		*Liabilities & Capital*	
	Book		
Cash	$150		
Land	150		
	$300	*Capital Accounts*	
			Book
		C	$150
		D	150
			$300

C's initial balance in her capital account is $150, the fair market value of the land. D's initial balance in her capital account is $150, the cash contributed.

Now let's re-create the CD opening balance sheet, adding some additional information which relates to tax, not book, accounting. Note that when C contributed the land, C's book capital account was credited with a contribution of $150, the full fair market value of the land. But we know that for tax purposes the partnership will inherit C's basis in the land, $100, under § 723. So although C's contribution to the partnership's book capital is the full $150, it could be said that C's contribution to the partnership's inside *tax* basis is only $100. This is also the amount that C is given credit for in determining her outside basis under § 722 as a result of the contribution of the land. If we add to the balance sheet this tax information, we can learn even more about the partnership: we will add to the asset side a column for tax basis, and to the capital accounts a column which is referred to as "tax capital" to which we will credit the partnership's basis inherited from C and D under § 723. Our revised balance sheet is as follows:

	Assets		**Liabilities & Capital**
	Basis	Book	
Cash	$150	$150	Liabilities = None
Land	100	150	
	$250	$300	

Capital Accounts

	Tax	Book
C	$100	$150
D	150	150
	$250	$300

By examining this revised balance sheet we can observe two important relationships that generally hold true in the absence of liabilities. First, the total balance in the partners' tax capital accounts equals the partnership's inside basis. In essence, the balance in each partner's tax capital account is that partner's "share" of inside basis, i.e., the contribution that she has made to inside basis.[12] Second, each partner's tax capital account equals her outside basis. As we shall see in *Chapter Eight*, the existence of liabilities complicates these relationships because liabilities are reflected in the partnership's inside basis and in the partners' outside bases, but *not* in the partners' tax capital accounts.[13]

You are undoubtedly asking why it is necessary to complicate the balance sheet with this information. Compare C's contribution of the land to D's contribution of cash. D's contribution was treated consistently for book and tax purposes: The cash is carried on the partnership's book and tax accounts at $150; D's outside basis, share of inside basis and the balance in her capital account are all $150. Thus, D's tax and book capital accounts are equal.

Now consider C's contribution of the land. The land is carried on the partnership's books at $150, and C's book capital account is credited with $150 by virtue of the contribution, yet for tax purposes the land has a basis of $100. If the partnership sells the land for its fair market value of $150, it will have a taxable gain of $50, and a corresponding increase in its inside basis. Who should report

12. The concept of tax capital had been embedded in the regulations since the 1980's without being defined. In 1999, Treasury issued regulations defining "previously taxed capital," a new term which is used to determine a particular partner's share of inside basis. § 1.743-1(d). A partner's share of previously taxed capital in most cases is simply the balance in her tax capital account. This term is discussed in detail in *Chapter Ten*.

13. For example, if the partnership borrowed $100, this amount would increase CD's inside basis by $100, and increase C's and D's outside basis by $50 apiece, but would have no effect whatsoever on the partners' tax capital accounts. It would of course increase the partnership's liabilities by $100. Thus, when liabilities are present, inside basis generally equals tax capital plus liabilities.

that gain for tax purposes, or put another way, who should get credit for that increase in inside basis?

As you will learn in *Chapter Seven*, § 704(c) requires the partnership to allocate the $50 gain to C, but you should also be able to see why that must be true by looking at the balance sheet: there is a disparity between C's tax and book capital accounts because C contributed land with a basis different from its value; put another way, at the time of contribution C recognized the $50 gain in the property for book purposes, but the tax gain was deferred because of § 721. Elimination of the book/tax disparity is necessary to avoid shifting some of C's $50 built-in gain to D. The easiest way to eliminate that disparity is to tax C on the full $50 gain from sale of the land. Because there is tax gain of $50, but no book gain (the land was sold for its book value), taxing C on the gain will raise her tax capital account to $150, now equal to her book capital account. Lest the point still be unclear consider this general proposition: **We maintain tax capital accounts because tax/book disparities highlight and help keep track of § 704(c) allocation problems.**

Revaluations

The contribution of property is not the only transaction that can result in the partners' having disparate shares of inside basis. As we discussed at the beginning of this chapter, assets are normally reflected on a partnership's balance sheet at historical cost, rather than fair market value. Nevertheless, contributed property is "booked" at fair market value, rather than the contributing partner's cost; effectively the property is revalued at the time of the contribution, even though no tax gain or loss results because of § 721. The partnership capital accounting rules describe other circumstances when a partnership may revalue its existing assets, or "book-up" (or down) the assets to their current fair market value.[14] These circumstances generally are limited to those transactions in which the partners have significant non-tax reasons for determining the values of their assets, and the partners have adverse interests.[15] Thus, revaluations are permitted when a new or existing partner contributes money or property to a partnership as consideration for an interest in the partnership, and when money or property is distributed to a partner in liquidation of all or a part of his interest.[16] In both cases, the partners will have independent

---

14. § 1.704–(1)(b)(2)(iv)(f).

15. Revaluations are also permitted under certain circumstances if substantially all the partnership's property is readily tradeable on established markets. § 1.704–(1)(b)(2)(iv)(f)(5)(iii).

16. Another event which one might expect would permit revaluation is the sale by one partner of his interest in the partnership. Yet, presumably because of the lack of adverse interest between the partnership and the purchasing partner,

reasons to want an accurate valuation of all of the partnership's assets.[17]

If a partnership revalues its assets, the partnership recognizes for book, but not tax, purposes any inherent gain or loss in its assets. These gains and losses must be allocated among the partners *as if* the partnership had sold the assets for fair market value. To illustrate, assume that several years ago E and F formed an equal partnership. On January 1 of the current year, the partnership holds cash of $50, equipment with a basis of $50 and a fair market value of $210, and land with a basis of $100 and a value of $140. EF's balance sheet looks as follows:

Assets		*Liabilities & Capital*	
	Book		
Cash	$50		
Equipment	50		
Land	100		
	$200	*Capital Accounts*	
			Book
		E	$100
		F	100
			$200

On January 1, G contributes $200 cash and becomes a full one-third partner in all income, gains and losses of the partnership, and the partnership elects to book up its assets under § 1.704–1(b)(2)(iv)(f). Therefore, the partnership must recognize for book purposes the $160 book gain in the equipment, and the $40 book gain in the land. According to the partnership agreement, these gains are allocated equally between E and F, increasing the balance in their capital accounts by $100 each. Thus far into the process, the balance sheet would appear like this:

Assets			*Liabilities & Capital*	
	Basis	*Book*		
Cash	$250	$250		
Equipment	50	210		
Land	100	140		
	$400	$600	*Capital Accounts*	
				Book
			E	$200
			F	200
			G	200
				$600

the regulations do not permit a revaluation in such event.

17. For example, if a entering partner contributes $50 for a 1/3 interest in a partnership, presumably the value of the partnership assets before the contribution is $100.

This balance sheet does not, however, provide us with all of the information we need. If the partnership sells the land for its current fair market value, it will incur a $40 tax gain, but no book gain. As you will learn in *Chapter Seven*, the regulations require that the § 704(c) principles described briefly above govern to tax E and F on that tax gain, because the book gain was allocated to them at the time of the revaluation. Therefore, just as we did above, we can add a tax capital column to the balance sheet which will indicate how the partners should share in the partnership's inside basis. Therefore, after the revaluation, the partnership's completed balance sheet is as follows:

Assets

	Basis	Book
Cash	$250	$250
Equipment	50	210
Land	100	140
	$400	$600

Liabilities & Capital

Capital Accounts

	Tax	Book
E	$100	$200
F	100	200
G	200	200
	$400	$600

As you will see in *Chapter Seven*, a "reverse § 704(c)" allocation problem is created when a partnership revalues its assets in connection with a contribution or distribution. Tax capital accounts are helpful in these situations as well. So we will expand the general proposition offered above to state: **We maintain tax capital accounts because tax/book disparities highlight and help keep track of § 704(c) and "reverse § 704(c)" allocation problems.**

Our concern here is limited to setting up tax and book accounts. The rules for using those accounts to solve § 704(c) and § 704(c) type problems are discussed in detail in *Chapter Seven*.

Chapter Five

PARTNERSHIP ALLOCATIONS: SUBSTANTIAL ECONOMIC EFFECT

Background

As noted in the preceding chapters, Subchapter K taxes a partnership's items of income and loss on an aggregate basis to its member partners. We have seen that in order to accomplish this, the partnership itself is treated as an entity for purposes of calculating the income, gains and losses of the partnership business enterprise. In fact, the role of the partnership for tax purposes might best be viewed as an accounting one; the rules discussed in *Chapter Three* require calculation of partnership level income, but do not dictate to whom it will be taxed. Because it is the partners, and not the partnership, who must report the income for tax purposes, the obvious critical question still left unanswered is how the partnership's income and loss will be divided among the various partners.

Consistent with Subchapter K's stated goal of treating partnership operations flexibly, the general rule regarding the division of partnership taxable income and loss in § 704(a) states: "A partner's distributive share of income, gain, loss, deduction or credit shall, except as otherwise provided in this chapter, be determined by the partnership agreement." Thus, absent some overriding rule, the partners are permitted to agree among themselves as to how the partnership taxable income and loss will be allocated. Nevertheless, this flexibility is not without limitation; Subchapter K was not intended to permit taxpayers to circumvent general principles prohibiting tax avoidance and assignment of income and losses.

The factors which partners may take into account while striking their deal with regard to the sharing of profits and losses are many. In the simplest case of a two person partnership in which the partners contribute equally to the capital and management of the enterprise, chances are the partners will share taxable income, deductions and losses equally as well. Yet there might be some reason why the partners might agree to an unequal sharing of some partnership item. For example, in a law partnership, the partners might agree that their shares of profits will depend, in part, on the number of clients brought to the firm each year. Perhaps one of the partners guarantees a partnership nonrecourse liability for which she receives a larger share of partnership profits. Perhaps one of the partners acts as the managing partner for which she receives additional compensation. However the partners agree to divide the economic profits of the enterprise, it is appropriate (and, as we shall see, necessary) that the corresponding *taxable* income be divided similarly, in order to avoid the shifting of income (or loss) from one partner to another. As a general proposition, § 704(a) of the Code provides that the partners' agreement regarding allocation of partnership income and deductions, including "special allocations" (i.e., those which deviate from the partners' proportionate interests in capital), will be respected.

There might be other reasons that the partners would choose to specially allocate some item of partnership income or loss which, unlike the reasons described above, are grounded solely in the desire to reduce income tax. For example, suppose one of the partners in our two person partnership is a corporation with substantial net operating losses which will expire in three years. To take advantage of this NOL, the partners agree to allocate 90% of the partnership's taxable income to the corporation for the next three years, and then to allocate 90% of its taxable income to the noncorporate partner for the following three years. The obvious consequence of these special allocations is to reduce the aggregate tax liability of the partners by utilizing the expiring NOL. Will these allocations be respected? The answer is maybe, and the result will depend on whether or not these allocations are significant independent of the tax savings. The framework for analysis is found in § 704(b), which overrides § 704(a) and permits the IRS to reallocate the partnership income and loss in accordance with the "partners' interests in the partnership" if it determines that the partners' agreed method of sharing these items lacks "substantial economic effect."

"Substantial Economic Effect"

The determination of whether a particular allocation has substantial economic effect (which we will frequently refer to by the acronym of "SEE") is made under some of the most detailed and complex regulations ever promulgated under the Internal Revenue Code. Due to their extraordinary complexity, it is very easy for the neophyte to get lost in the trees and lose sight of the forest. For this reason, it is helpful to be familiar with how the phrase has evolved.

The phrase "substantial economic effect" first appeared in the Senate Finance Committee report accompanying the 1954 Code. Subchapter K of the newly enacted Code was designed to give partners flexibility in allocating items of income, loss and deduction among themselves. As originally proposed (and subsequently enacted) in 1954, § 704(b) provided that the partners' agreement as to allocation of these items was to be respected for tax purposes, unless "the principal purpose" of an allocation was tax avoidance or evasion. If tax avoidance was the principal purpose (or if the partnership agreement made no allocation), each partner's distributive share of each item would be determined in accordance with her interest in the partnership. To allay fears that the IRS would assert that the principal purpose of every special allocation that reduced taxes was tax avoidance, the Senate Finance Committee report states that if a special allocation " ... has substantial economic effect and is not merely a device for reducing the taxes of certain partners without actually affecting their shares of partnership income, then [the allocation] will be respected for tax purposes."[1]

Treasury adopted the phrase "substantial economic effect" in its regulations interpreting the original version of § 704(b). Those regulations based the determination of whether an allocation had tax avoidance as its principal purpose on all of the facts and circumstances, including, most significantly "... whether the allocation has 'substantial economic effect,' that is, whether the allocation may actually affect the dollar amount of the partners' shares of the total partnership income or loss independently of tax consequences...."[2] Although under the regulations the presence of SEE technically was neither necessary nor sufficient to prove lack of tax avoidance, courts applying the regulations latched on to the concept and as a practical matter this factor became the touchstone for the determination.

As we already know, the capital accounts of a partnership typically reflect the equity that each partner has in the venture: the balance in each partner's capital account is the amount that she would be entitled to if the partnership were to sell all of its assets for their book value, pay off all its liabilities and liquidate. For this reason, the courts found it useful to analyze the capital accounts of a partnership to determine if a particular allocation was meaningful

1. S. Rep. No. 1622, 83d Cong., 2d Sess., 379 (1954).   **2.** § 1.704–1(b)(2)(superceded).

apart from its tax consequences. If the allocations were not reflected in the capital accounts, they lacked independent significance, and hence could not have "substantial economic effect."

The Significance of Capital Accounts: The Orrisch Case

An excellent illustration of how the early regulations were applied as well as the emerging importance of capital accounts is *Orrisch v. Commissioner.*[3] Orrisch was a partner in the O–C Partnership. For the years at issue, Orrisch had large amounts of taxable income from other activities, while his partner, Crisafi, had none. The partners agreed to divide all items of income, loss and deduction equally *except* depreciation, which was allocated entirely to Orrisch. This special allocation clearly resulted in significant tax savings for Orrisch, but he nevertheless argued the allocation must be respected because it was reflected in the capital accounts. After analyzing the capital accounts of the partnership, however, the Tax Court disagreed.

To evaluate the court's analysis, let us make an heroic simplification of the facts. Assume that Orrisch and Crisafi each contributed $500 to the O–C partnership which used the $1,000 to acquire a building. Assume further that, aside from depreciation, each year the O–C partnership broke even and had a zero cash flow. Finally assume that the partnership had $200 in depreciation, all of which was allocated to Orrisch.

Upon formation, each partner would have had a capital account of $500. At the end of the first year's operations, after adjusting for the depreciation, O–C's basis in the building would be $800 and Orrisch's capital account would have been reduced to $300. Crisafi's capital account would have stayed at $500.

In its analysis, the Court considered two possible outcomes to see if either might affect the dollar amounts ultimately received by either partner. The court first considered what would happen if the partnership sold the building for more than its original purchase price. In this case, since the partnership agreement contained a "gain charge-back provision," the partners would end up economically in precisely the same position they would have been in the absence of the special allocation of the depreciation.[4]

---

3. 55 T.C. 395 (1970).

4. This is easy to demonstrate. Under a gain chargeback provision, all partnership gain attributable to depreciation taken is allocated to the partner who was allocated the depreciation. Therefore, on our simplified facts, if the partnership were to sell the property for $1,000 or more, the first $200 of taxable gain would be entirely allocated to Orrisch, while any additional gain would be split equally. In such a case, the special allocation of depreciation will always be offset by the gain and the balance in the partners' capital accounts will always be precisely the same as they would have been in the absence of the allocation.

The court then examined what would happen if the building declined in value and was sold for less than its original purchase price. Stated somewhat differently, the court sought to determine who was bearing the burden of the theoretical decline in value represented by the depreciation on the building. Orrisch insisted that he was bearing the burden as evidenced by the partnership's capital accounts:

	Orrisch	Crisafi
Original contribution	$500	$500
Depreciation	(200)	0
	$300	$500

According to these capital accounts, if the partnership sold the building for $800 and liquidated, Crisafi would receive $500 and Orrisch only $300. Orrisch insisted that this proved that he was bearing the burden of depreciation on the building and the special allocation could indeed affect the dollar amounts that the partners might eventually receive.

The court would have undoubtedly agreed with Orrisch except for one small matter: based on the evidence at trial, the court concluded that in the above scenario the partners had no intention of distributing liquidation proceeds per the capital accounts, but instead intended that all distributions should be made equally. Testimony indicated that the partners viewed the capital account entries as "mere paper entries,"[5] and that their actual agreement was that all distributions would be equal. In other words, the capital accounts were meaningless. For this reason, the court held

To illustrate, suppose O–C sold the building for $1,100 and then liquidated. In the absence of the special allocation, each partner would be entitled to $550. This would have been reflected in their capital accounts as follows.

	Orrisch	Crisafi
Original contribution	$500	$500
Depreciation	(100)	(100)
Gain	150	150
	$550	$550

In the alternative, if the special allocation of depreciation and the gain chargeback provision of the agreement were followed, the adjustments to the capital accounts would be different, although the ending balances in the accounts would be identical with those reached above. As a result of the special allocation of depreciation, Orrisch's capital account would be $300 at the time of the sale. Of the $300 gain on the sale, the first $200 would be allocated to Orrisch

while the remaining $100 would be split $50 each. The partners' capital accounts would be adjusted as follows:

	Orrisch	Crisafi
Original contribution	$500	$500
Depreciation	(200)	0
Gain	250	50
	$550	$550

Based on the above analysis, the court recognized that in all cases where the building was sold for more than its original purchase price, the sole effect of the special allocation would be to reduce Orrisch's tax liability without any correlative reduction in his economic benefit from the partnership operations.

5. As evidence of this, the court noted that Orrisch's counsel distinguished between capital account entries relating to cash and those "paper entries relating to depreciation." *Orrisch* at 404, n.8.

that the allocations of depreciation to Orrisch lacked substantial economic effect. Consequently, it determined that the depreciation should be shared consistently with the partners' general profit and loss sharing ratio, i.e. fifty-fifty.

Codification of Substantial Economic Effect

As a result of cases such as *Orrisch*, the importance of capital account analysis in identifying whether allocations have SEE became apparent. In 1976, § 704(b) was amended by codifying the phrase "substantial economic effect." The 1976 amendment makes clear that § 704(b) governs the special allocation of "bottom line" income and loss allocations (i.e., those under § 702(a)(8)), as well as allocations of specific items. It also makes clear that a special allocation cannot be respected unless it has substantial economic effect; despite the language of the original regulations treating SEE as one of several factors to consider, there is now no other alternative.

In 1985, Treasury promulgated new regulations under § 704(b). Although the regulations are basically consistent with prior case law interpretations of SEE, they are extremely detailed, and hence require an analysis much more complicated than under earlier law, and to the neophyte, more painful. Nevertheless, except for that portion dealing with nonrecourse debt, these regulations have precisely the same underlying rationale as earlier law: A special allocation will be respected for tax purposes as long as it reflects the economics of the partners' deal. If it is merely a device to reduce the aggregate taxes of the partners, the allocation will not be respected and the item will be reallocated in a manner that does reflect the true economics of the partners' deal.

The § 704(b) Regulations

In General—Structure

It is important to note at the outset that § 704(b) is not the only provision of Subchapter K that governs allocations. For example, as we will see in *Chapter Seven*, the allocation of gain or loss inherent in contributed property is governed by § 704(c), which essentially requires that it be allocated to the contributing partner. Other sections that may impact upon allocations include § 706(c) and § 704(e).[6] Nevertheless, § 704(b) governs the vast majority of partnership allocations, and is at the heart of Subchapter K.

The regulations under § 704(b) are comprised of four distinct parts:

6. Section 704(e) is discussed at the end of this chapter.

(i) The first part, found in § 1.704–1(b)(2), defines SEE and establishes the safe harbor. Normally, if an allocation has SEE, it will be respected; if it does not, the item will be reallocated in accordance with the partners' economic interests, i.e., in accordance with each "partner's interest in the partnership."[7]

(ii) The second part describes what is meant by the term "partners' interests in the partnership." This section, § 1.704–1(b)(3), establishes the default rules for allocations which fail to meet the safe harbor.

(iii) The third part contains certain special rules to deal with specific situations where the concept of SEE is inapplicable for reasons discussed below. The most important of these rules concern nonrecourse liabilities (§ 1.704–2) and revaluations of partnership assets in connection with certain partnership transactions (§ 1.704–1(b)(4)).

(iv) Finally, the fourth part consists of very useful examples illustrating the application of the rules set forth in the first three parts. These are found in § 1.704–1(b)(5) and § 1.704–2(m).

Under the § 704(b) regulations, there are three different ways in which a particular allocation can be sustained. First, the allocation will be sustained if the allocation satisfies the definition of SEE in § 1.704–1(b)(2). The regulations use the term SEE to create a safe harbor; that is, as long as each and every specific requirement of the safe harbor rule is met, the partnership can be assured that its allocations will be respected. Many partnerships choose to comply with the safe harbor to obtain the benefit of this certainty. Second, an allocation that does not have SEE (within the meaning of the regulations' safe harbor) may still be sustained if it is in accordance with the partners' interests in the partnership as described in § 1.704–1(b)(3). Finally, allocations governed by the special rules of § 1.704–1(b)(4) (revaluations) and § 1.704–2 (nonrecourse deductions) cannot have SEE within the meaning of the regulations. Nevertheless, they will be "deemed" to be in accordance with the partners' interests in the partnership, and therefore will be valid, if the special rules are followed. These special rules are discussed in later chapters.[8]

Substantial Economic Effect

In General

The phrase "SEE" has quite a different technical meaning under the current regulations than it did under prior law. Under

---

7. § 1.704–1(b)(1)(i).

8. The special rules relating to revaluations are discussed in *Chapter Seven* and those relating to nonrecourse deductions in *Chapter Six*.

prior law, finding that an allocation did not have SEE was tantamount to holding that the allocation was not consistent with the underlying economics of the partnership deal and therefore would not be respected for tax purposes. In such a case, the item would be reallocated among the partners in accordance with their interests in the partnership. This is not true under the current regulations. A finding that an allocation lacks SEE under the current regulations means *only* that the partnership is outside the safe harbor. It may still be true that the allocation is consistent with the partner's interest in the partnership, and no reallocation is required. Thus, allocations which would have substantial economic effect under the pre–1985 regulations might fail the safe harbor under the current rules, yet they would still be respected as being in accord with the partners' interests in the partnership.

The test for whether a given allocation has SEE (and is therefore within the safe harbor) is bifurcated into two separate tests, both of which must be met. The first test is quite mechanical and determines whether the allocation has "economic effect."[9] Generally speaking, an allocation will have economic effect if the partnership keeps meaningful capital accounts and maintains them in accordance with a strict set of rules.[10] The second test is whether the economic effect of an allocation is "substantial."[11] This test is necessarily more subjective. In general, for an allocation to be substantial, there must be a reasonable possibility that the allocation will affect substantially the dollar amounts received by partners *independent* of tax considerations.

If the partnership fails the safe harbor, the allocation lacks SEE and it must be tested to see if it is consistent with the partners' interests in the partnership (i.e., under part two of the regulations). If it is not, then it will be reallocated in accordance with those interests.[12]

Economic Effect

The fundamental principle underlying the concept of economic effect in the regulations is as follows:

> "In order for an allocation to have economic effect, it must be consistent with the underlying economic arrangement of the partners. This means that in the event there is an economic benefit or economic burden that corresponds to an allocation, the partner to whom the allocation is made must receive such economic benefit or economic burden."[13]

---

9. § 1.704–1(b)(2)(ii).

10. § 1.704–1(b)(2)(iv). These rules are discussed extensively in *Chapter Four*.

11. § 1.704–1(b)(2)(iii).

12. § 1.704–1(b)(3).

13. § 1.704–1(b)(2)(ii)(a).

To effectuate this principle, Treasury imposed rigorous capital accounting rules on partnerships to ensure that the economic benefit or burden follows the allocation. Although these rules are at times quite complex and at other times arbitrary, their general purpose is quite clear: To have economic effect, the partnership's capital accounts must be meaningful and kept in accordance with a strict set of uniform rules with which the Service's personnel are familiar.

Three alternative tests determine whether a given allocation has economic effect. The first two, the Basic Test and the Alternate Test, are both quite important and are dealt with extensively. The third, "Economic Effect Equivalence Test," is of limited significance and is dealt with summarily.

Basic Test for Economic Effect

Under the Basic Test, which is found at Reg. § 1.704–1(b)(2)(ii)(b), an allocation will have economic effect only if the partnership agreement meets the following three requirements:[14]

1. *Capital Account Requirement.* The partnership must maintain its capital accounts in accordance with the rules found in § 1.704–1(b)(2)(iv), which are discussed in *Chapter Four.*[15]

2. *Liquidation Requirement.* Upon liquidation, liquidating distributions must be made in accordance with the positive balances in the partners' capital accounts.[16]

3. *Deficit Makeup Requirement.* If after liquidation any partner has a deficit in her capital account, she must be unconditionally obligated to restore that deficit.[17]

As long as a partnership fulfills all three requirements, both the Service and the courts can be assured that the partnership's allocations of income, loss or deduction for tax purposes will be consistent with the economic benefits and burdens corresponding to those items.

While the first two requirements are quite straightforward, the deficit makeup requirement deserves some additional examination. This requirement can be satisfied by a clause in the partnership agreement or an unconditional obligation imposed under state or local law. As long as a partner has an unconditional obligation to restore a deficit in her capital account, allocations of losses and deductions will be considered to have economic effect even though they create or increase a deficit in her capital account. Since the partner must at some point contribute sufficient capital to elimi-

---

14. These requirements must be met throughout the entire term of the partnership.

15. § 1.704–1(b)(2)(ii)(b)(1).

16. § 1.704–1(b)(2)(ii)(b)(2).

17. § 1.704–1(b)(2)(ii)(b)(3).

nate any deficit, she is in a very real way bearing the burden of these losses or deductions. This would not be true in the absence of the deficit makeup rule, or one similar in effect.

To develop this more fully, consider the following examples. Assume throughout this section that the allocations described would satisfy the substantiality requirement.

Example #1: G and L form a general partnership to which each contributes $70. The partnership agreement satisfies all three requirements of the Basic Test, allocates all partnership losses 80% to L and 20% to G, and allocates all income and gains 50% to L and 50% to G. The partnership loses $50 in each of its first two years of operations. After the second year, GL's balance sheet is as follows:

	Assets	*Liabilities & Capital Accounts*
	Book	
Assets	$40	*Liabilities:* None

		Capital Accounts	
		G	*L*
		$70	$70
	1st year loss	(10)	(40)
	2nd year loss	(10)	(40)
		$50	($10)

Since all three of the requirements of the Basic Test are met, the loss allocations have economic effect and will be respected. Note that the capital accounts accurately reflect how the partners are sharing the economic burden of the $100 loss that the partnership has experienced. This can be demonstrated by considering what would happen if the partnership sold all of its assets for their book value and liquidated. On liquidation, L would be required to make up the deficit in her capital account by contributing $10 to GL. Together with the $40 from the sale of the assets, G would have the $50 necessary to distribute to G an amount equal to G's balance in her capital account. Therefore, L would have lost $80 on the venture and G $20. These are precisely the amounts of the losses that were allocated to the partners.

Example #2: Assume the same facts in *Example #1* except that GL is a limited partnership in which G is the general partner and L is the limited partner. The partnership agreement provides for the first two requirements of the Basic Test, but not the third. Consistent with her status as a limited partner, L has no obligation to contribute any additional capital to the partnership and has no obligation to restore any deficit in her capital account.

Note that if the allocations for both years were respected in this variation, GL's balance sheet at the end of Year 2 would be precisely the same as in ***Example #1***, but the capital accounts would not reflect the manner in which the economic burden of the losses is being shared. If the partnership were to sell its assets for book value and liquidate, the partnership would have only $40 to distribute to G, even though the balance in her capital account would be $50. This means that G has borne the economic burden of $10 of the $80 loss that was allocated to L. This is precisely the result that the economic effect rules were designed to prevent. Because the partnership agreement does not have an unlimited deficit makeup obligation, none of GL's allocations will have economic effect. GL's losses for ***both*** years must be allocated in accordance with the partners' interests in the partnership or "PIP," discussed below.[18]

Alternate Test for Economic Effect

The principal reason that most limited partnerships are formed is to limit the financial exposure of its limited partners. An unlimited deficit makeup obligation is antithetical to this goal. For this reason, allocations made to limited partners would never have economic effect under the Basic Test. In recognition of this reality, Treasury created an "Alternate Test for Economic Effect." Under the Alternate Test, an allocation is considered to have economic effect as long as:

(1) the partnership agreement satisfies the first two requirements of the Basic Test (i.e., the capital account and liquidation requirements),

(2) the agreement contains a "qualified income offset" ("QIO") provision, and

(3) the allocation does not create (or increase) a deficit in a partner's capital account in excess of the partner's obligation to restore a deficit.[19]

The Alternate Test is based on the premise that as long as the first two requirements of the Basic Test are met, even in the absence of an unlimited deficit makeup provision, one can still *generally* rely on an allocation having economic effect so long as it does not create a deficit in a partner's capital account that she is not obligated to restore. Although these rules prohibit an allocation that creates such a deficit in a partner's capital account, they contemplate that such a deficit might be created by other events, such as an unexpected distribution. This is where the "qualified

18. As we will see, the PIP rules contain a special rule that will apply in this case.

19. § 1.704–1(b)(2)(ii)(d).

income offset", or "QIO", comes into play. The QIO provision protects the integrity of the prior allocations and the partnership's capital accounts by requiring the partnership to eliminate such an unexpected deficit as quickly as possible through income allocations. To illustrate how the Alternate Test works, consider the following:

> *Example #3*: Same as *Example #2*, except that the partnership agreement provides for a "qualified income offset" provision, or "QIO." As of the end of the second year, GL does not anticipate making any distributions.

In this example, the allocations of the losses are considered to have economic effect under the Alternate Test as long as the allocation does not reduce L's capital account below her deficit makeup obligation, which in this case is zero.[20] Therefore, the entire first year's loss allocation will be respected, reducing L's balance in her capital account to $30. Only a portion of the second year's allocation will have economic effect: Since L's balance in her capital account is now only $30, no more than $30 of the second year's loss can be allocated to her. As discussed more fully below, under the PIP rules, the balance of the loss must be allocated to the partner(s) who are bearing the burden of the loss. In this case, since L's capital account has already been reduced to zero and L does not have a deficit makeup obligation, the remaining $20 must be allocated to G.[21] The adjustments to the partners' capital accounts would be as follows:

	G	**L**
	$70	$70
1st year loss	(10)	(40)
Balance as of 1/1/2	$60	$30
2nd year loss	(20)	(30)
	$40	$0

Note that these capital accounts are meaningful and reflect the way that G and L are bearing the burden of the losses: If GL were to sell its assets for book value and liquidate after the second year, G would receive a distribution of $40 and L would receive nothing.

You may wonder why a separate "alternate test" was necessary, when Treasury might have incorporated the concept of a limited deficit make-up provision into the Basic Test. As written, the Basic Test isn't satisfied absent an unlimited deficit make-up provision. Treasury considered and rejected the idea of having in

20. Note that there are no adjustments required in this case because GL has no plans to make a distribution.

21. As a technical matter, $37.50 of the second year's loss has economic effect and would be allocated $30 to L and $7.50 to G.

the Basic Test a rule that would have simply permitted allocations to have economic effect *to the extent* that there was an obligation to restore deficits. The problem with this approach is that events *other than* loss allocations cause reductions in capital accounts, most notably partnership distributions. If the Basic Test permitted loss allocations to create deficits only up to the amount of the restoration obligation, and a partnership then made a distribution, planned or unplanned, that increased the deficit balance in a partner's capital account in excess of the amount of her deficit make-up obligation, the capital accounts would be rendered meaningless. The partner would have a negative balance in her capital account beyond that which she was required to restore.

To illustrate the problem and Treasury's solution, consider the following example:

> **Example #4:** Same facts as in **Example #3**. In Year 3, the partnership breaks even. In addition, the partnership borrows $20 on a recourse basis and distributes $10 to each partner. Its balance sheet at the end of Year 3 is as follows:

Assets		*Liabilities & Capital Accounts*	
	Book		
Assets	$40	*Liabilities:* $20	
		Capital Accounts	
		G	*L*
		$70	$70
1st year loss		(10)	(40)
2nd year loss		(20)	(30)
		$40	($0)
3rd year distr.		(10)	(10)
		$30	($10)

The $10 distribution in Year 3 reduces L's capital account below zero even though L does not have a deficit makeup obligation. This undermines the validity of the capital accounts: If GL were now to liquidate by selling all of its assets for $40 and paying its liability, it would only have $20 to distribute to G. In effect, the burden of $10 of the previously allocated loss deductions has been shifted from L to G.

Treasury addressed this possibility with two rules, one for those future events that the partnership reasonably anticipates might reduce the balance of a partner's capital account below the partner's deficit makeup obligation, and a second for those events that are not anticipated but actually do reduce the balance in the capital account below that obligation.

Under the Alternative Test, an allocation has economic effect as long as it does create or increase the deficit in a partner's capital account in excess of the partner's deficit makeup obligation, *as adjusted*. It is through these adjustments that Treasury takes into account those events that are reasonably expected to reduce a partner's capital account. There are three adjustments required, the most important of which is that the deficit makeup obligation must be reduced by any future distributions that are reasonably expected to be made to that partner in excess of any reasonably expected offsetting allocations (e.g., income allocations).[22] These latter allocations are only taken into account to the extent they are expected to occur during or prior to the year of the expected distribution.[23]

To illustrate, reconsider *Example #4*. Suppose that the end of Year 2, GL expected to break even in Year 3, and also expected to borrow $20 and distribute $10 to each of its partners. If this were the case, then L's deficit makeup obligation, *as adjusted*, would have to take into account the anticipated $10 distribution. Since GL expects to break even for the year, an allocation to L will not have economic effect to the extent that it reduces the balance in L's capital account below a positive balance of $10. Therefore, on these facts, the maximum amount of the second year's loss that could be allocated to L and have economic effect under the Alternative Test is $20; under PIP, the balance must be allocated to G. At the end of Year 2, the partners' capital accounts would be as follows:

	G	*L*
	$70	$70
1st year's loss	(10)	(40)
Balance as of 1/1/2	$60	$30
2nd year's loss	(30)	(20)
	$30	$10

As you can see, now L has a sufficient amount in her capital account so that the anticipated distribution will not result in a deficit.

It would seem that these rules would require the partnership to have a crystal ball in order to predict what income it will have to offset distributions. Yet clearly, the partnership's expectations may not match reality. In this case, an unexpected deficit may arise, and this is when the qualified income offset, or QIO, comes into play. A QIO provision states that if a partner ends up with an unexpected deficit in her capital account in excess of the amount she is required to restore, the partnership *must* allocate items of income

---

22. The other two adjustments are for depletion allowances and certain other mandatory allocations under §§ 704(e), 706(c) and 751. § 1.704–1(b)(2)(ii).

23. § 1.704–1(b)(2)(ii)(d)(6).

and gain (including gross income) to that partner sufficient to eliminate that excess as quickly as possible.[24]

To illustrate how and when a QIO operates, once again consider another variation of *Example #4*. Suppose that at the end of Year 2, GL reasonably expected to have net income for the year of $40, of which $20 would be allocated to L. It also planned to borrow $20 and distribute $10 to each of its partners. Since the partnership reasonably expects the distribution to L to be offset by her allocation of income for the year, under the Alternate Test no adjustment is made to L's deficit makeup obligation. Therefore, in Year 2, L is allocated $30 of the partnership's loss for the year, reducing the balance in her capital account to zero. During Year 3, GL borrows $20, which it distributed to its partners as planned, but due to a downturn in the economy, the partnership does not earn the expected $40 but only breaks even, with gross income and deductible expenses of $30 each. In the absence of a QIO, the balance sheet at year end would be as follows:

	Assets	*Liabilities & Capital Accounts*	
	Book		
Assets	$40	*Liabilities:* $20	
		Capital Accounts	
		G	L
		$70	$70
1st year loss		(10)	(40)
2nd year loss		(20)	(30)
		$40	($0)
3rd year distr.		(10)	(10)
		$30	($10)

As a result of the distribution, L now has an unexpected deficit of $10 in her capital account that she has no obligation to restore. This will trigger the QIO provision, which mandates that GL specially allocate income and or gain to L as quickly as possible to eliminate the unexpected deficit. On these facts, GL would be required to specially allocate $10 of its gross income to L. This special allocation results in a bottom-line loss of $10 (i.e., $20 of remaining gross income less $30 of expenses), all of which must be allocated to G. After taking into account the QIO, GL's balance sheet would be as follows:

24. § 1.704–1(b)(2)(ii)(d)(6) (flush language).

	Assets	*Liabilities & Capital Accounts*	
	Book		
Assets	$40	**Liabilities:** $20	
		Capital Accounts	
		G	*L*
		$70	$70
1st year loss		(10)	(40)
2nd year loss		(20)	(30)
		$40	($0)
3rd year distr.		(10)	(10)
QIO			+ 10
3rd year loss		(10)	0
		$20	($0)

Economic Effect Equivalence Test

Even though a partnership may not satisfy the Basic Test or the Alternate Test, it is still possible for it to come within the safe harbor rules for economic effect if its allocations are "deemed" to have economic effect within the meaning of § 1.704–1(b)(2)(ii)(i). This last test for economic effect is designed for a general partnership that does not technically comply with the requirements of the Basic Test, but whose practices would produce the same economic results to the partners that would have been generated if they had complied with all of the requirements of the Basic Test. Allocations made by such a partnership will be "deemed" to have economic effect. It is highly unlikely that a partnership that satisfies the economic equivalence test would need to rely upon the SEE safe harbor; its allocations would seem almost by definition to be consistent with the partners' interests in the partnership. For this reason, this last test for economic effect is clearly the least significant of the three.

Reallocation based upon the Partners' Interests in the Partnership

If an allocation lacks substantial economic effect, the regulations require that the item be reallocated in accordance with the partners' interests in the partnership ("PIP").[25] In general, this means that the item will be allocated to those partners who are actually bearing the economic burden, or enjoying the economic benefit, of that item, taking into account all relevant facts and circumstances. The regulations state that among the factors to be considered are the following:[26]

(i) relative contributions;

(ii) interests in economic profits and losses (if different from taxable income and loss);

(iii) interests in cash flow and other nonliquidating distributions; and

---

25. § 1.704–1(b)(3).   **26.** § 1.704–1(b)(3)(ii).

(iv) rights to distribution on liquidation.

As you might imagine, this is a fairly open-ended inquiry that can breed uncertainty. Fortunately, the regulations provide a somewhat more concrete special rule for allocations that do not have economic effect for failure to meet the third requirement of the Basic Test, the deficit makeup requirement. Under this rule, referred to in the regulations as "certain determinations," the regulations compare the amount that each partner would receive if the partnership were liquidated at the end of the current year with what each would have received if the partnership were liquidated on the last day of the prior year.[27] In this way the regulations attempt to determine who was actually burdened by, or benefitted from, the item.[28] This special rule only applies if the allocations so determined are substantial within the meaning of § 1.704–1(b)(2)(iii).

To illustrate the special "certain determinations" rule, reconsider *Example #2*, above. Recall that in that example the partnership agreement allocated its losses 80% to L and 20% to G and the partnership had losses of $50 in each of its first two years. In that example we determined that these allocations lacked economic effect because L had no deficit makeup obligation and the partnership agreement had no QIO provision; therefore, the losses had to be reallocated in accordance with the PIP rules. As you recall, the original balance sheet was as follows:

	Assets	*Liabilities & Capital Accounts*	
	Book		
Assets	$140	*Liabilities:* None	
		Capital Accounts	
		G	L
		$70	$70

Under the PIP rules, since the partnership meets the first two requirements of the Basic Test, one can determine how the losses should be allocated under the special "certain determinations" rule. That rule provides a mechanism for determining how the partners share the economic burden of a deduction or loss incurred in the course of a year. We compare the amount that each partner would have been entitled to receive if the partnership had liquidated on the last day of the *prior* taxable year (which under our facts would be the date of formation) with the amount that each would be entitled to receive if the partnership liquidated at the end of the *current* year. As applied to our facts, if the partnership had liqui-

---

27. § 1.704–1(b)(3)(iii).

28. Of course, if there were a distribution during the year, this would have to be taken into account.

dated immediately after formation each partner would simply receive back her $70 contribution. During the first year's operations, GL incurs a $50 loss, which the partnership agreement states should be allocated $10 to G and $40 to L. If we were to respect that agreement then the allocation would reduce the partners' capital account balances to $60 and $30 respectively. The partnership's balance sheet at year end would be as follows:

Assets		**Liabilities & Capital Accounts**	
	Book	**Liabilities:** None	
Assets	$140		
1st Year loss	(50)		
	$90	**Capital Accounts**	
		G	L
		$70	$70
		(10)	(40)
		$60	$30

If the partnership were to liquidate at year end, G would be entitled to $60 and L to $30. Therefore, as an economic matter, G and L will have shared the economic burden of the first year's loss consistently with the manner in which it was allocated under the agreement ($10 by G and $40 by L), and that allocation will be respected as consistent with the partners' interests in the partnership. Note that in this case we reach the same result as we would have had the partners included a QIO agreement and satisfied the alternate test for economic effect!

The allocation of the second year's $50 loss would be determined in the same way. As demonstrated above, if GL had liquidated at the end of year one, G would have been entitled to $60 and L to $40. According to the partnership agreement, the second year's loss should also be allocated $10 to G and $40 to L. With these allocations, GL's balance sheet at the end of year 2 would be as follows:

Assets		**Liabilities & Capital Accounts**	
	Book	**Liabilities:** None	
Assets	$140		
1st Year loss	(50)	**Capital Accounts**	
	$90	G	L
2nd Year loss	(50)	$70	$70
	$40	(10)	(40)
		$60	$30
		(10)	(40)
		$50	($10)

Now consider what the parties have agreed will happen if the partnership were to liquidate at the end of year 2. According to the capital accounts, G should receive $50, and L should contribute $10. Yet L is not obligated to make that contribution, and the partnership will only have $40 available to distribute to G. That means that in fact L is only bearing the economic burden of $30 of the year 2 loss, the remaining $10 that was allocated to her is in fact suffered by G. Therefore, under PIP, the second year's $50 loss must be reallocated consistent with this economic reality: $20 to G and $30 to L. Note again that we reach precisely the same result that we would have had the partnership satisfied the alternate test.

Drafting Allocation Provisions: A Real World Perspective

The task of drafting partnership agreements that satisfy the requirements of the regulations is a daunting one. The extreme complexity of the regulations breeds long and complex contractual language, most of which is beyond the understanding of most clients and many lawyers who are not schooled in the niceties of Subchapter K. Frustration with this complexity has led many practitioners over the last decade to look for alternative ways to draft allocation provisions that focus more on the economics of the deal and less on tax items. One type of provision that has become popular calls for "targeted allocations."[29] In contrast with traditional tax allocation provisions, targeted allocations focus on those provisions in the partnership agreement dealing with cash flows (i.e., contributions and distributions), and simply state that the taxable income and loss of the partnership will be allocated among the partners as necessary to conform their capital accounts to the amounts that they would be entitled to receive if the partnership liquidated at year end. These provisions essentially leave it up to the accountants to figure out how to allocate the partnership's various items of taxable income and loss.

What is interesting about targeted allocations is that, although they are completely consistent with the economics of the business deal, it is not clear that they have "substantial economic effect" within the meaning of the safe harbor in § 1.704–1(b)(2). The technical problem is that the partnership agreement does not explicitly provide that the partnership will liquidate in accordance with the positive balances in the partners' capital accounts, but

---

29. For an excellent description of targeted allocations, see William G. Cavanagh, Targeted allocations or "Why I don't liquidate partnerships in accordance with capital accounts (much) anymore" and other real world partnership tax allocations, Tax Forum No. 615 (2009). See also Terrence Floyd Cuff, Several Thoughts on Drafting Target Allocations Provisions, 87 Taxes 171 (2009).

rather in accordance with various distribution percentages. Even if targeted allocations do not come within this safe harbor, it seems very likely that if the allocations do track the economics of the deal, they should be respected as being consistent with PIP. There are many variations of these provisions out there, and at this point they have not been blessed by the government. Nevertheless, an IRS spokesman recently was quoted as indicating that guidance on the use of such alternative allocation provisions may be forthcoming.

Substantiality

To come within the regulations' safe harbor, partnerships must do more than reflect special allocations in their capital accounts. They must be able to demonstrate that the special allocation has some effect *other than* tax savings, i.e., the economic effect of the allocation must be "substantial."[30] The role of the substantiality requirement of the safe harbor is to identify those allocations that have little significance except to reduce the government's share of the partnership operations. The regulations adopt both a pre-tax and after-tax test for substantiality. The general rule is a pre-tax test and requires that there be a "reasonable possibility that the allocation (or allocations) will affect substantially the dollar amounts received by partners *independent* of the tax consequences."[31] Under this rule, if the only effect of an allocation is to reduce taxes without substantially affecting the partners' pre-tax distributive shares, the economic effect of the allocation will not be substantial. Merely satisfying this general rule is not sufficient to establish substantiality. The regulations provide an "after-tax exception" to the general rule which focuses on the after-tax consequences to the partners.[32] Under this exception, if the after-tax effect of an allocation is to enhance the economic consequences of one or more partners without adversely affecting any other partner, the allocation will not be substantial. This exception is discussed in detail below.

In contrast with the mechanical test for determining if an allocation has economic effect, the determination of substantiality is far more subjective. The regulations, however, give some guidance by describing two common situations where an allocation will not be substantial under the general (pre-tax) rule. These two situations, "shifting tax consequences" and "transitory allocations," are very similar to one another. They both deal with situations where one or more special allocations have a negligible effect on the net adjustments to the partners' capital accounts,

30. § 1.704–1(b)(2)(iii).

31. § 1.704–1(b)(2)(iii)(a)(first sentence, emphasis added).

32. § 1.704–1(b)(2)(iii)(a)(second sentence).

while significantly reducing taxes. The rule for shifting tax consequences deals with one or more allocations that occur within a single taxable year, while the rule for transitory allocations deals with allocations that occur over two or more taxable years.

Shifting Tax Consequences[33]

An allocation lacks substantiality under the shifting tax consequences rule if the partners have allocated types of income or loss among themselves within a given year solely to reduce their total tax liability. The economic effect of such allocations is not substantial if at the time the allocations become a part of the partnership agreement there is a strong likelihood that

1.   The net effect on the capital accounts of the partners will not be significantly different from what it would be in the absence of the allocations, AND

2.   The total tax liability of all of the partners (taking into account their individual circumstances) will be less than it would be in the absence of the allocation.

At the end of the taxable year, if these two results come to pass, the regulations presume (rebuttably) that at the time the allocation was originally agreed to there was a strong likelihood that they would occur.[34]

To illustrate, consider the following two examples:

Example #5: A, who is in the 40% bracket, and B, who is in the 0% bracket, are equal general partners in a partnership that has both taxable and tax exempt income. The partnership agreement satisfies all three requirements of the Basic Test for economic effect. Although their partnership agreement calls for A and B to share all income equally, A is to be allocated all of the partnership's tax exempt income up to her 50% share of overall income. During the taxable year, the partnership has $200 of income, $110 tax exempt and $90 taxable. A is allocated $100 of the tax exempt income and B is allocated the $90 taxable and the remaining $10 of tax exempt income.

Although this allocation has economic effect, under the shifting tax consequences rule, the effect is not substantial. On these facts, there is more than a strong likelihood that the allocation 1) will not affect the net balances in the partners' capital accounts and 2) will reduce the total tax liability of the partners. Indeed, this case could not be clearer: This allocation cannot possibly affect the balances in the partners' capital accounts; in all events, each partner gets

33. § 1.704–1(b)(2)(iii)(b).   **34.** § 1.704–1(b)(2)(iii)(b)(flush language).

credited with 50% of the partnership's economic profits. For this reason, the only effect this allocation could have is to reduce the joint tax liability of the partners. Since the allocation is not substantial, both the tax exempt and taxable income must be reallocated in accordance with the partners' interests in the partnership.[35]

> *Example #6*: C and D are equal partners in the CD partnership. C is in the 40% tax bracket and has a capital loss carryover in excess of $100,000, and D is in the 20% tax bracket and has no capital losses. Capital gains are taxed at a maximum rate of 15%. The partnership agreement satisfies all three requirements of the Basic Test for economic effect. This year CD expects to recognize a $100,000 capital gain, and there is a strong likelihood that the CD partnership will have operating income well in excess of $100,000. At the beginning of the year, the partnership agreement is amended to allocate the capital gain entirely to C and an equal amount of operating income to D. Any net income in excess of this amount will be split 50:50.

Although this allocation has economic effect, under the shifting tax consequences rule the effect is not substantial. It is clear that at the time the allocation is made, there is a strong likelihood that 1) the allocation will have no effect on the balances in the partners' capital accounts, and 2) the total tax liability of C and D will be reduced.

Once again, this an easy case. As long as the net operating income of the CD partnership equals or exceeds the capital gain, the adjustments to the capital accounts of the partners will be identical to what they would have been in the absence of the allocation. The only effect of the allocation will be to reduce the partners' joint tax liability. On the assumption that CD has operating income of exactly $100,000, then in the absence of a special allocation, each partner would receive $50,000 of operating income and $50,000 of capital gain. Therefore, C would owe $20,000 in taxes ($20,000 on her share of the operating income and $0 on her share of capital gains) and D would owe $17,500 ($10,000 on her share of the operating income and $7,500 on her share of the capital gains) for a total of $37,500. If the allocation were respected, C would owe no taxes (because of the capital loss carryover) and D would owe $20,000 on the operating income for a total tax of $20,000. As you can see, the only effect of the allocation has been to reduce the government's share of the partnership's operations.

---

35. This allocation is made on the basis of all the pertinent facts and circumstances. § 1.704–1(b)(3). On these facts, each partner would be allocated $55 in tax exempt and $45 in taxable income. See § 1.704–1(b)(5)Ex. 5.

Transitory Allocations[36]

Transitory allocations are quite similar to the allocations intended to shift tax consequences except that transitory allocations cover more than one year. A transitory allocation occurs when a partnership makes an "original allocation" in one year, and then cancels out the economic effects of that allocation in a later year when the partnership makes an "offsetting allocation."

Under the rule for transitory allocations, if a partnership provides for both original and offsetting allocations, and at the time these allocations become part of the partnership agreement, there is a strong likelihood that:

1. the net effect of the original and offsetting allocations on the partners' capital accounts will not differ substantially from what it would have been in the absence of these allocations, AND

2. the total tax liability of the partners will be reduced from what it would otherwise be, THEN

the allocations will not be substantial and the items will have to be reallocated in accordance with the partners' interests in the partnership.[37] As was the case with shifting tax consequences, if the offsetting allocation(s) result in the above two conditions being met, it will be presumed that there was a strong likelihood at the time the allocations were made a part of the agreement that they would occur.

When determining whether a transitory allocation exists, the regulations create two extremely important presumptions. These are:

1. *Five-year rule*: If at the time the original and offsetting allocations are made part of the partnership agreement there is a strong likelihood that the original allocation will not be "largely" offset within 5 years after the original allocation is made, then it shall be presumed that the economic effect of the allocations is not transitory.[38]

2. *Value-equals-basis rule*: A partnership's assets are irrebuttably presumed to have a value equal to their basis (or book value, if different from basis).[39]

36. § 1.704–1(b)(2)(iii)(c).

37. The reallocation rules are in § 1.704–1(b)(3).

38. This rule is found in § 1.704–1(b)(2)(iii)(c), midway through the flush language, and begins with the words "Notwithstanding the foregoing..."

The allocation still might be subject to the after-tax exception discussed below.

39. This rule in also in the flush language of § 1.704–1(b)(2)(iii)(c), immediately following the five year rule. This presumption also applies to the after-tax exception.

To illustrate the transitory allocation rule, consider the following two examples. In each one, assume that the allocations in question have economic effect.

Example #7: A and B are partners in an equal partnership. The AB partnership has relatively stable net income of $100 per year. A has an NOL that will expire this year in an amount in excess of $100. For this reason, A is effectively in the 0% bracket this year. Next year, however, A expects to be in the 40% bracket. B is, and expects to remain, in the 40% bracket. On January 1 of this year the AB partnership agrees to allocate all of the current income to A and all of the following year's income to B.

If there is a strong likelihood that the partnership's net income this year and next will be about the same, then these allocations will be considered transitory and their economic effect not substantial. Even though they will have economic effect, because they are appropriately reflected in capital accounts, this year's allocation of $100 to A will be effectively offset by next year's allocation of $100 to B. The capital accounts at the end of next year will be identical to what they would have been had the partners simply split the income equally each year. Yet the tax liability of the partners is significantly different: had they split the income equally, A's tax liability for the first year would be zero, and B's would be $20, and each would have owed $20 for year two, for a total of $60 for the two years. The two offsetting allocations eliminate B's liability in the first year, and leaves unchanged aggregate tax for the second year, for a total of $40. Thus, only the government has suffered from this allocation.

Example #8: C and D are partners in an equal partnership that acquired an apartment building for investment. There is a strong likelihood that the apartment building will increase in value. C is in the 40% bracket and D is in the 0% tax bracket. C and D agree to share all items equally, except C is allocated all depreciation on the building. The partnership agreement also has a "gain chargeback" provision, which allocates all gain on the sale of the building attributable to previously taken depreciation deductions to C.

These allocations might be considered transitory allocations, if there was a substantial likelihood that the property would be sold at a gain within 5 years. However, it would be difficult to reconcile that result with the capital accounting rules requiring reduction in C's capital account by the amount of the depreciation deduction: that capital account adjustment is made because it is assumed that it represents a real decline in the value of C's interest. Indeed, the capital accounts are used as a surrogate for economic reality. To avoid this conflict, Treasury incorporated the value-equals-basis rule in the capital accounting regulations. Because of that rule, there cannot be a strong likelihood that the gain chargeback provision will offset the original allocation of the depreciation, because it is presumed that each dollar of depreciation reflects a dollar decline in the value of the property. Therefore, the economic effect of the allocation of depreciation is substantial, in spite of the gain chargeback provision.

After-Tax Exception[40]

When drafting the regulations, Treasury was well aware of the increasing sophistication of the partnership tax bar, and the ability of talented tax planners to take advantage of the time value of money to significantly alter the pre-tax consequences of a transaction. For example:

> **Example #9:** A and B are equal partners in a partnership that generates $100 of net taxable income each year which they normally share equally. The partners expect this amount of income for the foreseeable future. At all times, B is in the 40% bracket. A has an NOL that will expire at the end of next year. Therefore, for the next two years, A is effectively in the 0% tax bracket. After the expiration of the NOL, A expects to be in the 40% bracket. Assume all allocations have economic effect.
>
> A and B agree that A will be allocated all the partnership's income for the next two years and that B will be allocated all of the partnership's income for the following three years. Thereafter, A and B will once again share all partnership income equally.

This arrangement does not appear to violate the transitory allocation rules because the adjustments to the partners' capital accounts (which are made pre-tax) would differ substantially from what they would have been in the absence of the allocations. Assuming that the partnership earns $100 a year for each of the 5 years at issue, under the agreement A's capital account will be increased by $200 and B's by $300. In the absence of these allocations, both capital accounts would be increased by $250 apiece.

Even if a given allocation satisfies the general pre-tax rule, i.e., there is a reasonable possibility that a given allocation may substantially affect the dollars that the partners will receive, the allocation might nevertheless be considered insubstantial under the after-tax exception: The regulations state that the economic effect of an allocation is not substantial if, at the time the allocation becomes part of the partnership agreement,

40. § 1.704–1(b)(2)(iii) (second sentence).

1. the allocation may enhance the after-tax economic consequences of one partner, in present value terms, AND

2. there is a strong likelihood that the after-tax economic consequences of no partner will be diminished.

In making this determination, the value-equals-basis rule applies.[41]

Notice that the focus of this exception is different from the general rule in two quite meaningful ways. First, the exception focuses on the after-tax consequences to the partners, not the pre-tax effects on capital accounts. Second, in contrast with the transitory allocation rule, the exception tells us to take present values into account.

Under the after-tax exception, the economic effect of the allocations in *Example #9* may be found to be insubstantial. Let's take a look at the after-tax consequences to A and compare them with what they would have been in the absence of these allocations. Under the allocation, A would receive $200 on which A would owe no tax as a result of the NOL. In the absence of the allocations, A would have $50 of income in each of the 5 years, for a total of $250. A would have had to pay taxes of $20 in years 3, 4 and 5 for a total of $60. Therefore, in the absence of the allocations, A would have ended up with only $190 after taxes as compared with $200 with the allocation. The benefit to A is even greater when one considers the time value of money: the present value of $200 to be received in years one and two is significantly greater than the present value of $190 to be received over 5 years.

B also does quite well under the allocation. Without the allocation, B would receive $50 each year for a total of $250 (less total taxes of $100, B would be left with $150 after-tax). As a result of the allocation, B receives $300 pre-tax, and $180 after-tax. The benefit to B would be somewhat less than the $30 after-tax difference, because the allocation postpones B's receipt of the income until years three through five. Undoubtedly the partners took this time value of money into account in arriving at the allocation. The result is that each is treated the same or better after-tax, and the government is treated worse. It is fairly clear on these facts that at the time of the allocations:

1. A's after-tax economic consequences may be enhanced by the allocation, AND

2. there is a strong likelihood that B's after-tax economic consequences will not be diminished.

---

41. As a technical matter, the 5–year rule does not apply to the after-tax exception. Nevertheless, the after-tax exception was not mentioned in § 1.704– 1(b)(5)Ex.2 on facts to which it might apply. It is unclear what, if anything, to glean from this omission.

Therefore, under the exception to the general rule, the economic effect of these allocations is not substantial.

The after-tax exception was designed to combat at least some of the innovative allocation schemes that sophisticated tax planners generate. It is obviously much more subtle, and has the potential to apply in far more situations than the pre-tax rule, which appears to be limited to the shifting and transitory schemes described above.

Taking a Step Back

As we noted at the outset, the SEE regulations are among the most complicated ever promulgated by Treasury, so complicated and detailed, in fact, that it is easy to focus exclusively on the rules and lose sight of their purpose. These regulations were not intended to prevent taxpayers from forming a partnership and allocating income and deductions in any way they deem appropriate *so long as* the allocations are not simply a tax play. This is important to keep in mind when evaluating allocations because the substantiality rules, particularly the transitory allocation rule and the after-tax rule, if applied literally, could invalidate many allocations that should be respected. Consider the following:

> ***Example #10.*** X, Y and Z form a partnership to create a new product. X and Y contribute $100 each to the venture; Z contributes her expertise. As a result of marketing research, the partners believe there is an excellent chance that the partnership will break even after 3 years and begin to show an overall profit in the fourth year. The partnership agreement satisfies the three requirements of the basic test for economic effect under § 1.704–1(b)(2)(ii)(b). It provides that all initial income and losses are to be shared equally by X and Y until the aggregate income and gain of the partnership equals its losses in prior years. Thereafter, the profits and losses of the partnership will be shared equally among the three partners. For the first two years of operations, X and Y are in the 35% tax bracket and Z in the 15% bracket. Thereafter, all three partners are in the 35% tax bracket. During each of the first two years of its operations, the partnership loses $80. In its third year it earns $100, and in its fourth year it earns $180.

If the allocations are respected, the capital accounts of the partners are adjusted as follows:

	X	**Y**	**Z**
Original Contributions	$100	$100	0
Year 1 Loss	(40)	(40)	0
Year 2 Loss	(40)	(40)	0
Year 3 Profit	+50	+50	0
Year 4 Profit (first $60)	+30	+30	0
Year 4 Profit (balance of $120)	+40	+40	+40
	$140	$140	$40

Read literally, the transitory allocation rule and the after-tax rule present a serious problem: Since the special allocations did not have any net effect on the partners' capital accounts but did reduce their total tax liability, the regulations presume that there was a strong likelihood when the allocations were made that these results would occur, and the economic effect of the allocations therefore is not substantial.

In our view, neither the transitory allocation nor the after-tax rule was intended to apply to allocations like those in *Example #10*. Treasury was concerned with allocations made by a partnership with a stable, predictable income stream that presents little risk of not playing out as expected, solely to save taxes (e.g., rental payments from a long-term lease).[42] The allocations in *Example #10*, by contrast, are commercially motivated and are quite common. The early expected losses are allocated to those partners who actually invest their capital in the venture and, therefore, bear the loss if the venture is not successful. Allocating income first to those partners enables them to recoup their capital if the venture just breaks even.[43] That the venture is successful and ends up saving taxes should not undermine the allocations. Neither the transitory allocation rule nor the after-tax rule should apply in this case and the allocations should be respected.[44]

A Limitation—Family Partnerships

Even though a partnership complies with all of the requirements of § 704(b), its allocations still might not be respected if it is a family partnership. Historically, our tax system has had a progressive rate structure and has treated each individual as a separate taxpayer. In an effort to avoid high marginal rates, taxpayers have come up with a myriad of devices to split income among family members. In response to these devices, the courts developed

42. See, e.g., § 1.704–1(b)(5)Ex. 2 (long-term triple net lease of 5–year recovery property with triple A credit lessee).

43. If income were split equally among X, Y and Z from the first dollar, it would take income of $240, i.e., an overall profit of $80, for X and Y to break even.

44. There is support for this view in two examples in the regulations. § 1.704–1(b)(5) Exs. 3 (research and development) & 19(ii) (oil and gas exploration). Both examples hold that offsetting allocations of loss and income are substantial as a matter of law if the nature of the venture, by experience and common knowledge, entails a high degree of risk. In considering the spectrum of risk, these two examples on the one hand, and Example (2) (the financially secure lease) on the other, are polar extremes. The regulations do not give any guidance as to the degree of risk that is required to place a particular case under the protection of Examples (3) and (19)(ii). We believe, however, that the uncertainties of life are such that virtually any ordinary commercial venture will present a meaningful risk that the offsetting allocations of income will not materialize rather than a substantial likelihood that they will.

the assignment of income doctrine, which generally holds that income must be taxed to the person who earns it, or to the person who owns the income-producing capital.[45] One of the devices used by taxpayers to split income was the family partnership. Using the flexible allocation rules generally available to partnerships, the owner of the capital or the provider of the services could form a partnership with family members and allocate income to them, thereby avoiding both the higher marginal rates on income and reducing the size of her estate.

Prior to the enactment of the predecessor of § 704(e), it was unclear whether family partnerships would be respected under the tax law. The Service took the position that for a family member to be respected as a partner, the member would have to supply "original capital" or "vital services" to the partnership. The Supreme Court in *Commissioner v. Culbertson*[46] rejected this view and held that the appropriate question was "whether, considering all the facts and circumstances ... the parties in good faith and acting with business purpose intended to join together in the present conduct of the enterprise."[47] Some lower courts, however, continued to apply the original capital doctrine by not recognizing donees of capital interests as partners.[48]

Section 704(e)(1) effectively overrules these cases for any partnership in which capital is a material income-producing factor by providing that a person shall be recognized as a partner if she owns a capital interest, no matter how acquired.[49] Nevertheless, § 704(e)(2) limits the extent to which income allocations can be made to such partners. In an effort to backstop the assignment of income doctrine, if one family member has acquired a capital interest from another, by gift or purchase,[50] the "donee" may report her distributive share as long as the "donor" has received reasonable compensation for all services rendered to the partnership. The obvious purpose of this rule is to prevent the conversion of what should be the service income of one family member into the capital income of another.[51]

Section 704(e) does not address family partnerships in which capital is not a material income-producing factor. Whether these

---

45. See, e.g., *Lucas v. Earl*, 281 U.S. 111 (1930) and *Helvering v. Horst*, 311 U.S. 112 (1940).

46. 337 U.S. 733 (1949).

47. Id. at 742. See discussion in *Chapter One*.

48. See, e.g., *Harkness v. Commissioner*, 193 F.2d 655 (9th Cir.1951).

49. Although entitled "Family Partnerships," this provision can apply to anyone.

50. § 704(e)(3).

51. The importance of these rules has been significantly reduce with the advent of the "kiddie tax" which taxes the income of minor children at the parents' rate. See § 1(g).

partnerships (and their partners) will be respected by the tax law continues to depend on the application of *Culbertson*.

Conclusion

Although somewhat daunting in their detail and complexity, the § 704(b) regulations have given certainty, as well as a good deal of flexibility, to an area of partnership taxation which was unclear for many years. Those partnerships which choose to avail themselves of the safe harbor know precisely what they must do to accomplish that, and those partnerships remaining outside the safe harbor have more guidance than ever before on what the term "partners' interests in the partnership" means. Although some may argue that these regulations are too complex, no one argues that they are too restrictive concerning the allocations they permit.

Chapter Six

THE ALLOCATION OF NONRECOURSE DEDUCTIONS

Background

In the preceding chapter we examined the "substantial economic effect" rules, which require that a partnership allocate its income and deductions for tax purposes to the partners who enjoy the benefit of the income, or bear the economic burden associated with the deduction. However, those rules are of no help in allocating deductions attributable to nonrecourse financing. When partnership property is pledged as security for a nonrecourse loan, it is the lender, not the partnership, who bears the economic risk that the value of the property will not satisfy the loan. Therefore, the allocation of the deductions generated by the property to the partners cannot have substantial economic effect.[1]

Nevertheless, the Code (as interpreted by the Supreme Court) permits the owner of property to take depreciation and other deductions which may be economically borne by a nonrecourse lender (these deductions are referred to in the regulations as "nonrecourse deductions").[2] After completing the substantial economic effect regulations, Treasury turned to drafting rules for applying these principles in the partnership setting. The rules

---

1. See § 1.704–2(b)(1), which states that because they cannot have substantial economic effect, allocations of nonrecourse deductions must be allocated in accordance with the partners' interests in the partnership.

2. The regulatory definition of the term "nonrecourse deductions" is quite

complex, and will be discussed later in this chapter. For present purposes, it is enough to understand that the most common type of nonrecourse deduction is depreciation on property which is acquired or improved with the proceeds of nonrecourse financing.

appear in § 1.704–2, and are commonly referred to as the "nonrecourse deduction regulations."

To illustrate why the allocation of nonrecourse deductions cannot have substantial economic effect, and the problems faced by Treasury in establishing rules for the allocation of these deductions, consider the following fact pattern based on the Supreme Court decision in *Commissioner v. Tufts*:[3]

> **Example #1:** A and B form a general partnership to construct and operate an apartment complex. They agree to allocate all income, deductions, gains and losses 60% to A and 40% to B. AB obtains construction financing of $1,850 from a local bank for the entire project by giving a mortgage secured by the property; the partners invested negligible capital of their own. The building is depreciable at the rate of $100 per year. During the first four years of the partnership's operation, the partnership's rental income precisely offsets its out-of-pocket expenses, resulting in annual losses of $100 (as a result of the depreciation). At the end of the fourth year, the partnership's balance sheet looks as follows:

	Assets	*Book*	*Liabilities & Capital*	
Building		1,850	Mortgage	$1,850
Less four years depreciation		(400)		
		$1,450	***Capital Accounts***	
				Book
			A	($240)
			B	(160)
			Total	($400)

Let us first assume that the mortgage is recourse. By examining this balance sheet we can discern three things:

1.   First, the AB partnership has lost $400 during its four years of operation, consisting of the decline in value of the building which the depreciation represents. This decline in value is reflected in the book value of the building and in the capital accounts of the partners.

2.   Second, this loss has been allocated 60% to A and 40% to B, reducing their capital account balances to ($240) and ($160) respectively.

3.   Third, if the partnership were dissolved at this time, a sale of the building at its presumed value of $1,450 would leave the

---

3.   461 U.S. 300 (1983). For a detailed discussion of the *Tufts* case, see Laura E. Cunningham and Noël B. Cunningham, *The Story of Tufts: The 'Logic'* *of Taxing Nonrecourse Transactions* in Business Tax Stories (Foundation Press 2005).

partnership shy by $400 of the cash necessary to repay the lender. A and B, as general partners, must make good on the partnership's debts. The negative balances in their respective capital accounts represent the amount that each must contribute to pay the lender.

The bottom line is that the $400 loss described by this balance sheet will be economically borne by A and B, and the § 704(b) regulations mandate that the partnership allocate its depreciation deductions between its partners in proportion to the burden each will bear, i.e., 60% to A and 40% to B. Any other allocation would be disregarded as without substantial economic effect.

If we assume instead that the mortgage is nonrecourse (as it was in *Tufts*) and reexamine the balance sheet, it is clearly misleading. In portraying the partners' capital accounts as negative, it implies that if the partnership dissolves after selling the building for its book value, A and B will contribute the amount of the deficit balances in their capital accounts to satisfy the lender. That is clearly not the case. Since the loan is without recourse, A and B need contribute nothing; neither will suffer any of the burden associated with the decline in the value of the building below the amount of the debt. That entire loss will be borne by the lender, who must discharge the $1,850 liability even though it receives only $1,450 in repayment. In this context, the partnership's capital accounts are meaningless (or at best misleading) in that they do not accurately reflect the partners' economic burdens.

In the last chapter we learned that the basic underlying principle on which all partnership allocations are based is that tax deductions must be allocated to the person who bears the economic burden associated with those deductions. Here that person is the lender. To be consistent with this principle, shouldn't we allocate the cost recovery deductions to the lender? The answer is unequivocally yes. Nevertheless, ever since the Supreme Court's decision in *Crane v. Commissioner* (which the Court reaffirmed in *Tufts*) it has been the law that when property is purchased with the proceeds of a nonrecourse mortgage, the purchaser is the sole owner of the property, and the only party entitled to deduct depreciation with respect to it.[4]

Now the problems faced by Treasury in drafting rules to govern the allocation of nonrecourse deductions should be apparent: These deductions must be taken by the partnership as the sole owner of the property, even though none of the partners are economically at risk. In theory, therefore, the partnership might

---

4. *Crane v. Commissioner*, 331 U.S.   U.S. 300 (1983), see especially fn. 5.
1 (1947); *Commissioner v. Tufts*, 461

allocate the deductions among the partners in any way they agree. No allocation scheme would be more rational than another, since none would be anchored to the economic burden borne by any partner. The theory, if taken to its limits, would permit the partners to allocate these deductions arbitrarily to whichever partner might gain the greatest tax advantage.[5]

Fortunately, given the reality that no nonrecourse lender will extend credit on an unsecured basis, the analysis and holding of *Tufts* suggests a solution. In *Tufts*, the Supreme Court held that when property subject to a nonrecourse mortgage is disposed of in a taxable transaction, the full amount of the liability must be included in the amount realized, regardless of the value of the property at that time. The Supreme Court reasoned that since a nonrecourse mortgage was treated as "true debt" when it was incurred (generating full basis credit in the acquired property, even though the proceeds are tax-free), the mortgage must be treated as true debt when it is discharged. Hence, even though the debtor is not legally obligated to satisfy any shortfall between the amount of the loan and the value of the security, consistency requires us to treat it as if it received consideration for the property sufficient to pay the debt in full. Failing to do so would permit the debtor to receive the funds tax-free when the loan is taken out, yet never pay tax on those funds when the loan is discharged. The result of *Tufts* is that when property is transferred subject to a nonrecourse liability which exceeds the property's basis, the debtor will be forced to include in income an amount equal to the difference. This inclusion offsets the nonrecourse deductions previously allowed to the debtor, i.e., those for which the lender ultimately bore the economic burden.

To illustrate, on the facts of **Example #1**, this means that by looking at the balance sheet at the end of the partnership's fourth year of operations, we can see that if the partnership disposed of the property subject to the mortgage in a taxable transaction, including transferring it to the lender, the partnership would have to include the full amount of the mortgage, $1,850, in its amount realized. Subtracting its basis of $1,450 would yield a gain of $400. Because of *Tufts*, we know that no matter what the value of the underlying property, the partnership would have a gain of at least $400 (if you will, a "minimum gain"), the difference between the principal amount of the mortgage and the partnership's adjusted basis. This "minimum gain" is at the heart of the regulations governing allocations of nonrecourse deductions. As we shall see, the regulations permit partnerships to allocate nonrecourse deduc-

---

5. Indeed, this is precisely the position that was taken by the proposed regulations.

tions in virtually any way the partners agree, so long as the minimum gain is allocated in the same fashion.

In drafting the regulations dealing with nonrecourse deductions, Treasury's task was not to revisit the question of who should be entitled to these deductions, the owner/partnership or the lender. Rather, its task was to determine how much flexibility partnerships should be given in allocating these deductions among their partners. The regulations take a very liberal and flexible approach to the allocation of nonrecourse deductions, but are quite strict with respect to how the resulting *Tufts* gain must be allocated. They were drafted in tandem with the regulations that allocate nonrecourse debt for basis purposes,[6] and together combine to permit the allocation of nonrecourse deductions with few constraints and ensure that the partners have sufficient basis to make use of those deductions.[7]

Regulations

Introduction

Like the SEE regulations, the nonrecourse deduction regulations adopt a safe harbor approach. If the partnership agreement complies with all of the requirements of the safe harbor, then the allocations of nonrecourse deductions will be respected, i.e., they are deemed to be in accordance with the partners' interests in the partnership.[8] If the partnership does not comply with the requirements of the safe harbor, then the Service has the authority to reallocate the deductions under the facts and circumstances rules of § 1.704–1(b)(3). Because the PIP analysis focuses on the economics of the partners' deal, and nonrecourse deductions are actually borne economically by the lender, it is not at all clear how the rules should apply in this context.[9]

The safe harbor is found in § 1.704–2(e), and its requirements are as follows:

(1) The partnership agreement must satisfy either the basic or the alternate test for economic effect;[10]

---

6. § 1.752–3. These rules are discussed in *Chapter Eight*.

7. The partners themselves may be subject to further limitations. See e.g., §§ 465 and 469.

8. § 1.704–2(b).

9. Prior to 2009, the regulations created a presumption that that nonrecourse deductions should be shared equally by the partners, on a per capita

basis. In 2009, the regulations were amended and this presumption was eliminated.

10. § 1.704–2(e)(1). The nonrecourse debt safe harbor is actually a safe harbor within a safe harbor: if the partnership chooses not to comply with the safe harbor for SEE under § 1.704–1, then the nonrecourse debt safe harbor is unavailable to it.

(2) Nonrecourse deductions must be allocated by the partnership agreement in a manner that is "reasonably consistent" with allocations of some other "significant" partnership item attributable to the property securing the debt;[11]

(3) The partnership agreement must contain a "minimum gain chargeback" provision;[12] and

(4) All other material allocations and capital account adjustments must be respected under § 1.704–1(b).[13]

In general, the safe harbor requirements are relatively straightforward. You should already be familiar with requirements (1) and (4) and have a general understanding of (2). The third requirement, requiring the partnership agreement to contain a minimum gain chargeback provision, is really the heart of the regulations. In the simplest case, this provision simply requires those partners who received allocations of nonrecourse deductions to report an offsetting amount of gain when the partnership disposes of the property. However, it is not possible to fully understand how the minimum gain chargeback works without examining several new terms used in the regulations. As we examine these terms, we will revisit *Example #1.*

Definitions

"Partnership Minimum Gain" (PMG).[14] PMG can be thought of as (and we will sometimes refer to it as) *"Tufts* gain," i.e., the minimum amount of gain that the partnership would realize were it to make a taxable disposition of property secured by nonrecourse financing.[15] At any given time, that gain is the excess of the amount of the loan over the property's basis. As you will recall, when the partnership in *Example #1* disposed of the property, the partnership had a gain of $400, the amount by which the principal amount of the mortgage ($1,850) exceeded the partnership's basis ($1,450), even though the value of the property had fallen below the amount of the mortgage.

---

11. § 1.704–2(e)(2).

12. § 1.704–2(e)(3), and 1.704–2(f).

13. § 1.704–2(e)(4). This requirement seems somewhat redundant given the first requirement.

14. § 1.704–2(d).

15. Although PMG is normally equal to the difference between the amount of the nonrecourse liability and the basis of the property securing it, when the property's book value differs from its basis, either because it was contributed to the partnership at a value different from its basis, or because it was revalued and "booked up or down" to reflect changes in its value, the regulations use book value, rather than basis, in measuring PMG. This is because, under the principles of § 704(c) (discussed in *Chapter Seven*), any inherent gain (including *Tufts* gain) which exists at the time appreciated property is contributed to the partnership must be allocated to the contributing partner, and any inherent gain (including PMG) which exists at the time of a revaluation must be allocated to the partners whose book capital accounts were adjusted to reflect the change in book value.

Measurement of PMG is important to the regulatory scheme governing nonrecourse deductions for two primary reasons. First, the regulations measure the amount of nonrecourse deductions for a given year *indirectly* by reference to the increase in PMG during the year. Second, a decrease in a partner's share of PMG may trigger a minimum gain chargeback.

Because PMG at any given time is the spread between the loan and the property's basis, there are two principal events that will cause it to increase, cost recovery deductions and secondary financing. Cost recovery deductions will increase the amount of PMG if they reduce the partnership's adjusted basis in the secured property faster than the principal of the nonrecourse liability is repaid. To illustrate, in ***Example #1*** the partnership's original basis in the apartment complex was $1,850, an amount exactly equal to the principal of the mortgage. At that time, there was no PMG. During its first year of operation, the partnership took $100 of depreciation, reducing its basis to $1,750. Since the partnership did not repay any portion of the principal of the mortgage, $100 of PMG was created during that first year, or phrased somewhat differently, there was an increase in PMG of $100. If the partnership had repaid $40 of principal during that first year, then the increase in PMG would have been only $60.

PMG may also increase if a partnership borrows funds without incurring personal liability, using its property as security for the loan. To illustrate, suppose a partnership that holds unencumbered land with a value of $500 and a basis of $200 borrows $350 without recourse, using the land as security. Prior to the borrowing, the partnership has no PMG; after the borrowing, since the principal amount of the nonrecourse liability exceeds the partnership's basis by $150, it has $150 of PMG, an increase of $150. If the proceeds of such a borrowing are distributed to the partners, then to the extent that the borrowing caused an increase in PMG (here $150), we will refer to it as a **"nonrecourse distribution."**[16]

An increase in PMG for a particular year generally will equal the sum of the nonrecourse distributions and nonrecourse deductions for that year. The total amount of partnership minimum gain at any time represents the total of deductions taken by the partnership and distributions made by the partnership for which the lender has borne the burden. Although the tax law permits the partnership to take these deductions, and permits these distributions, it requires that, upon disposition of the underlying property, the partnership recognize an offsetting minimum gain.

"Nonrecourse Deductions" (NRDs).[17] Nonrecourse deductions are those deductions attributable to nonrecourse financing

---

16.   §§ 1.704–2(c) & 1.704–2(h).   **17.**   § 1.704–2(c).

and represent amounts for which no partner bears the economic burden. NRDs are measured annually and are equal to the "net increase in the partnership's minimum gain" during the taxable year, less any nonrecourse distributions made during the year. In *Example #1*, for example, since there was an annual increase in PMG of $100 and no nonrecourse distributions, the partnership had NRDs of $100 each year.

Normally, NRDs are comprised of the cost recovery deductions taken on the encumbered property. This is sensible because the most common source of an increase in PMG is cost recovery. For a number of reasons, however, the cost recovery deductions of the partnership may be less than the increase in PMG.[18] Therefore, the regulations create the following ordering rule to determine which of the partnership's deductions are characterized as nonrecourse:

i. first, depreciation or cost recovery deductions with respect to the encumbered property, and

ii. then, if necessary, a pro rata portion of the partnership's other expenses (including deductible items and non-deductible § 705(a)(2)(B) expenses) for the year, and

iii. finally, if there are insufficient deductions for the year, the excess nonrecourse deductions are carried over to the following year.[19]

As a practical matter, in the absence of secondary borrowing, there will always be sufficient cost recovery deductions, because those deductions will have been responsible for the increase in partnership minimum gain. Therefore, the NRDs in *Example #1* are exclusively cost recovery deductions.

"Partner's Share of Partnership Minimum Gain."[20] The ultimate objective of the regulations is to ensure that each partner will eventually report an amount of income or gain equal to her share of nonrecourse deductions and distributions. Treasury did not want one partner to be allocated all of the NRDs and another all of the *Tufts* gain. For this reason, the regulations require partnerships to keep track of each partner's share of PMG. Thus, each year's increase in PMG is allocated among the partners in accordance with the amount of NRDs allocated to each and the amount of nonrecourse distributions made to each. If there has been a net decrease in PMG during the year, it too will be allocated among the partners and may trigger the minimum gain chargeback provision. Thus, at any given point in time each partner's share of the total PMG of the partnership will be equal to the excess of:

18. For example, the increase in PMG may be attributable to secondary financing which is not distributed, but used to pay partnership expenses.

19. §§ 1.704–2(j)(1)(ii) & (iii).

20. § 1.704–2(g)(1).

(1) the sum of the NRDs allocated to her and nonrecourse distributions she has received, OVER

(2) that partner's share of net decreases in PMG.

In effect, these shares represent the amount by which each partner has benefitted from nonrecourse financing, through deductions or distributions, without incurring risk. On the facts of *Example #1*, A's share of PMG is $240, and B's share is $160.

"Minimum Gain Chargeback Provision."[21] Although the rules with respect to the allocation of nonrecourse deductions are quite liberal, they are quite strict in how the resulting *Tufts* gain is allocated. The underlying principle is that the partner who enjoyed the benefit of a nonrecourse deduction (or distribution) should be required to report a corresponding share of the partnership's minimum gain. This principle is implemented by the minimum gain chargeback provision, which generally requires that if there is a "net decrease in PMG" for a taxable year, each partner must be allocated an amount of income or gain equal to her share of the decrease.

Although there are many possible causes for a decrease in PMG, the most common cause is the disposition of the encumbered property. For example, in *Example #1*, at the beginning of the year in which the partnership disposed of the property, the partnership had $400 in minimum gain; after the disposition, its minimum gain is reduced to zero, resulting in a net decrease of $400. Under the minimum gain chargeback provision, the partnership would be required to allocate the $400 gain from the disposition of this property in an amount equal to each partner's share of the decrease in PMG. As a technical matter, a partner's share of a net decrease in PMG equals the amount of the decrease times each partner's share of the total PMG. On the facts of *Example #1*, this means that the partnership would be required to allocate $240 ($400 times 60%) of this gain to A and $160 ($400 times 40%) of it to B.

Although the disposition of the underlying property is the most common cause of a decrease in partnership minimum gain, there are several other possible causes, four of which Treasury found to be inappropriate to trigger the minimum gain chargeback provision. In each of these cases, Treasury concluded that it was not necessary to trigger the gain chargeback to protect the basic principle that each partner must report her share of PMG. These four exceptions are:

    1. *Conversions and refinancing.*[22] A decrease in PMG can result simply from the conversion of a nonrecourse obligation into one on which one or more of the partners are personally

---

21. § 1.704–2(f).   **22.** § 1.704–2(f)(2).

liable. As to those partners who become personally liable there is no reason to trigger the minimum gain chargeback since these partners are now actually bearing the economic burden associated with the deductions they have already taken. The minimum gain chargeback, however, applies with full force to any partner who does not incur personal liability.

2. *Contributions of capital.*[23] A decrease in PMG may result from a partner's contribution of capital that is used either to repay the principal of a nonrecourse liability or to make a capital improvement to the encumbered property. The repayment reduces the liability, and the improvement increases basis, either of which will reduce the spread between basis and the amount of the liability. In either case, since the decrease is caused by an actual investment in the property, it is inappropriate to trigger the gain chargeback.

3. *Revaluations.*[24] Although a decrease in PMG can result from the revaluation of a partnership's assets, the minimum gain chargeback provision will not apply. The reason for this exception, as we shall see in the next chapter, is that a revaluation has the effect of converting each partner's share of PMG into "§ 704(c)-type gain" for which the partners remain personally responsible.[25]

4. *Waiver.*[26] Finally, Treasury recognized that under certain other circumstances the minimum gain chargeback could distort the economic arrangement among the partners. In such a case, the partnership may request a waiver of the provision.

Illustrations

The following examples illustrate these rules.

Example #2: On January 1, 2010, G and L formed a limited partnership to acquire and operate a rental apartment building. L, the limited partner, contributed $135 and G, the general partner, contributed $15. The partnership obtained a nonrecourse loan from an unrelated financial institution for $850 and purchased a building for $1,000 on leased land. The loan is secured by the building. The loan requires interest to be paid currently, but does not require any principal payments for 25 years. The building is depreciable over 10 years at the rate of $100 per year.

The partnership agreement satisfies the first two requirements of the basic test for economic effect (i.e., the capital account

---

23. § 1.704–2(f)(3).
24. § 1.704–2(d)(4).
25. § 1.704–3(a)(6).

26. § 1.704–2(f)(4). For an example of when a distortion may be created, see § 1.704–2(f)(7) Ex.1.

and liquidation requirements). L has no obligation to make up any deficit in her capital account. The partnership agreement, however, does have a QIO provision. It also has a "minimum gain chargeback" provision as described in § 1.704–2(f). The partners agree that nonrecourse deductions will be shared equally. Finally, the agreement provides that all items of income, deduction and loss, *other than nonrecourse deductions*, will be allocated 90% to L and 10% to G until the first time that income and gain exceed losses taken in prior years. Thereafter, all items of income, gain, and loss will be allocated equally between the partners.

For the taxable years 2010–2012, the partnership has $70 of gross rental income and $70 of out of pocket expenses ($60 in interest and $10 in operating expenses). As a result of the depreciation deduction on the building, the partnership has an annual net tax loss of $100 each year. During this period, the partnership makes no distributions.

The partnership's initial balance sheet is as follows:

Assets		*Liabilities & Capital*	
	Book		
Building	$1,000	Mortgage	$850
		Capital Accounts	
			Book
		G	$15
		L	135
			$150

Example #2 raises several different issues which we will explore.

Issue #1: How much flexibility does the partnership have in allocating the nonrecourse deductions that the partnership expects to have?

The partnership is permitted to allocate these deductions in any way it wishes *as long as* the allocation is "reasonably consistent" with the allocation of another significant item relating to the property that has SEE. At the outset, all significant items other than nonrecourse deductions are to be allocated 90/10. Assuming there is a reasonable likelihood that income and gain will eventually exceed prior losses and deductions, these items will eventually be allocated 50/50. Therefore, according to the regulations, the allocation of NRDs would be respected if the sharing ratio is anywhere within the range of 90/10 to 50/50.[27] A sharing ratio outside this

---

27. See § 1.704–2(m)Ex.1 (ii).

range may be attacked by the Service.[28] In this example, we shall assume that the partnership allocates all nonrecourse deductions equally. This will allow us to distinguish the partnership's nonrecourse deductions from its other deductions.

Issue #2: What are G's and L's initial bases in the partnership?

Their initial bases depend on how they share the nonrecourse debt. On these facts, it is probable that the partners will share the debt equally, or $425 each.[29] On this assumption, G's initial outside basis is $440 and L's is $560.

Issue #3: How should the $100 loss for 2010 be allocated between G and L? Phrased somewhat differently, are there any NRDs in 2010?

At the end of 2010, the book value of the building still exceeds the principal amount of the mortgage; therefore, this partnership has neither minimum gain nor any NRDs. According to the agreement, the $100 loss is to be allocated $10 to G and $90 to L. For reasons discussed in the preceding chapter, this allocation has SEE and will be respected.[30] On January 1, 2011, the partnership's balance sheet would look as follows:

Assets		*Liabilities & Capital*	
	Book		
Building	$900	Mortgage	$850

	Capital Accounts	
		Book
G		$5
L		45
		$50

Issue #4: How should the $100 loss for 2011 be allocated? Are there any NRDs in 2011?

At the end of 2011, the adjusted basis of the building is now $800 while the balance of the mortgage remains at $850; therefore, $50 of PMG has been created—a net increase of $50. Since there are no distributions, $50 of the depreciation deduction is characterized as a NRD and is allocated equally between the partners, $25 each. In addition, the partnership has a $50 loss (calculated without taking into account the NRDs), that is allocated $5 to G and $45 to

---

28. § 1.704–2(m)Ex.1(iii)(on similar facts held that a sharing ratio of 99/1 was not reasonably consistent).

29. See § 1.752–3 for the rules allocating nonrecourse debt. These rules are discussed in *Chapter Eight.*

30. As you will recall, this is because the alternate test for economic effect is satisfied and the allocation is not transitory because of the value equals basis rule.

L; this allocation has SEE. The adjustments to the partners' capital accounts for 2006 are as follows:

	Capital Accounts	
	G	**L**
Balance (as of 1/06)	$5	$45
NR Deduction	(25)	(25)
Loss (w/o NRDs)	(5)	(45)
	($25)	($25)

Issue #5: What are G's and L's shares of the $50 partnership minimum gain?

Since G and L each received $25 of the NRD, each has a $25 share of the PMG.

Issue #6: Normally, a QIO is triggered whenever a deficit in a partner's capital account is created in excess of the amount that a partner is obligated to restore. At the end of 2011, L's balance in her capital account is ($25). Since she does not have a deficit make-up obligation, is the partnership's QIO provision triggered?

No. Essentially, each partner's share of PMG is treated as a limited deficit make-up obligation.[31] This is a sensible rule for two reasons: First, in the absence of such a rule, few limited partners would be able to benefit from an allocation of NRDs: the allocation would trigger the QIO, which would offset the benefit. Second, in a very real way, the integrity of the alternate test is not threatened by this rule, because the minimum gain chargeback provision ensures that a partner who is allocated NRDs is obligated to eventually include a similar amount in income, thereby restoring the deficit in her capital account.

Issue #7: How should the $100 loss for 2012 be allocated?

At the beginning of 2012, there was $50 of PMG. During 2012, the partnership's basis in the building is reduced to $700 while the balance of the mortgage remains $850. As a result, at the end of 2012, there is $150 of PMG, a net increase of $100. Therefore, the entire $100 depreciation deduction is a NRD which is allocated equally between the partners in accordance with the partnership agreement, i.e., $50 each. This increases each partner's share of PMG to $75, and reduces the balance in her capital account to ($75). The partnership's balance sheet on January 1, 2013 would look as follows:

---

31. § 1.704–2(g)(1).   See   also § 1.704–1(b)(2)(ii)(d).

Assets		*Liabilities & Capital*	
	Book		
Building	$700	Mortgage	$850

Capital Accounts

	Book
G	($75)
L	(75)
	($150)

Example #3: Assume the same facts as in ***Example #2***. In addition, assume the following ALTERNATIVE events occur during 2013. Ignore any possible depreciation deduction for 2013.

Alternative #1: On January 1, 2013, the partnership transfers the building to the lender in complete satisfaction of its obligation under the mortgage.

Under *Tufts*, the partnership realizes a gain of $150 on the disposition of this building. As a result of the disposition, the partnership has a net decrease in PMG of $150 for the year.[32] This decrease in PMG triggers the minimum gain chargeback provision, which requires the partnership to allocate to each partner her share of that decrease. On these facts, the partnership MUST allocate $75 to L and $75 to G, even though they generally share gains 90/10. The minimum gain chargeback provision, in other words, establishes an overriding layer of profit sharing.

Alternative #2: On January 1, 2013 the partnership sells the building for $100 cash, the buyer taking the building subject to the $850 mortgage.

On the sale of the building, the partnership has $250 of gain. As in ***Alternative #1***, the disposition of the building results in a net decrease in PMG of $150. This triggers the minimum gain chargeback provision, and, for the same reasons as in ***Alternative #1***, $150 of this gain must be allocated equally between G and L in accordance with their share of the decrease in PMG. The $100 balance represents real partnership profit, not just a restoration of the lender's notional earlier losses. According to the agreement, this profit is allocated $10 to G and $90 to L, restoring to each partner a portion of her initial capital contribution. This allocation will have substantial economic effect.

Alternative #3: On January 1, 2013, G personally guarantees the mortgage.

As a result of the guarantee, the mortgage changes its character from a partnership nonrecourse liability to a partner nonrecourse debt.[33] Essentially, a partner nonrecourse debt is one that is

32. Since there is no longer a nonrecourse liability, there can't be any PMG.

33. § 1.704–2(b)(4). Partner nonrecourse debt is debt that is technically nonrecourse with respect to the partnership, but is recourse with respect to one or more of the partners. Here, G has undertaken the entire economic burden represented by the difference between the value of the building and the face amount of the debt. As in each of the other alternatives, the guarantee results in a net decrease in PMG of $150. Nevertheless, the regulations recognize that this would be an inappropriate time to trigger the minimum gain charge back with respect to G, since G now is personally liable on the obligation.[34] This is not true for L. At the beginning of 2013, the balance in her capital account was a negative $75, even though she had no deficit restoration obligation. This $75 represents NRDs allocated to L but whose economic burden was being borne by the lender. Now that G has undertaken that burden, it is not appropriate for L to have a negative balance for amounts for which G is responsible. Therefore, the minimum gain charge-back provision applies to her. Note, however, that there is no gain to "charge-back." In this situation, the regulations require a pro rata portion of the partnership's other items of gain and income for that year be allocated to L.[35]

Conclusion

From the foregoing discussion it should be clear that the safe harbor created by the regulations gives partnerships enormous flexibility in allocating nonrecourse deductions among their partners. If a partnership does not come within the safe harbor, its nonrecourse deductions will be allocated in accordance with the partners' interests in the partnership under § 1.704–1(b)(3). Because the burden represented by these deductions is being borne by the lender, and not the partnership, there is no certainty as to exactly how these deductions would be allocated.[36] Since this type of uncertainty makes many investors uneasy, for many years most limited partnerships opted for the safe harbor. As we mentioned at the end of *Chapter Five*, many partnerships are now using targeted allocations, allocations that may or may not have substantial economic effect under § 1.704–1(b)(2). If they do not, then the safe harbor under § 1.704–2(e) is not available. Even if that is the case, it is our understanding that many practitioners believe that their

---

nonrecourse under § 1.1001–2, but for which one or more partners (or related parties) are personally liable. Under § 1.704–2(i), the deductions and distributions attributable to partner nonrecourse liabilities must be allocated among those partners who are liable under rules parallel to those for nonrecourse liabilities.

34. § 1.704–2(f)(3).

35. § 1.704–2(f)(6). See also § 1.704–2(j)(2)(i) and (iii). Cf. § 1.704–1(b)(2)(iv)(the rules relating to qualified income offsets).

36. This was especially true when the regulations created a presumption that all partnership interests were equal.

allocation of nonrecourse deductions will be respected *as long as* they are allocated in the same way as other partnership items. As we shall see in *Chapter Eight*, the rules governing the sharing of nonrecourse liabilities are designed to work in tandem with these allocation rules to ensure that the partner who is allocated nonrecourse deductions will in most cases have sufficient basis to benefit from these deductions.

Chapter Seven

CONTRIBUTIONS OF PROPER-
TY: SECTION 704(c) AND SEC-
TION 704(c) PRINCIPLES

Introduction

The last two chapters have shown that partnerships are given great flexibility in allocating items of income or loss, so long as the allocation has substantial economic effect or is determined to be in accord with the partners' interests in the partnership. Underlying these rules is the mandate that, however a partnership allocates its book items, it must allocate its corresponding tax items in the same manner. In other words, "tax must follow book."

The "tax follows book" principle generally works fine when a partnership purchases an asset and reflects it on the books at cost for both tax and book purposes. In that case, the partnership's gain, loss, or depreciation with respect to that asset will be the same for book and tax purposes, so that the partnership can comply with the tax follows book mandate.[1]

There are, however, certain events which predictably create a disparity between a partnership's book and tax accounts. Two events that have this effect are (i) the contribution to a partnership of "§ 704(c) property," i.e., property whose fair market value differs from its basis (resulting in "built-in gain" or "built-in loss") and (ii) the revaluation of a partnership's assets as permitted by § 1.704–1(b)(2)(iv)(f) (because the book/tax disparity resulting from revaluing partnership assets is so much like that caused by the contribution of § 704(c) property, allocations with respect to revalued assets are referred to as "reverse § 704(c) allocations"). The book/tax disparity is created because, at the time of contribution or

---

1. This assumes that the partnership elects to follow the capital accounting rules prescribed in § 1.704–1(b)(2)(iv) which are discussed in *Chapter Four*.

revaluation, the property must be reflected on the partnership's books at its fair market value even though no gain or loss is recognized for tax purposes. In effect, the gain or loss inherent in the property is recognized for book purposes but not for tax purposes. As a result, when the partnership makes a taxable disposition of the property there will be tax gain (or loss) for which there is no corresponding book gain (or loss). In the case of depreciable property, the partnership's book depreciation will not match its tax depreciation. For this reason, with respect to the disparity, tax *cannot* follow book, and it is impossible for the tax allocations to have substantial economic effect. The allocation of these tax items is governed by the special rules (and principles) of § 704(c) and the regulations thereunder.[2]

Section 704(c)(1)(A) requires that "income, gain, loss, and deduction with respect to property contributed to the partnership by a partner shall be shared among the partners so as to take account of the variation between the basis of the property to the partnership and its fair market value at the time of contribution." Thus, if appreciated or depreciated property is contributed to a partnership, the built-in gain or loss (when realized by the partnership) must be taken into account for tax purposes by the contributing partner, i.e., the partner to whom the gain or loss was allocated for book purposes at the time of contribution. This requirement is consistent not only with assignment of income principles, but also, in a very fundamental way, with the "tax follows book" principle that underlies § 704(b). Because the capital accounting rules require that contributed property be reflected on the books of the partnership at its fair market value,[3] all built-in gain or loss is economically allocated to the contributing partner. By requiring that the corresponding tax gain or loss be allocated to the contributing partner, § 704(c) can be thought of as requiring tax to follow book, albeit on a deferred basis, i.e., when the tax gain or loss is recognized by the partnership.

While the principles of § 704(c) appear relatively simple, their implementation can be quite complex. In this chapter we examine

2. Section 1.704–1(b)(2)(iv)(f)(4) requires that allocations of tax items with respect to revalued property must be governed by § 704(c) principles. The § 704(c) regulations explicitly describe allocations with respect to revalued property as "reverse § 704(c) allocations," and make clear that the principles of those regulations are applicable to those allocations. Thus, when a partnership revalues its assets as permitted by the capital accounting rules, § 704(c) principles require that the built-in gain or loss be allocated to the partners to whom the gain or loss was allocated for book purposes at the time of the revaluation.

3. § 1.704–1(b)(2)(iv)(b). When a partnership revalues its assets, it "books up" the assets on its balance sheet to fair market value, and must allocate that book gain or loss among the partners' capital accounts in the same manner as if it had been sold for fair market value. § 1.704–1(b)(2)(iv)(f)(2).

how the regulations implement these principles, first in the context of contributions of property, then in the context of revaluations.

Contributions of Property

Section 704(c) requires that tax items with respect to contributed property must be shared so as to take into account the built-in gain or loss at the time of contribution. The statute defers to the Secretary for guidance on how this should be accomplished. The regulations state that the partnership may use a "reasonable method which is consistent with the purpose of section 704(c),"[4] and go on to identify three methods that Treasury generally will find reasonable: the "traditional method,"[5] the "traditional method with curative allocations,"[6] and the "remedial allocation method."[7] We will first examine each of these as they apply to nondepreciable property, and then will tackle the more complex rules applicable to depreciable property.

Nondepreciable Property

To illustrate the various ways to account for built-in gain and loss inherent in nondepreciable property, we will consider several variations of the following fact pattern:

> ***Example #1:*** A and B form an equal partnership to which A contributes land with a basis of $60 and a fair market value of $100 and B contributes $100 cash. The land is a capital asset in the partnership's hands.

The partnership capital accounting rules of § 1.704–1(b)(2)(iv) require the partnership to account for this transaction for *book* purposes by giving A credit in her capital account for the land's full fair market value, and the land will be reflected on the asset side of the partnership's balance sheet at that value.[8] As a result, a disparity exists between the partnership's tax and book accounts, i.e., the land has a tax basis of $60 but a book value of $100. To reflect these disparities, and to assist in tracing them to the partner to whom they are attributable, the regulations contemplate maintenance of "tax capital" accounts for the partners, which essentially reflect each partner's share of the partnership's inside basis, net of

---

4. § 1.704–3(a)(1).

5. § 1.704–3(b).

6. § 1.704–3(c).

7. § 1.704–3(d).

8. § 1.704–1(b)(2)(iv)(d). Although partnerships are not required to follow the capital accounting rules of § 1.704–1(b)(2)(iv) unless they wish to rely upon the safe harbor for substantial economic effect under § 1.704–1(b)(2)(ii), the regulations governing contributed property under § 704(c) require that partnerships which do not do so must use book capital accounts "based upon the same principles." § 1.704–3(a)(3).

liabilities.[9] Thus, at formation, the partnership's balance sheet is as follows:

	Assets		**Liabilities & Capital**
	Basis	*Book*	
Cash	$100	$100	
Land	60	100	
	$160	$200	

	Capital Accounts	
	Tax	*Book*
A	$ 60	$100
B	100	100
	$160	$200

It is apparent from the balance sheet that if the partnership were to sell the land for $100, it would realize a tax gain of $40, but no book gain. A's book capital account reflects that she received the benefit of that book gain at the time she contributed the property. Thus, if any of the $40 tax gain were reported by B, the result would be to tax B on gain that was credited to A for book purposes.

Traditional Method

Under the "traditional method,"[10] the noncontributing partner is effectively treated as though she purchased an undivided interest in the property for its fair market value, and allocations of tax items are made consistent with that treatment. As a result, where the contributed property is nondepreciable, only tax gains (or losses) corresponding to book gains (or losses) will be allocated to her. Thus, in *Example #1*, if the partnership were to sell the property for $100, none of the $40 tax gain would be allocated to B because she sustained no book gain. A, on the other hand, has a $40 disparity in her tax and book capital accounts, reflecting the fact that she was credited with a book gain at the time of contribution, which has not yet been matched by a tax gain. Therefore all of the corresponding $40 tax gain will be allocated to her, fulfilling the basic mandate that tax must follow book, even though the tax allocation followed the book allocation on a delayed basis. To illustrate further, consider the following variation:

Variation #1: Assume the land in *Example #1* increases in value and AB sells it for $120. As a result of the sale, AB has a book gain of $20 and a tax gain of $60.

Under their agreement, A and B share the book gain equally, $10 apiece. Under the traditional method the tax gain is allocated as follows: B, the noncontributing partner, is allocated an amount of tax gain equal to her book gain of $10, and A is allocated the

---

9. These concepts were introduced in *Chapter Four.*

10. § 1.704–(3)(b).

balance, $50. By allocating the tax gain first to the noncontributing partner to match her book gain, the traditional method maintains the equality between B's book and tax capital accounts. Once this is accomplished, the remaining tax gain is necessarily allocable to the contributing partner, A. Note that, in this variation, this allocation has the effect of eliminating entirely the book/tax disparity on the partnership's books.

The regulations impose one important limitation on the principle prohibiting shifts of built-in gain: the so-called "ceiling rule."[11] Traditionally, the ceiling rule has imposed a limit upon the amount of any tax item that a partnership may allocate among its partners: that limit is the amount of tax gain, income, loss, or deduction that the partnership, as an entity, actually recognizes for the year. In operation, the ceiling rule can cause serious distortions, by shifting a portion of a built-in gain to the noncontributing partners. This is illustrated by **Variation #2.** Prior to 2004, the ceiling rule also could operate to shift built-in losses to noncontributing partners. However, § 704(c)(1)(C), enacted in 2004, explicitly states that a built-in loss can only be taken into account by the contributing partner. This provision would appear to override the regulatory ceiling rule with respect to built-in losses.[12] The tax consequences of this new rule are not entirely clear and are the subject of **Variation #3.**

> **Variation #2:** Assume the facts of **Example #1**, but that instead the land goes down in value and AB sells it for $70. As a result of this sale, although AB has a book loss of $30, it has a tax gain of $10.

For book purposes, A and B suffer a loss of $15 each; however, the partnership has no tax loss to match B's book loss. The result is a book/tax disparity in B's capital accounts. For tax purposes, the entire tax gain of $10 is allocated to A, but this amount is not sufficient to eliminate A's book/tax disparity. Immediately after the sale, AB's balance sheet appears as follows:

	Assets		*Liabilities & Capital*	
	Basis	*Book*		
Cash	$170	$170		
			Capital Accounts	
			Tax	*Book*
			A $70	$85
			B 100	85
			$170	$170

---

11. § 1.704–3(b)(1).

12. Section 704(c)(1)(C) also has the effect of preventing a purchaser of a partnership interest from being able to benefit from a built-in loss in property contributed by the seller. This is discussed in *Chapter Ten.*

Notice that, although the disparity between tax and book has been eliminated on the asset side of the balance sheet, a new one has been created between B's tax and book accounts. This is because B has recognized a real economic loss that has been taken into account for book purposes but not for tax purposes: her $15 economic loss has not been matched by a tax loss. A, on the other hand, who enjoyed a book gain of $40 at the time she contributed the property (and was given a book capital credit of $100) and sustained an offsetting loss of $15 when the property was sold, (for a net gain of $25), has only reported $10 of tax gain, effectively (albeit temporarily) shifting $15 of that gain to B (via the deferred loss deduction). This result is compelled by the ceiling rule, and these effects will presumably be offset one day, when the partnership liquidates or when A and/or B sell their partnership interests.[13] In the meantime, however, B's unrecognized loss and A's unrecognized gain will be locked in.

Variation #3: Assume the same facts of *Example #1* except that A's basis in the land on the date of contribution is $150. At formation, the partnership's balance sheet is as follows:

	Assets		**Liabilities & Capital**
	Basis	*Book*	
Cash	$100	$100	
Land	150	100	
	$250	$200	

	Capital Accounts	
	Tax	*Book*
A	$150	$100
B	100	100
	$250	$200

From this balance sheet, it is clear that if the partnership were to sell the land for $100, although it would not have either a book gain or loss, the partnership would have to recognize a tax loss of $50. This loss has already been reflected in A's book capital account and under § 704(c) the partnership must allocate this loss to A. Suppose, however, that the partnership sells the land for $120, resulting in a book gain of $20 and a tax loss of $30. Under their agreement, A and B share the book gain equally, or $10 each. If the ceiling rule applied, B would not be taxed on this gain (because the partnership had no gain), and A would be allocated the entire $30 loss. In effect, this would result in a shift of $10 of A's loss to B.

---

13. If the partnership were immediately to liquidate, distributing cash of $85 to each partner, A would recognize a gain of $15 under § 731(a)(1) and B would recognize a $15 loss under § 731(a)(2). Similarly, if either were to sell his or her partnership interest, recognition of the deferred gain or loss under § 741 would result.

Section 704(c)(1)(C) prohibits this result and establishes two additional rules for determining tax allocations when property with a built-in losses is contributed to a partnership, one for the contributing partner and one for the noncontributing partners. These are:

1. Contributing partner: If a partner contributes property to a partnership with a built-in loss (as A did), then the partnership must allocate any tax item related to that loss to the contributor,[14] and

2. Non-contributing partner: To determine the amount of any item with respect to built-in loss property that is to be allocated to a noncontributing partner (such as B), the partnership shall be treated as having an initial tax basis in the property equal to its fair market value on the date of contribution.[15]

Under these rules, the tax consequences to B are clear: B has a $10 tax gain, an amount precisely equal to her book gain. The statute requires the partnership to use fair market value of the land on the date of contribution as its basis for determining B's gain or loss on the sale. Therefore, the partnership is treated as having a basis in the land of $100 and a gain of $20, of which B's share is $10.

The tax consequences to A are less clear. Economically A has experienced a $40 loss. She contributed land with a built-in loss of $50 and recouped $10 of this loss through her share of the land's subsequent appreciation. The problem is that the partnership apparently only has a $30 tax loss. Should a variation of the ceiling rule apply here? In our view, such a rule would treat A unfairly without any apparent justification. For this reason, we believe that future regulations will allow A a full $40 tax loss.

This result can be justified a couple of different ways. First of all, the partnership has a tax loss of only $30; it has no gain. If Congress believes it appropriate to tax B on her gain to prevent a shifting of losses from A to B, then it seems equally appropriate for A to retain those losses. Indeed, one might view the partnership's $30 loss as a net loss made up of a $40 loss and a $10 gain. Viewed this way, if B is required to include $10 gain, then A must be entitled to a $40 loss. As we shall see below, this is precisely what Treasury prescribes under the "remedial allocation method." Additionally, one could view this simply as a question of how the partnership should allocate its $150 basis between A and B. Conceptually, A and B are each selling one-half interest in the land for $60. The statute requires B to use fair market value at the date of contribution ($50 for her ½ interest) which results in a $10 gain.

14. § 704(c)(1)(C)(i).   **15.** § 704(c)(1)(C)(ii).

The balance of the partnership's basis ($100) should be available for A, which would result in a $40 loss.

In sum, it is no longer possible to shift built-in losses. No one other than the contributor is entitled to benefit from them. On the other hand, built-in gains remain subject to the ceiling rule which tolerates shifts in built-in gains. As mentioned above, this can result in serious distortions.

Traditional Method with Curative Allocations[16]

Recognizing the problems caused by the ceiling rule, Treasury now permits partnerships to use the "traditional method with curative allocations".[17] Partnerships using this method may elect to make reasonable "curative allocations" to eliminate ceiling rule distortions. A "curative allocation" is an allocation of an item for tax purposes that differs from the allocation of the corresponding book item. The allocation is meant to "cure" the disparities caused by the ceiling rule and is available only if the ceiling rule creates an initial book/tax disparity. Curative allocations must be reasonable in amount and of the same type as the item that was subject to the ceiling rule.[18] Absent an appropriate item to allocate, a curative allocation cannot be made. To illustrate, consider the following:

> *Variation #4:* Assume the facts of *Example #1*. Further assume that AB invested the $100 cash in stock which appreciates in value to $150 and that the land declines in value to $70. AB sells the land for $70 (recognizing a $30 book loss and a $10 tax gain) and sells the stock for $150 (recognizing a $50 gain for both book and tax purposes). After these sales, in the absence of curative allocations, the capital accounts of A and B would look as follows:

	A Tax	A Book	B Tax	B Book
Initial Balance	$60	$100	$100	$100
Land Sale	10	(15)	–	(15)
Stock Sale	25	25	25	25
	$95	$110	$125	$110

Once again, the ceiling rule has created a disparity between book and tax capital of $15 for both partners. Realization of gain on the stock, however, presents an opportunity to eliminate the disparity by reallocating gain on the stock for *tax* purposes, $40 to A and $10 to B. The regulations permit this, so long as the reallocated amount does not exceed the amount of ceiling limited item for the taxable

16. § 1.704–3(c).

17. § 1.704–3(c)(1).

18. § 1.704–3(c)(3). In the case of depreciable property, the period of time over which the curative allocations are made must also be reasonable.

year, and is of the same type or character as that item. Since the amount of the curative allocation is precisely the amount of the distortion, and since both the land and the stock are capital assets, the curative allocation of gain on the stock can be expected to have the same effect as loss limited by the ceiling rule. The allocation, therefore, would be reasonable and would result in the following adjustments to the partners capital accounts:

	A		*B*	
	Tax	*Book*	*Tax*	*Book*
Initial Balance	$60	$100	$100	$100
Land Sale	10	(15)	–	(15)
Stock Sale[19]	40	25	10	25
	$110	$110	$110	$110

Remedial Allocation Method[20]

The third method blessed by the regulations is the "remedial allocation method," which provides an alternative method of curing ceiling rule distortions. In essence, the remedial allocation method permits partners to ignore the ceiling rule: tax allocations will always be available to match book allocations to the noncontributors because the partnership is permitted to manufacture them. The remedial allocation method authorizes the partnership to "create" offsetting tax allocations, with the result that the net amount allocated will equal the partnership entity's total gain, loss or deduction. Remedial allocations are fictitious, or notional, offsetting tax allocations; their only role is to precisely eliminate any disparities between book and tax accounts created by the ceiling rule. These allocations always exactly equal the disparity and are of a character identical to that of the item limited by the ceiling rule. Because they are notional and offsetting, they do not have any effect on the partnership's taxable income or adjusted bases.[21] Remedial allocations are treated as actual tax items by the partners, however, and therefore may affect both their tax liability and their outside bases.[22] As we shall see below in the context of depreciable property, the remedial allocation method treats the contribution of property to a partnership in some ways as if it were a sale, with the gain on that sale recognized by the contributing partner only as necessary to neutralize the application of the ceiling rule.[23]

---

19. Note that curative allocations violate what was thought to be an "inviolate principle:" tax allocations must follow book. As we will see below, these differ from remedial allocations which are solely offsetting tax allocations.

20. § 1.704–3(d).

21. § 1.704–3(d)(4)(i).

22. § 1.704–3(d)(4)(ii).

23. The remedial allocation method is based upon the so-called "deferred sale method" for accounting for built-in gains and losses which had been periodically considered and rejected by Con-

To illustrate how the remedial allocation method applies to nondepreciable property, reconsider **Variation #2**, where the land fell in value and the AB partnership sold it for $70, resulting in a $30 book loss and a $10 tax gain. The $30 book loss was allocated equally between A and B, $15 each. Since there was no tax loss, under the traditional method the ceiling rule prevented B from receiving a tax loss to match her book loss. Under the remedial allocation method, however, B would report a tax loss of $15 characterized as if it were from the sale of the land; A would receive an offsetting tax gain of $15 of the same character. A thus reports total gain of $25, B reports a loss of $15, netting out to the partnership entity's gain of $10: just the appropriate result which was prevented by the ceiling rule. The partners would adjust their capital accounts as follows:

	A		**B**	
	Tax	*Book*	*Tax*	*Book*
Initial Balance	$60	$100	$100	$100
Land Sale	10	(15)	–	(15)
Remedial Allocation	15	0	(15)	0
	$ 85	$85	$ 85	$ 85

Notice that, in contrast with the traditional method with curative allocations, remedial allocations do not depend on the existence of other items of income or loss. If this partnership had used the traditional method with curative allocations, the lack of other capital gains would have prevented elimination of the disparity created by the ceiling rule.

Depreciable Property

When the contributed property is depreciable, allocation of built-in gain is more complex. Unlike the case of nondepreciable property, simply waiting until sale to allocate the gain or loss will not ordinarily accomplish the purpose of taxing the contributing partner on the built-in gain. This is so because, in the normal course, depreciable property does not generate gain on sale if held for its useful life; instead its value is realized by the owner during the property's life in the form of the ordinary income that it generates. In such a case, the only way to ensure that the contributor will be taxed on the built-in gain is to increase her share of current income from the property. This is accomplished under the traditional method by allocating depreciation *away* from the con-

gress and the Treasury since 1954. For a discussion of the history of the method and an argument that the deferred sale method be made mandatory, see Laura E. Cunningham and Noël B. Cunningham, *Simplifying Subchapter K: The Deferred Sale Method,* 51 SMU L. Rev. 1 (1997).

tributing partner: i.e., the noncontributing partner receives tax depreciation up to her share of book depreciation, and only if tax depreciation remains thereafter is it allocated to the contributing partner. The result is to tax the contributing partner on more than her book share of income from the property, thereby resolving the book/tax disparity over the life of the asset. To illustrate:

> **Example #2:** C and D form an equal partnership to which C contributes equipment with a basis of $80 and a value of $120 and D contributes $120 cash. The equipment originally had a 10 year recovery period and C elected to use the straight-line method. Although there are only 4 years remaining in its recovery period, if CD had purchased the equipment on the date of formation, it would have had a 10 year recovery period. C and D agree to share all book items equally. Upon formation, CD's balance sheet would be as follows:

Assets			Liabilities & Capital
	Basis	*Book*	
Equip't	$ 80	$120	
Cash	120	120	
	$200	$240	

	Capital Accounts	
	Tax	*Book*
C	$ 80	$120
D	120	120
	$200	$240

Before looking at the various ways to account for this built-in gain, there are two additional rules with which you must be familiar. First, when a partner contributes depreciable property to a partnership, the partnership steps into the shoes of the partner for purposes of cost recovery; the partnership must recover its transferred basis in the property over the remaining recovery period using the same method as the contributor.[24] Second, for book purposes under the capital accounting rules, a partnership must recover the same percentage (proportion) of basis for book purposes as it does for tax purposes.[25] Applying these rules to **Example #2**:

> 1) CD must recover its $80 tax basis using the straight-line method over its remaining recovery period of 4 years (i.e., $20/yr.), and therefore,

> 2) CD *must* also recover its $120 book basis using the straight-line method over the same 4 year period (i.e., $30/yr.).

The Traditional Method

Consistent with the traditional method's general intent to treat noncontributing partners as if each purchased an undivided inter-

24. § 168(i)(7). **25.** § 1.704–1(b)(2)(iv)(d), (g)(3).

est in contributed property for cash, the noncontributors are allocated (if possible) the same amount of cost recovery for tax purposes as they are for book purposes; if the partnership's cost recovery deduction exceeds the noncontributors' share, the contributing partner must be allocated the balance. On the facts of *Example #2*, since each partner suffers $15 of depreciation for book purposes, of the $20 tax depreciation $15 is allocated to D and only $5 to C. This means that, although C and D have the same book income, C will have $10 more in taxable income than D. If we assume for the moment that book income is a surrogate for economic income, C is being "overtaxed" by $10 each year. In this way, C takes into account (i.e., is taxed on) the built-in gain over the life of the property. After 4 years, C will have taken into account all $40 of built-in gain and the disparity between book and tax capital will have been entirely eliminated.[26]

The ceiling rule prevents the traditional method from completely eliminating the contributor's book/tax disparity, and allows some of the built-in gain to be shifted to the noncontributing partner, when there is insufficient tax basis to fully cover the noncontributor's share of book basis. In those circumstances, there will not be sufficient tax depreciation to allocate to the noncontributing partner.[27] To illustrate, consider the following:

> *Example #3:* The same as *Example #2*, except C's adjusted basis in the equipment at the time of contribution is only $40. Thus, CD's initial adjusted basis in the equipment is also $40 and CD is permitted only $10 of annual depreciation for tax purposes. In addition, each year for the first four years, CD has $20 of ordinary business income *before* taking depreciation into account.

Although D's share of the equipment's initial book value is $60, the total tax depreciation available under the ceiling rule is the $40 tax basis at the time of contribution. Thus, it will be impossible to treat D as though she purchased an undivided one-half interest in the property: although CD still has $30 of annual book depreciation, $15 of which is allocable to D, CD now only has $10 of annual tax depreciation. Under the traditional method, all $10 of tax

---

26. A similar analysis would apply to depreciable property that is contributed to a partnership with a built-in loss. To illustrate, suppose C's basis in the property contributed in *Example #2* was $160. Under § 168(i)(7), CD is required to recover its $160 basis over the remaining recovery period of 4 years, $40 per year. CD must still recover its book basis of $120 over the same period using the straight-line method, or $30 per year. Each year D will be entitled to $15 of depreciation for both book and tax purposes, while C will be entitled to $15 for book purposes but $25 for tax purposes. In this way C will get the benefit of the $40 built-in loss over the property's remaining recovery period.

27. There might be a ceiling rule problem, however, if the partnership sold the property during its useful life for a book loss and a tax gain.

depreciation is allocated to D. Nevertheless, since this allocation is insufficient to match D's share of book depreciation, it creates a disparity between D's tax and book capital accounts that will grow at the rate of $5 per year. After the first year, the partners' capital accounts are:

	C		**D**	
	Tax	*Book*	*Tax*	*Book*
Initial Balance	$40	$120	$120	$120
Depreciation		(15)	(10)	(15)
Ordinary Income	10	10	10	10
	$50	$115	$120	$115

Notice that a $5 disparity has been created in D's capital accounts. This disparity eventually will grow to $20 after 4 years and thereafter will be locked in until D sells or retires her partnership interest. In effect, the ceiling rule causes D to be overtaxed in the amount of $5 per year for 4 years, thereby taxing D on a portion of C's built-in gain. Resolution of these disparities will be deferred until liquidation of the partnership, or sale by C and D of their partnership interests.

Traditional Method with Curative Allocations

If the partnership in ***Example #3*** elected to use the traditional method with curative allocations, the partnership could eliminate this annual distortion by making curative allocations of its ordinary income. In ***Example #3***, CD has $20 of ordinary income that the partners share equally—$10 each. By allocating $15 of this income for tax (*not* book) purposes to C and $5 to D, the ceiling rule distortion would be "cured." Since this allocation would be reasonable in both amount and type it would be respected. If this were done, the partners' capital accounts would be adjusted as follows:

	C		**D**	
	Tax	*Book*	*Tax*	*Book*
Initial Balance	$40	$120	$120	$120
Depreciation		(15)	(10)	(15)
Ordinary Income	15	10	5	10
	$55	$115	$115	$115

The purpose of curative allocations is easy to see in the context of depreciable property: under the traditional method, the built-in gain in the property is amortized over the life of the property, as it produces income. When the ceiling rule applies, in the absence of curative allocations, the noncontributor is reporting more than his or her economic share of the property's income. The curative allocation of additional income to the contributing partner solves this inequity.

Remedial Allocation Method

A partnership that adopts the remedial allocation method for depreciable property must use a special rule to determine the amount of book depreciation with respect to that property. The partnership then uses the traditional method to allocate the related tax items, i.e., tax allocations will follow book allocations. If the ceiling rule prevents the noncontributing partner from receiving a tax allocation equal to the corresponding book allocation, the partnership makes offsetting remedial allocations of the appropriate character and amount to both the contributing and noncontributing partners.

The special rule for determining book depreciation with respect to the property is loosely based on the notion that the contributing partner sold the property on a deferred basis to the partnership on the date of contribution for its fair market value. To the extent of its transferred basis, the partnership steps into the shoes of the contributing partner for both book and tax purposes and must continue to use the contributing partner's cost recovery method. The value of the property in excess of its basis is treated for book purposes as if the partnership had purchased the property for this amount.[28] With respect to this latter amount, the partnership may use any method of cost recovery that is allowed for property of that type.[29]

To illustrate, assume the partnership in ***Example #3*** adopted the remedial allocation method. For book purposes, the partnership would be treated as if it acquired two pieces of equipment, one that was contributed by C with a value and a basis of $40, and one that it purchased with a value of $80. With respect to the contributed portion, the partnership would step into C's shoes and therefore would be required to use the straight-line method over the remaining four years of that property's life, resulting in depreciation of $10 per year for both book and tax purposes. With respect to the notionally purchased portion, the partnership may adopt any appropriate method of cost recovery permitted by the Code for property of that type. Ignoring conventions, if CD chooses the straight-line method over 10 years, the purchased portion will provide CD with $8 of book (but not tax) depreciation each year for 10 years. Therefore, CD would have a book cost recovery deduction of $18 per year ($10 from the contributed portion and $8 from the purchased portion) for the first 4 years, and $8 per year for the remaining 6 years. CD's initial balance sheet would look as follows:

---

28. If the basis of the contributed property is equal to or greater than its value, then this special rule has no application.

29. The partnership must also use the appropriate first year convention. See § 1.704–3(d)(2) and § 168(d).

	Assets		**Liabilities & Capital**
	Basis	*Book*	
Equip't[30]	$ 40	$120	
Cash	120	120	
	$160	$240	

Capital Accounts

	Tax	*Book*
C	$ 40	$120
D	120	120
	$160	$240

During each of its first four years of operation, CD would have $2 income for book purposes, and $10 of income for tax purposes determined as follows:

	Tax	*Book*
Net ordinary income	$20	$20
Depreciation	(10)	(18)
	$10	$ 2

For each of these years, for book purposes, C and D would each be entitled to one-half of both the ordinary income ($10) and the depreciation ($9), a net of $1 per year. For tax purposes each would be allocated $10 of ordinary income. However, under the traditional method, D would be allocated $9 of depreciation and C only $1. Therefore, D would have $1 of taxable income and C $9, thus

	C		**D**	
	Tax	*Book*	*Tax*	*Book*
Net ordinary income	$10	$10	$10	$10
Depreciation	(1)	(9)	(9)	(9)
	$ 9	$ 1	$ 1	$ 1

At the end of the first four years, the capital accounts of the partnership would be as follows:

	C		**D**	
	Tax	*Book*	*Tax*	*Book*
Initial Balance	$ 40	$120	$120	$120
Aggregate Adj. first 4 years	36	4	4	4
	$ 76	$124	$124	$124

Notice that during this period of time, the book/tax disparity in C's capital account has declined from $80 to $48. This is a result of the fact that C has taken only $1 a year in depreciation even though for book purposes she was entitled to $9. In effect, C has

30. In fact, CD only acquired one piece of equipment, and that by contribution. The two-item, or bifurcation, model is a fiction created by the remedial allocation regime.

over reported her tax income by $8 for each of four years, thereby taking into account $32 of the $80 built-in gain that was inherent in the property when it was contributed. Also notice that, to this point, the ceiling rule has not caused any book/tax disparity for D (because tax depreciation was sufficient to match D's book depreciation each year) and the partnership has not used any remedial allocations.

The analysis changes in year 5. During years 5 through 10, the partnership continues to have $20 of ordinary income. But the calculation of depreciation is changed because the partnership has entirely recovered the portion of basis inherited from D. Now the book depreciation is only $8 and there is no tax depreciation. Therefore, the partnership's net annual book income is $12 (and each partner's share is $6). Although $4 of book depreciation is allocated to D, the ceiling rule prohibits any allocation of depreciation for tax purposes. Therefore, under the remedial allocation method, the partnership must make two offsetting remedial allocations of $4 each year. Each year the partners' capital accounts will have the following adjustments:

	C		**D**	
	Tax	*Book*	*Tax*	*Book*
Ordinary Income	$10	$10	$10	$10
Depreciation	0	(4)	0	(4)
Remedial Allocation	4		(4)	
Annual Net Adjust.	$14	$ 6	$ 6	$ 6

Notice that each year C reports $8 more taxable income than she has for book purposes. This reduces the disparity between her tax and book accounts, so that by the end of year 10 the disparity will have disappeared.

Choice of Methods

The regulations are extremely flexible. Partnerships are permitted to choose a "reasonable method" for resolving book/tax disparities, and the Treasury has provided three examples of methods which may be reasonable. The choice of allocation method may be made on a property-by-property basis, so that a partnership is not bound to use one method with respect to all contributed or revalued property.[31] This flexibility is tempered, however, by the caveat that "the overall method or combination of methods [must be] reasonable based on the facts and circumstances and consistent with the purpose of section 704(c)."[32]

A partnership's choice of a particular method will depend on a variety of factors, most importantly the tax profiles of the individu-

---

31. § 1.704–3(a)(2).   **32.** *Id.*

al partners. Nevertheless, there are certain generalizations that can be made. First, each of the three methods yields precisely the same amount of annual net tax depreciation; they differ only in how that net amount is allocated among the partners.[33] For this reason, if all partners are in the same tax bracket, both the government and the partnership (as a whole) should not care which method is adopted; all methods result in the same aggregate tax savings. Yet because of the differences among the methods, the individual partners may care enormously.

If the partners are in different tax brackets, a partnership will probably choose the method that results in the largest aggregate tax savings for its partners. The most important factor in making this determination are the partners' tax brackets. To illustrate, reconsider *Example #3*. From C's point of view, the most beneficial method is the traditional method because C will never have to include any curative or remedial allocations. From D's point of view, however, the traditional method is the least favorable method, for she will only receive a total of $40 of depreciation rather than $60. Assuming that there are other items of the appropriate type and amount, the most beneficial method for D is the traditional method with curative allocations. Even though the traditional method with curative allocations and the remedial allocation method both provide D with $60 of depreciation, under the former it is spread over 4 years, rather than 10. Everything else being equal, the choice of methods should depend on the relative tax brackets of C and D. If C is in a relatively high bracket as compared with D, the traditional method will generate the most savings; if C is in a relatively low bracket, then the traditional method with curative allocations is best.[34]

33. To demonstrate, compare the annual depreciation to which each partner would have been entitled in *Example #3* under each of the three methods:

Method	Years				
	1	*2*	*3*	*4*	*5–10*
Traditional					
C	0	0	0	0	0
D	(10)	(10)	(10)	(10)	0
Net	(10)	(10)	(10)	(10)	0
Curative Allocations					
C	+5	+5	+5	+5	0
D	(15)	(15)	(15)	(15)	0
Net	(10)	(10)	(10)	(10)	0
Remedial Allocations					
C	(1)	(1)	(1)	(1)	+24
D	(9)	(9)	(9)	(9)	(24)
Net	(10)	(10)	(10)	(10)	0

34. Whichever method is chosen, the partner who bears the additional tax burden will have to be otherwise compensated.

Anti-abuse Rules

Treasury's blessing of the three alternative methods for making § 704(c) allocations is subject to the anti-abuse rule of § 1.704–3(a)(10). That rule states that an allocation method is *not* reasonable if

> "the contribution of property ... and the corresponding allocation of tax items with respect to the property are made with a view to shifting the tax consequences of built-in gain or loss among the partners in a manner that substantially reduces the present value of the partners' aggregate tax liability."

The regulations give two examples illustrating the anti-abuse rule. To understand Treasury's concerns, it is important to recognize that, ever since 1981, the Internal Revenue Code has provided very accelerated methods of cost recovery involving recovery periods that are generally much shorter than true economic lives. This was particularly true in the early 1980's when, for example, a taxpayer who purchased an airplane could recover its cost over 5 years even though the plane's economic useful life was in excess of 20 years. These methods of cost recovery have resulted in taxpayers holding valuable property with a low (or no) basis. This situation is central to both of the anti-abuse examples in the regulations.

In both of these examples, an equal partnership is formed with one partner ("P") contributing property with a value of $10,000 and an adjusted basis of $1,000 and the other partner ("O") contributing $10,000 cash. The property has only one year left in its recovery period, but has a substantially longer economic life.

The first example illustrates an unreasonable use of the traditional method.[35] In this example, P is in a high marginal bracket and O is in the zero bracket because of NOLs that are expected to expire unused. P contributes the property to the partnership with a view to shifting some of the built-in gain to O by selling the property in Year 2. Under the traditional method, the partnership takes $10,000 of depreciation for book purposes and $1,000 of depreciation for tax purposes in the first year. This reduces the partnership's basis in the property to zero for both book and tax purposes, eliminating all of the § 704(c) gain. The partners share the book depreciation equally, while O is allocated all of the tax depreciation. In year 2, the partnership sells the property at a $10,000 gain, which is shared equally for both book and tax purposes. If these allocations were respected, the capital accounts would be adjusted as follows:

---

35. § 1.704–3(b)(2)Ex. 2.

	P		O	
	Tax	*Book*	*Tax*	*Book*
Initial Balance	$1,000	$10,000	$10,000	$10,000
Depreciation	0	(5,000)	(1,000)	(5,000)
Sale	5,000	5,000	5,000	5,000
	$6,000	$10,000	$14,000	$10,000

The interplay of the one-year cost recovery period and the traditional method results in a shift for tax purposes of $4,000 of gain from P to O. The regulations find this to be an unreasonable use of the traditional method because it was used with a view to shifting built-in gain from a taxpayer in a high marginal rate to one with a lower marginal rate.

The second example involves the unreasonable use of the traditional method with curative allocations.[36] The facts of this example are strikingly similar to the first, but there are important differences: P is the zero bracket taxpayer who has NOLs, and O is in a high bracket; the partnership does not intend to sell the property; and the partnership has $8,000 of sales income. Under the traditional method with curative allocations, during its first year of operations, the partnership takes $10,000 of book depreciation which is shared equally, and $1,000 of tax depreciation which is all allocated to O. Due to an insufficient amount of tax depreciation, a curative allocation of sales income is made. For book purposes, each partner receives $4,000 of sales income, but for tax purposes, all $8,000 is allocated to P. If this were respected, the partners' capital accounts would be adjusted as follows:

	P		O	
	Tax	*Book*	*Tax*	*Book*
Initial Balance	$1,000	$10,000	$10,000	$10,000
Depreciation	0	(5,000)	(1,000)	(5,000)
Sale	8,000	4,000	0	4,000
	$9,000	$ 9,000	$ 9,000	$ 9,000

Notice that the curative allocation has eliminated the disparity between tax and book capital. Nevertheless, the regulations find this to be an unreasonable use of the traditional method with curative allocations. The abuse, it appears, is that O, the high bracket taxpayer, is essentially allowed immediately to deduct its entire cost of its share of the equipment ($5,000) at practically no cost to either P or the partnership. The "cost" is simply an acceleration of the built-in gain for which P should ultimately be responsible, but since P currently is in the zero bracket, P will owe no additional tax.

36. § 1.704–3(c)(4)Ex.3.

The role that this § 704(c) anti-abuse rule should play is unclear. By its terms, it could potentially apply anytime a ceiling rule shift of income to a lower bracket taxpayer has the effect of reducing the partners' aggregate income tax liability. We believe, however, that a more appropriate reading of the rule would limit it to situations like those in the two examples illustrating the rule, where the noneconomic capital accounting rules have the effect of accelerating a ceiling rule shift of income (as in § 1.704–3(b)(2)Ex.2), or permitting the noncontributor to expense her investment (as in § 1.704–3(c)(4)Ex.3).[37]

Revaluations

The second common event that predictably creates a disparity between book value and tax basis is the revaluation of partnership assets in connection with a contribution (or distribution) of money or other property to (or from) a partnership in exchange for an interest in that partnership.[38] When a revaluation occurs, all of the partnership's existing built-in gains and losses are recognized for book purposes and allocated among the existing partners in accordance with their agreement; the corresponding tax items, however, are not recognized. The resulting book/tax disparity is directly analogous to one created when § 704(c) property is contributed to a partnership, and raises the same issues. Indeed, the parallels are so striking that the regulations refer to allocations with respect to property that has been revalued as "reverse § 704(c) allocations," and require that these allocations be made in accordance with "§ 704(c) principles."[39] To illustrate, consider the following:

> ***Example #4:*** Several years ago, C and D formed an equal partnership. On January 1 of this year, CD's balance sheet is as follows:

Assets		*Liabilities & Capital*
	Book	
Cash	$ 50	
Equip't	50	
Land	100	
	$200	

		Capital Accounts	
			Book
	C		$100
	D		100
			$200

37. For a more complete analysis of the anti-abuse rule, see Laura E. Cunningham, *Use and Abuse of Section 704(c)*, 3 Fla. Tax Rev. 92 (1996).

38. Section 1.704(b)–1(b)(2)(iv)(f) permits revaluations only under certain circumstances. The reference to an interest in the partnership should be interpreted to mean any meaningful change in the profit or loss sharing ratios of the partners in response to a contribution or distribution of money or other property.

39. § 1.704–3(a)(6)(i).

On January 1, the equipment has a value of $210 and the land has a value of $140. The equipment originally had a 5–year recovery period and CD elected to use the straight-line method. Two years remain in its recovery period. On this date, E contributes $200 cash and becomes a full one-third partner in all income, gains and losses of the partnership. The partnership elects to book up its assets under § 1.704–1(b)(2)(iv)(f). After the revaluation, the partnership's balance sheet is as follows:

Assets			Liabilities & Capital	
	Basis	*Book*		
Cash	$250	$250		
Equip't	50	210		
Land	100	140		
	$400	$600		

	Capital Accounts	
	Tax	*Book*
C	$100	$200
D	100	200
E	200	200
	$400	$600

As a result of the revaluation, the built-in gains in both the equipment and the land have been recognized by the partnership for book purposes (but not for tax purposes) and allocated equally between C and D. A sale of the properties for their revised book values would result in tax gains, but no corresponding book gains. The only substantive difference between this and a contribution of § 704(c) property to a partnership is that the existing partners, not the contributor, are credited with the unrealized appreciation from the revaluation. Not surprisingly, the regulations require that those partners who shared the book gain be allocated the corresponding tax item "so as to take account of the variation between the adjusted tax basis and book value of such property in the same manner as under section 704(c) ..."[40] Thus, just as the revaluation creates the same type of book/tax disparity as a contribution of appreciated property, the principles of § 704(c) must be applied to resolve this "§ 704(c) type" situation.[41]

---

40. § 1.704–1(b)(2)(iv)(f)(4).

41. Another way to think about this revaluation is to recognize that its consequences are economically identical to those that would have resulted if the old partnership had been liquidated, and then a new partnership formed, with E contributing cash of $200 and C and D jointly contributing cash and property worth $400 with a basis of $200. If in fact CDE had been created in this manner, § 704(c) would have clearly applied.

Applying these principles to *Example #4*, the partnership must use one of the three allocation methods approved by the regulations to resolve the book/tax disparities with respect to the equipment and the land. As noted above, the partnership does not have to use the same method for both properties. In the three variations below, we make two simplifying assumptions: First, we assume the land is not sold (and therefore the method chosen for the land does not matter); second, we assume that during its first two years of operation the CDE partnership has $30 of net income from operations *before* taking into account depreciation. Consider how the equipment would be treated under each of the methods.

Variation #1: The partnership uses the traditional method.

Under the traditional method, CDE must recover its cost in the equipment for both book and tax purposes over 2 years, the equipment's remaining recovery period. For book purposes, it has $105 of annual book depreciation, which it allocates $35 to each partner. For tax purposes, there is only $25 depreciation. Under the traditional method, E, the new partner, must be allocated tax depreciation equal to her book depreciation, if possible. This is not possible in *Example #4* because of the ceiling rule: E's share of book depreciation is $35, but the partnership has only $25 of tax depreciation, all of which is allocated to E. This creates a $10 book/tax disparity in E's capital accounts at the end of the first year:

	C		D		E	
	Tax	*Book*	*Tax*	*Book*	*Tax*	*Book*
Initial Balance	$100	$200	$100	$200	$200	$200
Ordinary Income	10	10	10	10	10	10
Cost Recovery[42]	0	(35)	0	(35)	(25)	(35)
	$110	$175	$110	$175	$185	$175

In the second year of operations, the ceiling rule again will limit E's tax depreciation to $25, even though her share of book depreciation is $35. This will increase her book/tax disparity to $20, which will be locked in until she disposes of her interest in the partnership.

Variation #2: The partnership uses the traditional method with curative allocations.

As in *Variation #1*, the ceiling rule creates a book/tax disparity of $10 in each of the first two years of CDE's operations. Under the traditional method with curative allocations, CDE may allocate E's share of ordinary income for tax purposes, **not** for book purposes, equally between C and D to cure the disparity. This

---

42. The cost recovery allowance is separately stated because its allocation to E under § 704(c) principles in effect amounts to a special allocation. See § 1.702–1(a)(8)(i).

allocation is reasonable in amount and is of the same type as the depreciation that was limited by the ceiling rule. Under this method, the adjustments to the partners' capital accounts for the first two years would be as follows:

	C		**D**		**E**	
	Tax	*Book*	*Tax*	*Book*	*Tax*	*Book*
Initial Balance	$100	$200	$100	$200	$200	$200
Year 1 Adjustments:						
Ordinary Income	15	10	15	10	0	10
Cost Recovery	0	(35)	0	(35)	(25)	(35)
End of Year 1	$115	$175	$115	$175	$175	$175
Year 2 Adjustments:						
Ordinary Income	15	10	15	10	0	10
Cost Recovery	0	(35)	0	(35)	(25)	(35)
End of Year 2	$130	$150	$130	$150	$150	$150

Notice that this allocation precisely cures the book/tax disparity that otherwise would arise. Notice that C and D each has a $20 disparity in her capital account. This reflects the $40 built-in gain still inherent in the land.

> **Variation #3:** The partnership uses the remedial allocation method for the equipment.

If the remedial allocation method is used in this context, then the partnership must first compute its book depreciation under the special rule, and then use the traditional method for allocating tax items. If the ceiling rule prevents the new partner from receiving a tax allocation equal to her book allocation, the partnership makes the appropriate offsetting remedial allocations. On these facts, the special rule bifurcates the book value of the equipment ($210) into two portions. The first portion is equal to the partnership's basis in the equipment (i.e., $50) and must be recovered using the same method of cost recovery the partnership used immediately before the revaluation; therefore, CDE must recover this $50 using straight-line over two years (i.e., $25 per year). The second portion is equal to the excess of the equipment's fair market value over its basis, here $160,[43] and may be recovered using any method that would have been appropriate if the partnership had purchased the equipment for this amount. Ignoring conventions, if the partnership chooses to recover its cost in the "purchased" portion using the straight-line method over five years, the partnership will be entitled to $32 of book depreciation each year for 5 years. Therefore, the partnership will have a book cost recovery deduction with respect to the equipment of $57 per year ($25 + $32) for the first 2

43. $210 − $50 = $160.

years, and $32 per year for the remaining three years. It will have tax cost recovery of $25 for the first two years, and none thereafter.

Under the traditional method, for the first two years there is sufficient tax depreciation so that the ceiling rule does not come into play. For each of those years, the partnership has $57 of book depreciation, which is divided equally among the partners, and $25 of tax depreciation the first $19 of which is allocated to E, and the balance shared equally by C and D. The adjustments to the partners' capital accounts for depreciation (ignoring other adjustments) would be as follows:

	C		**D**		**E**	
	Tax	*Book*	*Tax*	*Book*	*Tax*	*Book*
Initial Balance	$100	$200	$100	$200	$200	$200
Depreciation						
Year 1	(3)	(19)	(3)	(19)	(19)	(19)
Year 2	(3)	(19)	(3)	(19)	(19)	(19)
End of Year 2	$94	$162	$94	$162	$162	$162

For years 3 through 5, however, since CDE is no longer entitled to any tax depreciation, the partnership must make remedial allocations equal to the amount of E's share of depreciation. The adjustments to the partners' capital accounts for depreciation and remedial allocations over the three year period would be as follows:

	C		**D**		**E**	
	Tax	*Book*	*Tax*	*Book*	*Tax*	*Book*
Balance (1/1/3)	$94	$162	$94	$162	$162	$162
Depreciation[44]	0	(32)	0	(32)	0	(32)
Remedial all[45]	16		16		(32)	
	$110	$130	$110	$130	$130	$130

The remaining disparity between C's and D's book and tax capital accounts reflects the built-in gain in the land.

44. Each partner would be entitled to book depreciation of ⅓ of $32 ($10.67) each year for three years.

45. E would be entitled to a remedial allocation of ($10.67) each year for three years. This is precisely offset by annual remedial allocations of $5.33 to both C and D.

Chapter Eight

PARTNERSHIP LIABILITIES

Introduction

It is well accepted for income tax purposes that when a person uses borrowed funds to purchase an asset or pay a deductible expense, she is treated just as if the funds were hers outright: she is given full "basis credit" for purchases, and is entitled to deduct the expense. This is true even though the funds are excluded from the tax base at the time of receipt, and will only be included if and when the taxpayer is relieved of the liability. These rules apply whether the liability is recourse or nonrecourse. The role of § 752 is to replicate these results in the partnership context.

Under the aggregate notion of partnership taxation, it is clear that credit for partnership liabilities must be divided among the partners. Section 752 accomplishes that by treating changes in a partner's share of partnership liabilities as contributions and distributions of cash to and from the partnership. Thus, partnership liabilities are included in a partner's outside basis under § 722. This can be important for two reasons. First, under § 704(d) a partner cannot deduct partnership losses in excess of her outside basis. Second, if a partner receives a distribution of cash from a partnership which exceeds her outside basis, she will have gain under § 731(a)(1). Although it is obviously important how partners share liabilities, it is not immediately apparent just how this should be done.

Until the early 1980's, the general rule was easily stated: Recourse liabilities were shared by general partners in accordance with their shares of partnership losses, while nonrecourse liabilities were shared by all partners in accordance with their profit shares. In most cases, this rule worked fairly well. As commercial lending practices became more and more sophisticated, however, it was sometimes difficult to distinguish between recourse and nonre-

114

course debt, and to determine who would bear ultimate responsibility for a particular liability. To illustrate, consider the following example based on the facts of *Raphan v. United States*:[1]

> **Example #1:** GL is a limited partnership to which G, the general partner, and L, the limited partner, each contribute $50. L has no obligation to contribute more capital to the partnership or to restore any deficit in her capital account. G and L agree to share profits and losses equally to the extent of each partner's basis; if L's basis is reduced to zero, G will be allocated all further losses. GL acquires a building for $1,000 by paying $100 in cash and giving a $900 nonrecourse mortgage for the balance. The lender, however, insists that G, in her personal capacity, guarantee the mortgage.

Should this mortgage be considered recourse or nonrecourse? If the mortgage were considered nonrecourse, G and L would share the mortgage in the same manner that they share profits, i.e., equally. Under this characterization, G and L would each have an initial outside basis of $500 and L could be allocated up to $500 of partnership losses. On the other hand, if the mortgage were considered recourse with respect to G, the entire liability would be allocated to G. In this latter case, L could only be allocated partnership losses to the extent of her capital contribution of $50.

As a technical matter, the mortgage is nonrecourse. As a matter of local law, a guarantor is not liable on a guaranteed debt until default. Therefore, one might argue that the mortgage should be considered nonrecourse for tax purposes unless, and until, there is a default. On the other hand, it is perfectly clear from the outset that if the property declines in value below the principal amount of the mortgage, it will be G, the guarantor, who will bear the loss. One might argue that characterizing this mortgage as nonrecourse would be the ultimate victory of form over substance.

Nevertheless, on facts similar to these, the Court of Claims held that, despite the guarantee, the mortgage should be treated as nonrecourse.[2] The decision permitted the limited partners to deduct losses borne economically by the guaranteeing general partner. Congressional reaction was immediate and swift. The following year it enacted legislation that prospectively overruled *Raphan* and directed the Treasury to revise the regulations under § 752 "to take into account current commercial practices and arrangements [including] assumptions, guarantees, indemnities, and similar ar-

---

1. 3 Cl.Ct. 457 (1983), *aff'd in part, rev'd in part*, 759 F.2d 879 (Fed.Cir. 1985).

2. The decision was based on an interpretation of old § 1.752–1(e), which was superceded in 1989.

rangements."[3] The current regulations are the product of this directive.[4]

A Preliminary Issue: What is a Liability?

Before examining the details of the regulations, it is important to recognize that they distinguish between two types of liabilities. The first type of liability is sometimes referred to as a "§ 1.752–1 liability," and, until recently, was the only type that was recognized under § 752. Section 1.752–1 liabilities are defined as only those obligations that, when incurred,

1. create or increase basis directly (e.g., a purchase money mortgage) or indirectly (e.g., a second mortgage or unsecured loan);[5] or

2. give rise to a deduction (e.g., accrued but unpaid expenses of an accrual method partnership);[6] or

3. give rise to expenditures described in § 705(a)(2)(B)(i.e., expenses that cannot either be deducted or capitalized, such as syndication fees).[7]

The general rules governing § 1.752–1 liabilities are the subject of this chapter.[8]

The second type of liability is known as a "§ 1.752–7 liability" and is defined as any partnership obligation that is not governed by the general rules.[9] This type of obligation is often contingent and includes environmental obligations, tort obligations, contract obligations, pension obligations, as well as various obligations that may arise under derivative financial instruments. All § 1.752–7 liabilities have one thing in common: although not reflected in basis, these liabilities do reduce the value of the property to which they relate. In this way, they are very similar to built-in losses. Until recently, they were not taken into account at all under § 752 and were used by aggressive taxpayers in questionable transactions. To

3. General Explanation of the Tax Reform Act of 1984, 251 (1985).

4. As a point of interest, *Raphan* was subsequently overruled on this issue. *Raphan v. United States*, 759 F.2d 879 (Fed.Cir. 1985).

5. The borrower will receive full basis credit for the asset purchased with the proceeds of the loan.

6. In contrast, the accrued but unpaid expenses of a cash method partnership are not "liabilities" for purposes of § 752. Rev. Rul. 88–77, 1988–2 CB 128.

7. § 1.752–1(a)(4)(i).

8. Section 1.752–1 liabilities also include certain obligations that would not technically constitute indebtedness. For

example, in Rev. Rul. 95–26, 1995–1 C.B. 131, the Service ruled that a short sale of securities by a partnership created a partnership liability for purposes of § 752. In a short sale, the short seller borrows securities from a broker-dealer that it sells to an unrelated buyer. The seller must return similar securities to the broker-dealer on demand. As a result of the short sale, the seller has additional assets equal to the sales price, but also an obligation to return the securities.

9. § 1.752–7(b)(3). § 1.752–7 liabilities also include the amount by which a § 1.752–1 obligation exceeds the amount taken into account under the general rules.

combat these transactions, Treasury decided that it must take these liabilities into account. Rather than subjecting them to the general rules of § 752, however, Treasury determined that § 1.752–7 liabilities should be governed by § 704(c) principles. For example, if a partner contributes property that is subject to a § 1.752–7 liability to a partnership, it is not reflected in either the partner's or partnership's basis. The liability is, however, reflected in the partner's capital account, creating the same type of disparity that would result from contributing property with a built-in loss.

Although a detailed examination of how § 1.752–7 liabilities are treated is beyond the scope of this book, to better understand the problem that they presented and Treasury's response, consider the following: A owns land that has a fair market value and a basis of $400. The land, however, may be subject to environmental liabilities that have an estimated value of $100.[10] As a result of the existence of these liabilities, if A were to sell the land, a buyer would pay only $300 and A would suffer a $100 loss on the sale. Suppose, however, that A were to contribute the land to a partnership in exchange for a partnership interest worth $300. These liabilities are § 1.752–7 liabilities and therefore are not reflected in either A's or the partnership's basis on contribution; they are, however, reflected in A's book capital account. After the contribution, A's capital accounts would be as follows:

A

Tax	Book
$400	$300

Notice that the disparity between the balances in A's book and tax capital accounts is precisely what it would have been if A had contributed property with a conventional built-in loss of $100. Treasury recognized this and the regulations require § 1.752–7 liabilities to be treated under § 704(c) principles.[11] Therefore, if the partnership were to sell the land for $300, under § 704(c) principles the partnership would be required to allocate the $100 tax loss to A. Similarly, if the partnership were to extinguish the liabilities by making a payment of $100, A would be allocated the deduction, if any, arising from that payment.

---

10. This is the amount a willing assignee would pay to assume the liability. § 1.752–7(3)(ii).

11. § 1.752–7(a). In many ways, the treatment of § 1.752–7 liabilities is similar to the treatment of accounts payable of a cash method contributor under § 704(c)(3).

The Regulations Governing
§ 1.752–1 Liabilities

Introduction

The regulations create two different sets of rules for allocating § 1.752–1 partnership liabilities among partners, one applicable to recourse liabilities and the other to nonrecourse liabilities. For this purpose, a partnership liability is recourse to the extent that any partner (or related person) bears the economic risk of loss associated with that liability.[12] Conversely, to the extent that no partner (or related person) bears such risk of loss, the partnership liability is a nonrecourse liability.[13]

The § 752 regulations work in tandem with the regulations under § 704(b). Recourse liabilities must be shared among partners in the same way that they share the economic risk of loss represented by the liability,[14] and to determine how that economic risk is shared one must first apply the allocation rules of the § 704(b) regulations. Nonrecourse liabilities generally must be shared, at least in part, in a manner consistent with the allocation of nonrecourse deductions, so that the partners to whom those deductions are allocated will have enough basis to use them.

Economic Risk of Loss

The concept of "economic risk of loss" is central to the regulations. Identifying the partner who bears the economic risk of loss associated with a partnership liability serves two essential purposes. First, it is used to characterize a liability as recourse or nonrecourse: if the economic risk of loss associated with a liability is borne by one or more of the partners, or persons related to the partners, the liability is characterized as recourse. If no partner or related person bears the economic risk of loss associated with the liability, then the liability is nonrecourse. Second, if the liability is recourse, it is shared among the partners in the same manner that they share the economic risk of loss associated with it. This requires a determination of ultimate responsibility for the liability.

The determination of who will ultimately bear the economic risk of loss requires an analysis not only of the partnership agreement, but also of those obligations created by other contractual arrangements or imposed by local law.[15] Side agreements among the partners or between a partner and a third party often provide for contributions, guarantees, indemnification, and other arrangements. These all must be taken into account. For example, recall the facts of *Raphan*, in which the general partners guaranteed an otherwise nonrecourse liability. Under these regulations, since the

---

12. § 1.752–1(a)(1). **14.** § 1.752–2(a).

13. § 1.752–1(a)(2). **15.** § 1.752–2(b)(3).

creditor has the right to look to the general partner for payment if the partnership defaults, the general partner, not the creditor, bears "the economic risk of loss" for the liability, and the liability would be treated as a recourse liability.

Local law also imposes certain obligations on partners that must be taken into account. Probably the most important of these are the joint liability for partnership obligations,[16] and the obligation to contribute towards the losses of the partnership,[17] which combine to create the equivalent of an unlimited deficit makeup obligation for general partners.

In determining whether a particular liability is recourse or nonrecourse, there is a de minimis exception that permits commercial lenders to hold minor interests (10% or less) in partnerships to which they lend money on a nonrecourse basis without the loan being recharacterized recourse. This exception only applies if the loan would constitute "qualified nonrecourse financing" (without regard to the activity financed) under § 465(b)(6).[18] There is a parallel exception for commercial lenders who guarantee third party nonrecourse loans.[19]

Sharing Recourse Liabilities

Partners share partnership recourse liabilities in the same way that they share the economic risk of loss associated with that liability.[20] The determination of who bears the economic risk of loss for any liability is based upon whose pocket the money would come from to satisfy the liability if the partnership went "belly up." In making that determination, the regulations posit a disaster scenario, called a "constructive liquidation" during which the following five events are deemed to occur:[21]

1. All partnership liabilities become due and payable in full;

2. All partnership assets, including cash, become worthless (solely excluding certain property held by the partnership in name only for the purpose of securing indebtedness);[22]

3. All partnership assets are disposed of in taxable transactions for no consideration (other than satisfaction of nonrecourse liabilities secured by the property);

---

16.   See UPA § 15.
17.   See UPA § 18(a).
18.   § 1.752–2(d)(1).
19.   § 1.752–2(d)(2).

20.   § 1.752–2(a).
21.   § 1.752–2(b)(1).
22.   § 1.752–2(h).

4.   The partnership allocates all items of income, gain, loss or deduction for its last taxable year ending on the date of the constructive liquidation;[23] and

5.   The partnership liquidates.

Following this "constructive liquidation," if, and to the extent that a partner (or related person) is *ultimately* responsible for paying a partnership liability, either directly to the creditor or by way of a contribution to the partnership or to her other partners, that partner bears the economic risk of loss for the liability and shares in the liability to that extent.[24]

In determining who will bear ultimate responsibility for a liability, an important assumption is made: in all but abusive cases,[25] all parties, regardless of actual net worth or financial condition, are assumed to live up to their obligations. For this reason, even though under state law each partner in a general partnership may be personally liable for all of the partnership's recourse liabilities, one must take into account all of her rights of contribution from the other partners, even those partners who are insolvent.

Illustration—Recourse Liabilities

The following basic example forms the basis for a series of variations we will use to explore how the regulations allocate recourse liabilities. In each variation, the question raised is how should the partners share the liability for purposes of § 752. Assume throughout that none of the variations are abusive.

> ***Example #2:*** On January 1 of this year, A and B form a general partnership to which A contributes $60 and B contributes $40. The partners agree to share all profits and losses 60–40. The partnership adopts the accrual method of accounting. The partnership agreement satisfies all three requirements of the basic test for economic effect: the capital account requirement, the liquidation requirement and the deficit makeup requirement. Upon formation, the partnership immediately purchases real estate for $1,000, paying $100 cash and giving a mortgage for the $900 balance. The mortgage calls for annual interest payments of $100 on December 31 of each year. No principal payments are due for 5 years. AB's initial balance sheet is as follows:

23. The allocations generally will consist of the losses triggered by the disposition of the worthless assets. If there are nonrecourse liabilities present, there also may be gains.

24. § 1.752–2(b)(6).

25. § 1.752–2(j).

Assets		Liabilities & Capital	
	Book		
Real Estate	$1,000	Mortgage	$900

Capital Accounts	
	Book
A	$60
B	40
	$100

Variation #1: Assume that the mortgage is fully recourse.

To determine each partner's share of this liability, we must posit a constructive liquidation during which the following five events are deemed to occur:

1.   the mortgage is due and payable;

2.   the real estate is worthless;

3.   the real estate is disposed of for no consideration, resulting in a $1,000 loss to the partnership;

4.   AB's taxable year ends and the $1,000 loss is allocated between A and B according to the partnership agreement, $600 to A and $400 to B. This allocation has substantial economic effect and reduces the partners' respective capital accounts to ($540) and ($360).

5.   The partnership liquidates.

In order to satisfy the partnership's liability to the creditor, A and B must make up the deficits in their capital accounts. These amounts, $540 and $360, respectively, represent each partner's share of the liability. Therefore, A's initial outside basis is $600 ($60 cash plus $540 of the liability) and B's is $400 ($40 cash plus $360 of the liability).

The result in this example should not be surprising. Since A and B share all items of income and loss 60:40, one might have guessed that they would also share the liability in the same way. This will usually be the case in a general partnership with no side agreements: if the partners share profits and losses in proportion to their capital account balances, recourse liabilities will be shared in the same proportion.[26] Indeed, the results of the regulations' constructive liquidation are intuitive in most cases.

---

26. Be careful of this generalization. To illustrate its limitations, consider the facts of ***Example #2***, except that A and B agree to share profits and losses 50:50, even though they contributed capital 60:40. Since they are not sharing profits and losses in the same proportion as their capital accounts, the generalization does not hold. In this variation the $1,000 loss upon the constructive liquidation would be allocated $500 to each partner, giving A a post-liquidation capital account balance of ($440) and B a balance of ($460). The liability would be allocated between A and B in those

Variation #2: Assume the mortgage is fully recourse, but there is no explicit deficit makeup obligation in the partnership agreement.

As you will recall from our discussion of economic effect,[27] even though the partnership agreement does not impose a deficit make-up obligation, local law typically does. Therefore, the analysis and allocation of the liability would be exactly as in *Variation #1*.

Variation #3: Assume the mortgage is fully recourse and A personally guarantees the partnership's obligation.

Under a typical guarantee agreement, a guarantor need not honor an obligation until the primary obligor defaults. Absent abuse, the constructive liquidation analysis assumes all parties live up to their obligations, regardless of net worth.[28] Therefore, in the constructive liquidation, A and B are assumed to contribute the funds necessary to satisfy the liability and the lender need not call A's guarantee. For this reason, A's guarantee is disregarded and the analysis and allocation of the liability are the same as in *Variation #1*.[29]

Variation #4: Assume that the mortgage is nonrecourse and there are no side agreements.

On these facts, only the creditor, and no partner (or related party), is bearing any risk of loss. Therefore, this is a nonrecourse liability and is allocated under the rules of § 1.752–3, discussed below.[30]

Variation #5: Assume the mortgage is nonrecourse, but is guaranteed personally by B.

In contrast with *Variation #3*, B's guarantee cannot be disregarded. Indeed, the guarantee converts this nonrecourse liability to a recourse liability for purposes of § 752 because B, one of the partners, bears the economic risk of loss associated with it. Furthermore, as we have already seen in the context of § 704(b), this obligation would be characterized as a "partner nonrecourse liability"[31] and all deductions and losses allocable to it must be allocated to partner B, who bears the economic risk of loss.[32] Under the constructive liquidation analysis,

---

amounts, and their outside bases would be $500 each.

27. See *Chapter Five*.

28. § 1.752–2(b)(6).

29. See § 1.752–2(f)(ex. 3).

30. Notice that, if we applied the constructive liquidation analysis to this liability, upon transfer of the real estate to the lender, the partnership's amount

realized would be $1,000 (*Tufts*), and the partnership would not have a loss.

31. § 1.704–2(b)(4).

32. § 1.704–2(i)(1). Although the liability is characterized as recourse for purposes of § 752, meaning that it will be entirely allocated to the guarantor partner, the § 704 regulations call it "partner nonrecourse debt," and require that all deductions with respect to it are

1. the mortgage is due and payable;

2. the real estate is worthless;

3. the real estate is disposed of for no consideration,[33] resulting in a $1,000 loss to the partnership.

4. AB's taxable year ends and the $1,000 loss must be allocated between A and B. The first $100 loss is allocated $60 to A and $40 to B in accordance with the partnership agreement. These allocations have substantial economic effect and reduce the partners' respective capital accounts to zero. The remaining $900 of the loss is a partner nonrecourse deduction which must be entirely allocated to B. This reduces B's capital account to ($900).

5. AB liquidates.

At this point, B steps into the shoes of the partnership and must satisfy the balance of the $900 obligation to the lender. Thus, B ultimately bears the risk of loss with respect to the entire liability and the liability must be allocated exclusively to her. Therefore, A's initial outside basis is $60, and B's is $940.

Once again, this result should not be surprising. If only one partner is personally liable for a partnership liability, that liability is entirely allocated to that partner.

Variation #6: Assume the mortgage is fully recourse and A agrees to indemnify B for any loss in excess of B's capital contribution of $40.

Under a typical indemnification agreement, one party agrees to reimburse another for all or part of a loss that the latter may incur. Thus, by virtue of this indemnification agreement, A has agreed to reimburse B for any losses she may otherwise incur in excess of her $40 contribution. Upon a constructive liquidation,

1. the mortgage is due and payable;

2. the real estate is worthless;

3. the real estate is disposed of for no consideration, resulting in a $1,000 loss to the partnership,

4. AB's taxable year ends and the partnership allocates the $1,000 loss, $40 to B and $960 to A. This will reduce the balance in B's capital account to zero, and A's to ($900).

allocated to the guaranteeing partner. This seems like a bit of unnecessary semantic confusion, that leads to a logical result.

33. Generally, nonrecourse liabilities are treated somewhat differently in the constructive liquidation scenario: gain or loss is recognized to the extent of the difference between the amount of the liability and basis. This rule does not apply, however, if the creditor may look beyond the property for repayment, as is the case here. § 1.752–2(b)(1)(iii), (2)(i).

Because B's maximum exposure is $40, an allocation of more than $40 of the $1,000 loss to B would not have SEE.[34]

5.   AB liquidates.

At this point, A must contribute $900 to the partnership to eliminate the deficit in her capital account. Therefore, the entire $900 liability must be allocated to A, resulting in initial outside bases of $960 for A and $40 for B. Once again, this result should not be surprising: Taking into account the indemnification, it is clear that A bears the entire risk of loss associated with the liability.

Partners Providing Property as Security for Partnership Debt

Sometimes a lender may require security for a loan in addition to the personal liability of the partners (as in the case of a recourse loan) or beyond the property which the partnership has pledged as collateral (as in the case of a nonrecourse loan), and in lieu of a personal guarantee one of the partners may pledge her individual property as collateral. This may be done directly (title to the property remains in the partner's name but the partner grants the lender a security interest to secure the partnership debt), or indirectly (the partner transfers the property to the partnership solely for purposes of giving the lender additional security). In the latter case the transfer to the partnership is in name only, and the regulations essentially ignore the transfer if substantially all items of income, gain, loss, and deduction attributable to the property are allocated to the contributing partner.[35] Where a partner thus puts her property at risk for a partnership liability, either directly or indirectly, she is treated as bearing the economic risk of loss for that liability up to the fair market value of the property at the time of the pledge. No promissory note of a partner is treated as property for this purpose unless it is readily tradeable on an established securities market.

To illustrate,

Variation #7: Assume the mortgage is nonrecourse, but the lender requires A to pledge stock with a basis of $100 and a fair market value of $400.

---

34.   For purposes of § 704(b), the indemnification agreement is treated as part of the partnership agreement. § 1.704–1(b)(2)(ii)(h). Thus B has no deficit make up obligation, in violation of the basic test for economic effect. Even if we were to assume it were possible to allocate more than $40, A would still be under an obligation to reimburse B for the excess, and therefore B would

still not be allocated any portion of the liability. § 1.752–2(b)(5).

35.   § 1.752–2(h). This "super allocation" is required to distinguish the case from a general contribution of property, and ensures that the partner is, for all practical purposes, the continuing economic owner of the property even though it is transferred to the partnership.

Since A has pledged her own personal property to secure the mortgage, the mortgage is considered recourse to the extent of the fair market value of the property ($400) and must be allocated exclusively to A.[36] The balance is a nonrecourse liability and will be allocated in accordance with the rules for nonrecourse liabilities discussed below.

Sharing of Nonrecourse Liabilities

A partnership nonrecourse liability is a partnership liability for which no partner (or related person) bears the economic risk of loss. For this reason, the constructive liquidation analysis used to determine a partner's share of partnership recourse liabilities is of no use in determining how to allocate nonrecourse liabilities. Instead, the regulations take a fairly liberal approach which is consistent with the approach taken by the § 704(b) regulations governing allocation of nonrecourse deductions.[37] Under the § 752 regulations, a partner's share of a partnership's nonrecourse liabilities is equal to the sum of:

1. her share of partnership minimum gain;[38]

2. her share of "§ 704(c) minimum gain" (the amount of gain that would be allocable to her under § 704(c) if the property were disposed of for no consideration other than satisfaction of the liability);[39] plus

3. her share of the "excess nonrecourse liabilities," i.e., those nonrecourse liabilities not allocated under (1) or (2).[40]

To understand this sharing arrangement more fully, let's examine each of these three amounts. First, as you will recall, each partner's share of partnership minimum gain is generally equal to the sum of the nonrecourse deductions allocated to that partner, plus any nonrecourse distributions made to her.[41] By allocating to each partner her share of partnership minimum gain, the regulations ensure that (i) a partner will have sufficient outside basis to prevent a nonrecourse deduction from being suspended under § 704(d),[42] and (ii) a nonrecourse distribution will not trigger gain under § 731(a)(1).

As we learned in *Chapter Seven*, when property is contributed to a partnership at a value that exceeds its basis, the resulting "§ 704(c) gain" must be taxed to the contributing partner. In this

---

36. Fair market value is determined as of the date of contribution or pledge. § 1.752–2(h)(3).

37. § 1.704–2. These rules are discussed in *Chapter Six*.

38. § 1.752–3(a)(1).

39. § 1.752–3(a)(2).

40. § 1.752–3(a)(3).

41. § 1.704–2(g)(1).

42. Of course, all partnership losses must also pass muster under § 465 and § 469, in that order.

context, "§ 704(c) minimum gain" is the term we use to describe the amount of gain that would be allocated to a partner under § 704(c) if the encumbered property had been disposed of in a taxable transaction for no consideration other than the satisfaction of the nonrecourse liability, i.e., the excess of nonrecourse liabilities encumbering contributed property over basis. By allocating this portion of the liability to the contributing partner, this rule prevents recognition of gain on the contribution of property to a partnership.[43] To illustrate:

> *Example #3:* A, B, and C form an equal partnership to which A and B each contributes $100 cash and C contributes Blackacre. Blackacre is real property worth $1,000, but is subject to a $900 nonrecourse mortgage. C's basis in Blackacre immediately before the formation of the partnership is $300.

Since the partnership is just being formed, there is no partnership minimum gain.[44] There is, however, $600 of § 704(c) minimum gain present, i.e., if Blackacre were to become worthless, the partnership would still have $600 of gain, all of which would be allocated to C under § 704(c). To prevent C from recognizing any gain on contribution, the regulations allocate the first $600 of the nonrecourse liability to C.[45] The balance of $300 is an excess nonrecourse liability which is allocated in accordance with the rules discussed immediately below.

"Excess nonrecourse liabilities" are the balance of nonrecourse liabilities remaining after each partner has been allocated her share of those liabilities based on partnership minimum gain and § 704(c) minimum gain.[46] On the facts of *Example #3*, there are $300 of excess nonrecourse liabilities.

The rules at § 1.752–3(a)(3) governing excess nonrecourse liabilities are extremely flexible. They approve multiple possible sharing arrangements, including:

> 1. The general rule calls for sharing based on profit shares, which under our facts would dictate that the $300 in excess

---

43. This rule also applies in the analogous reverse § 704(c) situation described in § 1.704–1(b)(2)(iv)(f) and § 1.704–1(b)(4)(i).

44. Recall that whenever property is reflected at different values for book and tax purposes, partnership minimum gain is defined as the excess of the nonrecourse liabilities secured by the property over the property's book value. § 1.704–2(f)(3). Since property must be reflected on the partnership's books at its fair market value when contributed, there is no partnership minimum gain.

45. If A and B together were allocated more than $300, C would have gain under § 731(a)(1). Thus, the allocation to C of the first $600 of the liability, leaving at most $300 to be allocated to A and B, protects C from recognizing gain as a result of the contribution. This § 704(c) minimum gain share could be viewed as an additional share of profits for purposes of allocating the liability.

46. § 1.752–3(a)(3).

nonrecourse liabilities would be shared equally by A, B and C. The regulations allow the partners to specify profit shares for this purpose, which will be respected so long as they are "reasonably consistent" with allocations of other items that have substantial economic effect.[47]

2. The regulations also permit the partners to agree to share nonrecourse liabilities in the same ratios that they share non-recourse deductions. If the partners have agreed to a special allocation of the nonrecourse deductions that differs from their profit shares, then if they relied on the general rule they would need to reallocate the liability among themselves each year as nonrecourse deductions are taken. This problem is illustrated in **Example #4**, below. Under our facts, we would reach the same result as above for ABC, because there is no special allocation of the nonrecourse deductions.

3. Finally, if the liability encumbers contributed property, the regulations allow the partners to allocate the excess nonre-course liabilities first to the contributor, in an amount of any § 704(c) gain in excess of the § 704(c) minimum gain that is allocated under § 1.752–3(a)(2).[48] If the entire excess nonre-course liability is not allocated under this alternative, the balance must be allocated under one of the other alternatives. Under the facts of **Example #3**, the partnership has $300 of excess nonrecourse liabilities. Blackacre had $700 of built-in gain at the time of contribution, $600 of which (the § 704(c) minimum gain) was allocated to C under § 1.752–3(a)(2). Un-der the third alternative of the excess nonrecourse liability rules, the partnership can elect to allocate the first $100 of the excess nonrecourse liabilities to C. The remaining $200 must be allocated under the first or second alternatives.

The second alternative offered by the regulations for sharing excess nonrecourse liabilities may be the most attractive to many partnerships, particularly if their agreement allocates nonrecourse deductions differently than profit shares. If that is the case, and the partnership doesn't take advantage of the second alternative, then the partnership will need to redetermine liability shares, and out-side bases, each year. To illustrate:

Example #4: G and L form a partnership to which G contrib-utes $60 cash and L contributes $40 cash. The partnership purchases a building for $1,000, using the $100 contributed capital and borrowing $900 on a nonrecourse basis. G and L agree to share profits and losses in accordance with their

47. This language should sound fa-miliar from our discussion of the nonre-course deduction rules in *Chapter Six*.

48. As we will see in *Chapter Fifteen*, this alternative is not available in apply-ing the disguised sales rules.

capital contributions, i.e., 60:40, except that nonrecourse deductions will be split 50:50. Assume that this latter allocation will be respected. The partners agree to share the excess nonrecourse liabilities in accordance with how they plan to share nonrecourse deductions, i.e., 50:50. During its first two years of operation, GL breaks even except for depreciation in the amount of $100 each year. No payment is made on the principal of the mortgage.

At the time of formation, there is no partnership minimum gain (PMG), nor is there any § 704(c) minimum gain. Therefore, according to their agreement, the $900 nonrecourse mortgage is allocated equally between G and L. L's initial basis is $490 (cash contributed of $40 plus $450 share of the liability). G's initial basis is $510 (cash contributed of $60 plus $450 share of liability).

During the first year of operations, GL has a $100 loss, and no increase in PMG. Thus, the first year depreciation deduction is allocated $40 to L and $60 to G; this allocation will have substantial economic effect. After the second year of operations, the PMG increases by $100 (the liability balance of $900 over adjusted basis of $800). As a result of the $100 increase in PMG, GL has $100 of nonrecourse deductions which are allocated 50:50 according to the agreement, or $50 to each. After taking into account these allocations, L's share of the liability is equal to her share of PMG, $50, plus her share of excess nonrecourse liabilities, $400 (½ of $800), or $450, precisely what it was when the partnership was formed. G's share is equal to her share of PMG plus her share of the excess nonrecourse liabilities ($50 plus $400) or $450, also unchanged.

If G and L had not specifically provided in the agreement that they would share nonrecourse liabilities in the same ratio in which they share nonrecourse deductions, their initial shares of the liability would be based on their shares of profits, i.e., 60:40, or $540 to G and $360 to L. After the second year of operations, however, their shares of that liability would have to shift to take into account their shares of PMG of $100. At that point in time, G's share of the liability would be $50 (her share of PMG) plus $480 (60% of the excess nonrecourse liability of $800), for a total of $530. L's share would be $50 (share of PMG) plus $320 (40% of excess) for a total of $370. Because PMG will increase each year, and the ratio in which it is shared differs from the manner in which the partners share profits (and hence excess nonrecourse liabilities), there will be an annual (needless) shift in the liability allocation, and a resulting recalculation of outside basis. Absent some desire to keep the partnership's accountants busy, this would seem to be an unnecessary complication.

Chapter Nine

TRANSACTIONS (OTHER THAN SALES) BETWEEN A PARTNERSHIP AND ITS PARTNERS[1]

Typically a partner's distributive share of partnership income compensates her for her efforts on the partnership's behalf, as well as for the use of her capital contribution, and the now familiar rules of § 704(b) govern the tax treatment of that amount. Nevertheless, partners often receive compensation for their services (or for the use of their property) in addition to their distributive share, so that their compensation is not entirely dependent upon the success of partnership operations. The tax treatment of those payments depends upon what is sometimes a difficult distinction: is the partner acting in her capacity as a partner (in which case the payments are governed by § 707(c)), or is the partner acting as a stranger vis a vis the partnership (in which case § 707(a) governs). The rules for distinguishing among distributive shares, § 707(c) payments, and § 707(a) payments, and the significance of the distinction, are the subject of the first part of this chapter.

The second part of this chapter is devoted to the related issue of the tax consequences which result when a taxpayer receives an interest in a partnership in exchange for services. This transaction is the subject of some recently proposed regulations that we will examine.

Sections 707(a) and 707(c)

Prior to 1954, the law was unclear as to whether it was possible for a partnership to pay a "salary" to a partner for tax

---

1. Sales between a partner and a partnership are the subject of *Chapter Fifteen*.

purposes; typically all amounts distributed to a partner were considered part of her distributive share. Theoretically, this was because a partnership was not viewed as an entity by the courts, but rather as an aggregate: how can one be employed by oneself? The aggregate approach also shed doubt on the appropriate treatment of a series of other transactions that often occur between partners and their partnerships. Is it possible for a partner to lease or sell property to her partnership (viz., to herself)? The courts were split on these issues.

In 1954, Congress resolved these issues by creating three different categories of partner-partnership compensation transactions:

1. Section 704(b) continues to apply aggregate treatment to payments for services or capital made to a partner acting in her capacity as such, if the amount of that compensation is determined with reference to the income of the partnership. Those payments will be treated as part of the partner's distributive share under § 704 and will be taxed under the general rules of Subchapter K.

2. Section 707(a)(1) governs transactions in which a partner is acting at arm's length with the partnership, and not in her capacity as a partner. Section 707(a) adopts the entity approach and, for most purposes, treats the transaction as if it were between strangers.

3. Section 707(c) governs transactions in which a partner, acting in her capacity as such, receives a fixed or "guaranteed payment"[2] for services (or for the use of capital). Section 707(c) adopts a hybrid approach: for purposes of §§ 61(a), 162(a) and 263 the payment is treated as though the recipient were not a partner; for all other purposes, the payment is treated as a distributive share.[3]

The threshold issue in categorizing a particular payment to a partner is the capacity in which the partner is acting: in the transaction in question, was the partner acting as a partner, or as a stranger? If she was acting as a stranger, the transaction is governed by § 707(a)(1). If she was acting in her capacity as a partner, then the payment will be a guaranteed payment if its amount is

2. That is, a payment that is not determined with respect to the income of the partnership. This could be a fixed dollar amount, or a percentage of the partnership's gross income.

3. E.g., a guaranteed payment is includible in the income of the recipient under the same rules as if it were part of the partner's distributive share. § 706(a).

determined without respect to the income of the partnership; otherwise it will be part of her distributive share. Although there is little guidance as to what types of services are generally rendered in one's capacity as a partner and what types are not,[4] a distinction is typically drawn between general managerial services (partner capacity) and services involving a partner's particular technical expertise (non-partner).[5]

Since the characterization of a given payment may be very significant, we will examine each of these in greater detail.

Distributive Share. Payments made to a partner acting in her capacity as such, which are determined with reference to the income of the partnership, are treated as part of the partner's distributive share of partnership income for the year. The character of a partner's distributive share flows through from the partnership, and the share must be included in the partner's income on the last day of the partnership's taxable year, whether or not received.[6] Technically, a distributive share is not deducted by the partnership in determining its income, but it can have the effect of a deduction: to the extent that income is allocated to one partner it is not included by the others. Yet the restrictions applicable to deductions do not apply to distributive shares; most significantly, they are not subject to the capitalization requirement.

Section 707(a)(1). Under § 707(a)(1), if a partner engages in a transaction with a partnership in a non-partner capacity, then the transaction will, for most purposes, be treated as occurring between strangers.[7] Section 707(a)(1) can encompass loans, leases, sales, and employment relationships. Thus, in contrast with pre–1954 law, § 707(a) allows a partner to be an employee of her own partnership.[8] The character of § 707(a)(1) payments will depend upon the underlying transaction: lease, compensation and loan transactions will result in ordinary income to the recipient, while sales may result in capital gain. The recipient's method of accounting will determine when she must include a § 707(a) payment in income, thus a cash method partner generally will include the amount on receipt. The partnership's tax treatment of the payment depends on the nature of the expense to which it relates: ordinary and necessary expenses are deductible under the partnership's method of accounting,[9] capital expenditures must be capitalized.

4. To date, no regulations have been promulgated under § 707(a)(2)(A).

5. See McKee et al., ¶ 14.02[2].

6. § 706(a).

7. They are not treated as strangers for all purposes. See, e.g., §§ 267(e), 707(b), 453(e) & (g) and 1239.

8. This can be quite important in certain cases because certain tax benefits are only available to employees, not partners. E.g., § 119 (exclusion of meals and lodging), § 79 (exclusion of premium for group-term life insurance), and § 132 (exclusion of fringe benefits).

9. These payments may be subject to § 267(a). § 267(e).

Guaranteed Payments. If a partnership makes fixed payments for services or the use of capital to a partner acting in her capacity as such, and if those payments are not dependent upon the partnership's income, then § 707(c) characterizes these payments as "guaranteed payments." Guaranteed payments are taxed under a hybrid approach. They are taxed like § 707(a) payments for services or capital in some ways: they are ordinary income to the recipient and are deductible by the partnership subject to the capitalization requirement of § 263. But they are taxed like distributive shares in other respects: they must be included in the income of the recipient under § 706(a) on the last day of the partnership's taxable year, whether or not actually received.[10]

The hybrid approach of § 707(c) was enacted to eliminate the conceptual and technical complexity that existed prior to 1954 when a partnership was unable to pay its partners a "salary" for their partnership services. This was true even though the partners agreed that the service partner was to receive compensation independent of the income of the venture. In cases where a partnership did not have sufficient income to cover the allocation, this regime created an accounting nightmare. To illustrate, consider the following:

> *Example #1*: ABC is a partnership in which all partners share income, gains and losses equally. In addition, A is entitled to a $10,000 payment for services she performs for the partnership, without regard to the income of the partnership. To the extent that ABC does not have sufficient income to make the $10,000 payment, B and C agree to bear the burden of that payment equally. Assume that A's services are ordinary and necessary in nature, the cost of which would have been deductible by the partnership if A were an employee. During the current year, ABC has $6,000 of income before taking into account A's $10,000 payment.

Under pre–1954 law, it was difficult to treat A (and ABC) in a sensible or rational way. Since A could not be an employee for tax purposes, the $10,000 payment must have been treated as part of her distributive share. If so, how much income would she have had? Since ABC only had $6,000 of income, did this mean that A only had $6,000 of income for the year? But she received $10,000. How should one have characterized the remaining $4,000 of the distribution? Return of basis? Capital gain? Did it matter that B and C were bearing the economic burden of this payment?

---

10. § 706(a). This timing rule is the chief difference in the treatment between a payment treated under § 707(a) and one treated under § 707(c): Under § 707(a), the payment is taken into account under the recipient's method of accounting.

These problems are resolved by § 707(c). The $10,000 payment is a guaranteed payment. It is therefore includible as ordinary income by A, and deductible (subject to § 263(a)) under § 162(a) by ABC. Therefore, ABC has a ($4,000) loss for the year, which is allocated between B and C under § 704(b).[11]

It is not uncommon for a service partner to be entitled to a certain minimum distributive share; that is, the partnership guarantees the service partner that her share of partnership income will equal some minimum amount. In such a case, if the service partner's distributive share exceeds the "minimum guarantee," no part of that share will be treated as a guaranteed payment.[12] To illustrate:

> *Example #2*: Same facts as *Example #1*, except that A is entitled to one-third of the partnership income, but not less than $10,000. ABC has $60,000 of income for the year.

Since A's distributive share of partnership income ($20,000) is more than her minimum guarantee ($10,000), no part of her distributive share is considered a guaranteed payment, and all is characterized as part of her distributive share under § 704(b).

> *Example #3*: Same as *Example #2*, except that ABC's income is only $12,000 for the year.

On these facts, before taking into account the minimum guarantee, A's distributive share of income will be $4,000. However, since A is guaranteed $10,000, A is treated as receiving a $6,000 guaranteed payment.[13] This $6,000 is deductible under § 162(a) and the deduction must be allocated to B and C equally under § 704(b).[14] In sum, A has $10,000 of income, and B and C each have $1,000 of income.[15]

Summary

The following table summarizes the different tax treatment applicable to the three categories of payments.

---

11. The loss is shared by B and C because they agreed to bear the burden of A's guaranteed payment. Compare § 1.707–1(c)Ex. 3, in which the service partner shares the burden of the guaranteed payment.

12. § 1.707–1(c) Ex. 2.

13. *Id.*

14. *Id.*

15. A includes $4,000 as her distributive share and $6,000 as a guaranteed payment; B and C each has $4,000 as a distributive share before taking into account the guaranteed payment, and a $3,000 deduction on account of the guaranteed payment.

	Character	Accounting Method	Payment subject to § 263
§ 707(a)	Ordinary or Capital	Partner's; § 267(e)	Yes
§ 707(c)	Ordinary	Partnership's; § 706(a)	Yes
§ 704	Flow Through	Partnership's; § 706(a)	No

Disguised Capital Expenditures: § 707(a)(2)(A)

Although there are many technical differences in the tax treatment of the various categories of payments, probably the most significant difference is the manner in which the capitalization requirement applies to each. Specifically, while § 707(a) payments and guaranteed payments are not deductible by a partnership if they are in the nature of capital expenditures, distributive shares under § 704(b) are in essence deducted by the partnership even if capital in nature. To illustrate the importance of this distinction, consider the following:

> *Example #4:* ABC is an equal partnership engaged in the construction of a building for its own use. A acts as general contractor in connection with the construction of the building. To compensate A for these services, the partnership allocates and distributes to A the first $60,000 of net income for the year. In fact, ABC only has $60,000 of income, all of which is allocated and distributed to A.

If A is acting in her capacity as a partner, A's distributive share would be $60,000; the other partners would have no income, and the basis in the building would not include the $60,000 distribution to A. In essence the partnership will have deducted a portion of the cost of its building. If, on the other hand, the payment is characterized as a § 707(a) payment because A is acting outside her capacity as a partner, then the payment would be nondeductible by the partnership (because the services relate to the construction of a long-lived asset) and would be capitalized as part of the cost of the building. The result: A would include the $60,000 payment as compensation income, and the partnership would still have $60,000 of income which must be allocated among the three partners, $20,000 to each! In sum, A would have $80,000 of income, and B and C would each have $20,000 for a total of $120,000.[16]

Because of the obvious advantages of characterizing what otherwise would have been capital expenditures as distributive shares, prior to 1984 it was not uncommon for architects, builders, brokers,

---

16. These tax consequences are quite similar to those that would have occurred if the partnership had hired an independent contractor to perform the services: The cost of the independent contractor would have been capitalized, and ABC would have had $60,000 of net income which would have been allocated $20,000 to each partner.

etc. to join partnerships for short periods of time so that their fees could be characterized as distributive shares. In 1984 Congress addressed this abuse and added § 707(a)(2)(A), which authorized Treasury to develop regulations which would identify disguised fees of the type described above. Under § 707(a)(2)(A), (i) if a partner performs services for a partnership[17] and (ii) there is a related allocation and distribution to that partner, and if these events, taken together, are properly characterized as a transaction between unrelated parties, the transaction will be treated under § 707(a) and the allocation/distribution will be recharacterized a disguised fee.

Section 707(a)(2)(A) did not change the law regarding characterization of services: the critical question remains whether the partner was acting in her capacity as a member of the partnership. Nevertheless, it did evidence Congressional concern and authorized the issuance of regulations. The legislative history of the 1984 Act sets out 5 relevant factors[18] to be considered in determining whether a given payment is made to a partner in her capacity as such, or as a stranger. These are:

1.   *Entrepreneurial Risk.* The most important factor is whether the amount of the payment is subject to any appreciable risk. As a general proposition, partners share in the success of the enterprise, while employees and independent contractors are paid in all events. Therefore, if the amount and fact of payment are subject to the entrepreneurial risk of the venture, then it is highly likely that the partner is acting as a member of the partnership and the payment will be treated as part of her distributive share.

2.   *Transitory Status.* If the recipient's status as a partner is only for a short period of time, this would be evidence that the payment is made to a stranger. For example, suppose the recipient were an architect who was to be a partner only for the first year of the venture at which time she would be retired. This would be evidence that amounts she received during that period were simply fees for architectural services rendered.

17. Section 707(a)(2)(A) also covers property transfers in exchange for allocation/distributions, although it is difficult to envision when such a transaction might occur. See McKee et al., ¶ 13.02[4][a]. For this reason, we will limit our discussion to service transactions.

18. 1 Senate Comm. on Finance, 98th Cong., 2d Sess., Deficit Reduction Act of 1984, at 227–228. See also *Gener-* *al Explanation of the Deficit Reduction Act of 1984* (*General Explanation*). Actually the legislative history lists a sixth factor that relates only to transfers of property and suggests that if the partnership's capital accounting rules are respected under § 704(b), then an income allocation and distribution are unlikely. This will be true except in the case of undervaluation.

3. *Timing of the Allocation/Distribution.* The closer in time the purported allocation and distribution are made in relation to when the services are performed, the more likely the payment allocation/distribution will be recharacterized as a fee. This factor is clearly related to entrepreneurial risk: the longer the period of time, the more likely that the payment will be deemed to be subject to the entrepreneurial risk of the venture.

4. *Tax Motivation.* If the recipient became a partner primarily to take advantage of the tax consequences of being a partner (either for herself or the partnership), then the allocation/distribution is more likely to be recharacterized as a fee paid to a stranger.

5. *The Relative Size of Suspect Payment.* The relative size of the purported allocation/distribution in relation to the recipient partner's long term interest in the partnership is also important. For example, an allocation/distribution of 50% of the partnership's net income to a particular partner for the first two years and only 5% thereafter would be suspect.

The relevance of these factors was illustrated in the **General Explanation of the Deficit Reduction Act of 1984** by the following example:

A commercial office building constructed by a partnership is projected to generate gross income of at least $100,000 per year indefinitely. Its architect, whose normal fee for such services is $40,000, contributes cash for a 25–percent interest in the partnership and receives both a 25–percent distributive share of net income for the life of the partnership, and an allocation of $20,000 of partnership gross income for the first two years of partnership operations after lease-up. The partnership is expected to have sufficient cash available to distribute $20,000 to the architect in each of the first two years, and the agreement requires such a distribution.

On these facts, the architect was found not to be acting in her capacity as a partner with respect to her architectural services. Therefore, the purported gross income allocation and distribution was a disguised fee under § 707(a). This conclusion was based primarily on the fact that the architect's fee was insulated from the risk of the joint venture. In reaching this conclusion, the most important factors were: (1) the special allocation is fixed in amount and there is a substantial probability that the partnership will have sufficient gross income and cash to satisfy it; (2) the distribution relating to the allocation is fairly close in time to the rendering of the services; and (3) it is not unreasonable to conclude from all the facts and circumstances that the architect became a partner with respect to the $40,000 gross income allocation primarily for tax reasons.

The *General Explanation* goes on to say that on somewhat different facts, the conclusion reached might be different. For example, if the special allocation were for 20 percent of gross income, without limitation, and the project was a "spec building," then the architect would have been assuming significant entrepreneurial risk with respect to the payment. Therefore, it is highly likely that the architect would have been found to be acting in her capacity as a partner and the allocation/distribution would have been respected.

Although entrepreneurial risk is the most important factor in determining whether a given payment is a disguised fee or part of a distributive share, certain purported allocation/distributions will not be respected, even though they are determined with reference to the net income of the partnership. This may occur whenever the partner performs services for the partnership which are normally compensated for in the market place on a contingent basis. For example,

> Suppose that a partnership is formed to invest in stock. The partnership admits a stock broker as a partner. The broker agrees to effect trades for the partnership without the normal brokerage commission. In exchange for his partnership interest, the broker contributes 51 percent of partnership capital and receives a 51 percent interest in residual partnership profits and losses. In addition, he receives an allocation of gross income that is computed in a manner which approximates his forgone commissions. It is expected that the partnership will have sufficient gross income to make this allocation. The agreement provides that the broker will receive a priority distribution of cash from operations up to the amount of the gross income allocation.

In this case, even though the broker/partner's special allocation appears contingent and not substantially fixed as to amount, it is computed by means of a formula like a normal brokerage fee and effectively varies with the value and amount of services rendered rather than with the income of the partnership. Thus, this contingent gross income allocation along with the equivalent priority distribution should be treated as a fee under § 707(a), rather than as a distributive share and partnership distribution.[19]

19. *General Explanation*. See also Rev. Rul. 81–301, 1981–2 C.B. 144.

Receipt of Partnership Interest in Exchange for Services

Section 721 affords nonrecognition treatment to exchanges of "property" for partnership interests, and it protects both parties to the exchange: neither the partner nor the partnership recognizes gain or loss. Suppose, however, that a person renders or promises to render services to a partnership (or a partner) and receives an interest in a partnership in exchange. Since services do not constitute property for purposes of § 721, the exchange of the partnership interest for services falls outside of the nonrecognition regime, and as a result there are potential tax consequences to both parties to the exchange. Just what those tax consequences should be has been the subject of much litigation and debate. Most of the issues are resolved, however, by regulations proposed by the Treasury in 2005.[20] We will give a nod to history, but because we expect that final regulations won't vary much from the proposed regulations, and because those rules substantially simplify the inquiry, we will concentrate on them.

Historically, the taxation of a partnership interest received in exchange for services depended on the type of interest received, whether it was a capital interest, which entitles the holder to a current claim on the partnership's assets, or a "mere" profits interest, which gives no claim to current assets but only to a share of future profits. Capital interests were taxable upon receipt, profits interests were not.[21] Under the proposed regulations, however, all partnership interests received in exchange for services will be taxed under the same regime. The proposed regulations tax the receipt of a partnership interest as a variation of a guaranteed payment. This means that the interest will be taxable to the recipient as ordinary income, and will be deductible by the partnership. But unlike most guaranteed payments, the timing of the inclusion is governed by § 83 rather than § 706(a).[22] Under § 83, the timing of the inclusion

---

20. See 70 Federal Register, 29675, May 24, 2005.

21. It has always been clear that a capital interest received in exchange for services was taxable, while the receipt of a profits interest in exchange for services has been a contentious issue for many years. In 1971, the Tax Court shocked the tax bar by holding that held that the receipt of a profits interest was taxable. *Diamond v. Commissioner*, 56 T.C. 530 (1971), aff'd, 492 F.2d 286 (7th Cir. 1974). Because of valuations issues, the Service was reluctant to push the issue. It did not do so again until *Campbell v. Commissioner*, 59 T.C.M. 236 (1990), aff'd in part and rev'd in part, 943 F.2d 815 (8th Cir. 1991), when the Tax Court held once again that receipt

of a profits interest was taxable. *Campbell* rekindled the academic debate as to how these interests should be treated. See, e.g., Laura E. Cunningham, *Taxing Partnership Interests Exchanged for Services*, 47 Tax L. Rev. 247 (1991) and Leo L. Schmolka, *Taxing Partnership Interests Exchanged for Services: Let Diamond/Campbell Quietly Die*, 47 Tax L. Rev. 287 (1991). In Rev. Proc. 93–27, 1993–2 C.B. 343, the Service largely settled the issue in favor of nonrecognition in the case of a transfer of a profits interest. This position was reaffirmed in Rev. Proc. 2001–43, 2001–2 C.B. 191. If the proposed regulations discussed in this section are finalized, these revenue procedures will be obsolete.

22. Proposed Reg. § 1.707–1(c).

and deduction depends upon when the interest is vested (i.e., transferable or not subject to a substantial risk of forfeiture).[23] Thus, if the interest is substantially vested at the time it is transferred, the service partner must include the fair market value of the interest in income (less any amount paid for the interest) upon receipt.[24] This amount will also be the initial balance in her capital account, and, in the absence of liabilities, her initial outside basis. If the interest is substantially nonvested, taxation of the interest is delayed until it vests, and during that time the service partner is not treated as a partner. However, if she makes an election under § 83(b), the non-vested interest will be immediately includible in income, and the service partner will be treated as a partner from that point on. These latter rules cause certain complications if the interest is subsequently forfeited, those rules are discussed below.

Valuing a partnership interest can be difficult. Recognizing this fact, the proposed regulations provide a safe harbor that permits a partnership to use the so-called "liquidation method"[25] to value the interests. Under this method, the value of the interest is deemed to be equal to the amount of cash the partner would receive if, immediately after the service partner receives her interest,

1. All partnership assets (including goodwill and other intangibles) are sold for their fair market value;

2. All the resulting gains and losses are allocated among the partners in accordance with the partnership agreement;

3. All partnership liabilities are satisfied; and

4. The remaining cash is distributed to the partners in accordance with the partnership agreement.

Under this method, a "mere" profits interests will have a zero value and therefore will not generate any current taxable income.

The tax treatment of the partnership (or in some cases, one of the other partners) is also governed by § 83. Under § 83(h), a deduction is generally permitted under § 162 (subject to § 263) to the person for whom the services were performed. The deduction is an amount equal to that included by the service partner, and is allowed for the same year that the service partner was required to include the amount in income.[26] If the services were performed for

---

23. § 1.83–3(b).

24. § 83(a).

25. Prop. Reg. § 1.83–3(*l*). This method had been used by the courts to determine if a service partner had received a capital interest or a profits interest. See, e.g., St. John v. United States, 84–1 USTC ¶ 9158 (D.C.Ill.1983).

26. If the partnership and the service partner have different taxable years, the partnership takes a deduction for the taxable year in which the service partner was required to include gross income.

the benefit of the partnership, the partnership is entitled to the deduction. However, if the services were performed for the benefit of a particular partner, then the partnership is not entitled to a deduction, although the partner may be.

Prior to the proposed regulations, many commentators thought that the issuance of a partnership interest for services should be treated as a taxable transfer by the partnership of an undivided interest in each of its assets to the service partner in satisfaction of an obligation.[27] The proposed regulations, however, take the position that this is not the case and afford nonrecognition to the partnership.[28] Essentially, they treat the transaction as if the partnership paid the service partner cash equal to the value of the transferred interest, which she immediately contributes to the partnership for her partnership interest. It should be noted that this nonrecognition rule does not extend to the transfer of a partnership interest that initially creates a partnership.[29]

These rules are illustrated in the following two examples,

Example #5: AB is an equal partnership with a fiscal year ending January 31. S, a calendar year taxpayer, has been working for the partnership for several years. On December 31, 2010, in recognition of her extraordinary service to the partnership, AB makes S a full 10% partner. Immediately before the transfer, the partnership's balance sheet was as follows (expanded to include fair market values):

27. For example, this was the position we took in the Second Edition of *The Logic of Subchapter K: A Conceptual Guide to the Taxation of Partnerships* (West 2000).

28. Prop. Reg. § 1.721–1(b)(2). Although some may argue that this is difficult to justify technically, we believe that the rule is justified from an administrative point of view and is consonant with the underlying policies of § 721. For early advocates of nonrecognition treatment in this context, see Cowan, *Substantial Economic Effect—The Outer Limits for Partnership Allocations*, 39 N.Y.U. Tax Institute 23.08 (1981), and Gunn, *Partnership Interests for Services: Partnership Gain and Loss?*, 47 Tax Notes 699 (May 7, 1990).

29. For example, in *McDougal v. Commissioner*, 62 T.C. 720 (1974), the owner of a race horse promised the horse's trainer that he would go into partnership with him if the trainer was able to cure an allergy that the horse had. The trainer did cure the allergy and an equal partnership was formed between the owner and the trainer. The court treated the transaction as though the owner transferred ½ of the horse to the trainer in satisfaction of his obligation, and then both the owner and the trainer contributed their portion of the horse to the newly formed partnership. The transfer of the ½ horse by the owner to the trainer was treated as a taxable exchange.

Assets	Basis/Book	FMV
Cash	$180	$180
Building	120	270
Equip't	90	150
Goodwill	0	150
	$390	$750

Liabilities & Capital
Mortgage $150

Capital Accounts

	Tax/Book	FMV
A	$120	$300
B	120	300
	$240	$600

The receipt of the partnership interest is treated as a guaranteed payment. Under the liquidation method, its value is deemed to be $60.[30] Under § 83(a), S must include the $60 as ordinary income in 2010. She is treated just as if she received $60 in cash and immediately contributed this amount back to the partnership in exchange for her 10% interest. Therefore, $60 is the initial balance in her capital account, and her initial outside basis is equal to $75 ($60 cash plus her $15 share of the mortgage).

The partnership recognizes no gain or loss on the transfer under § 721(a). Under § 83(h), it is entitled to a $60 deduction under § 162 for its fiscal year ending on January 31, 2011. Presumably, the burden of this deduction will be borne by A and B equally, and it should be allocated to them. If the partnership books up its assets and allocates the deduction for services equally between A and B, its balance sheet will be as follows:

Assets	Basis	Book
Cash	$180	$180
Building	120	270
Equip't	90	150
Goodwill	0	150
	390	750

Liabilities & Capital
Mortgage $150

Capital Accounts

	Tax	Book
A	$90	$270
B	90	270
S	60	60
	$240	$600

The historic partners, A and B, are responsible for the unrealized appreciation in the assets under § 704(c) principles.

Example #6: Assume the same facts as ***Example #5*** except that the partnership transferred the interest to S subject to the following condition: S must perform services for the partner-

30. If the partnership sold all of its assets (including the Goodwill) it would have $750 of cash. After paying off the $150 mortgage, it would have $600 to distribute to its partners. Since S is a full 10% partner, S would receive $60 on liquidation.

ship for the following three years. At the end of three years, the interest will fully vest. If S fails to fulfill this condition, then S must return the interest to partnership and forfeit any balance she may have in her capital account.

On these facts, S has received a substantially nonvested interest. Therefore, unless she makes an election under § 83(b), S will not include the value of the interest in her income unless and until the interest vests. When the interest vests, S will have income (and the partnership a deduction) in an amount equal to the fair market value of the interest at that time, and S will thereafter be treated as a partner under subchapter K.

If S does make a § 83(b) election, then the tax consequences are very similar to those in *Example #5*: S has immediate income and is treated as a partner under Subchapter K. This causes a potential problem, however. Because of the possibility that the partnership interest may never vest, allocations to S's capital account of income and loss during the vesting period cannot have substantial economic effect within the meaning of the § 704(b) regulations: If S does not fulfill her obligation, she will forfeit her capital and never enjoy the benefit of (or suffer the economic loss associated with) of those previous allocations. The regulations take the position, however, that the allocations will be considered to be in accord with the partners' interest in the partnership as long as the partnership agreement provides that, in the event of a forfeiture, the partnership will make allocations to rectify the partnership's capital accounts ("forfeiture allocations").[31]

A Final Note: Pending Legislation

At the time of this writing, legislation has been proposed that would change the tax treatment of certain profits interests. This legislation is a reaction to the use of so-called "carried interests" that are sometimes used to compensate private equity and investment fund managers. Carried interests are profits interests granted to fund managers as part of their compensation. Under current law, the character of the income from the profits interest flows through to the fund managers, so to the extent that the partnership's income is in the form of long term capital gains, the manager's compensation is taxed at a maximum rate of 15%. This treatment has been the subject of much discussion in the press, and has generated intense controversy in the academy and on Capitol Hill.[32]

31. Prop. Reg. § 1.704–1(b)(4)(xii)(b) & (c). There are limitations on this rule, including (i) all material allocations and capital account adjustments other than those relating to the service partner's non-vested interest must comply with § 704(b), and (ii) the rules do not apply if there is a plan at the time the § 83(b) election is made that the interest will be forfeited.

32. Professor Victor Fleischer brought attention to this issue with his

The current legislation is extremely complex and controversial.[33] For this reason, it is not clear that it will become law, and if it does, exactly what form it will take. Stay tuned for the Fifth Edition!

excellent article, *Two and Twenty: Taxing Partnership Profits in Private Equity Funds*, 83 NYU L. Rev. 1 (2008). See also, Noël B. Cunningham & Mitchell L. Engler, *The Carried Interest Controversy: Let's Not Get Carried Away*, 61 Tax L. Rev. 121 (2008).

33. In a recent article, one commentator described the current legislation as "... a horror of complexity." Howard Abrams, *The Carried Interest Catastrophe*, 128 Tax Notes 523 (2010).

Chapter Ten

THE SALE OF A PARTNERSHIP INTEREST

―――――――――

Overview

In no case is the tension between the entity and aggregate conceptions of partnerships more apparent than in the case of the sale of a partnership interest. An aggregate conception would treat the selling partner as if she sold an undivided interest in each and every partnership asset to the buyer. This would influence the character of gain or loss realized by the selling partner, and the buyer would receive a cost basis in each of the partnership's assets. An entity approach, on the other hand, would treat the sale much like a sale of corporate stock: the seller would realize capital gain or loss, and the basis of the partnership's underlying assets would be unaffected. At first glance it appears that Subchapter K takes an entity approach; the general rule of § 741 characterizes gain or loss on the sale or exchange of a partnership interest as capital, and under § 743(a) the sale has no effect on the inside basis of the partnership's assets. But the aggregate approach ultimately dominates: First, § 751(a) overrides § 741 and treats part of the gain or loss as ordinary to the extent it is attributable to certain ordinary income assets held by the partnership. Second, if the partnership makes (or has previously made) a § 754 election, or has a substantial built-in loss,[1] § 743 provides for a special adjustment to the basis of partnership assets to take into account the amount that the buyer actually paid for her interest in each of those assets. Thus, as with other areas of partnership tax law where the aggregate and entity notions conflict, Subchapter K takes a middle ground.

―――

1. § 743(d)(1). If a partnership would have an overall net loss of $250,000 or more if it sold all of its assets for their fair market value, then it has a "substantial built-in loss."

144

The basic rules applicable to a sale of a partnership interest can be summarized as follows:

(i) The seller must recognize gain or loss on the sale of her interest equal to the difference between her amount realized and her outside basis. The character of that gain or loss will be capital (§ 741) except to the extent it is attributable to certain ordinary income assets (§ 751(a)). The seller is entitled to use the installment method of reporting gain under § 453, with some modifications.

(ii) The buyer of a partnership interest takes a cost basis in that interest. The buyer generally inherits the seller's capital accounts (both tax and book) and her share of inside basis.[2] In almost all cases this will result in a disparity between the buyer's outside basis and her share of inside basis.

(iii) If the partnership makes (or has previously made) an election under § 754, or if the partnership has a substantial built-in loss, the partnership will make a special basis adjustment under the rules of § 743(b) and § 755 that is intended to eliminate the disparity between the buyer's outside basis and her share of inside basis. This adjustment relates only to the buying partner, and has no effect on the partnership's common basis in its assets.

(iv) Unless the sale results in a termination of the partnership under § 708,[3] there are no other tax consequences to the partnership.

After examining each of these rules in detail, we will consider a couple of related matters which arise whenever there is a change in the ownership of a partnership, specifically, how to allocate the partnership's income and deductions in a year in which the ownership of the partnership has changed.

The Seller

Statutory Scheme

Section 741 states that the sale or exchange of a partnership interest is treated as the sale or exchange of a capital asset, except as otherwise provided in § 751. Section 751(a), in turn, states that any portion of a selling partner's amount realized attributable to

---

2. This is not true if the selling partner contributed property with a built-in loss to the partnership. Under § 704(c)(1)(C), no one other than the contributor can benefit from this loss.

3. Under § 708(b)(1)(B), a termination occurs if there is sale of 50% or more of the total interests in partnership profits and capital within a 12 month period. Terminations are discussed more fully at the end of *Chapter Eleven.*

(1) unrealized receivables or (2) inventory items, shall be treated as being an amount realized from the sale or exchange of a noncapital asset. Only the excess, if any, will be treated as received in exchange for a capital asset. While the statute focuses on dividing the seller's amount realized between the two categories of assets, the ultimate result (which is accomplished through a mechanism provided in the regulations) is to characterize a portion of the seller's gain or loss as ordinary. The definition of "unrealized receivables" and "inventory items," those items we collectively refer to as "§ 751(a) property," is therefore critical to determining the tax consequences of the sale of an interest in a partnership.[4]

Section 751(a) Property

There are two categories of § 751(a) property. These are "unrealized receivables" and "inventory items". These terms are used throughout Subchapter K.[5] As this is our first encounter with them, we will examine them in some detail here.

Unrealized Receivables. The first category of § 751(a) property is "unrealized receivables," which are defined in § 751(c). Ordinarily, one might think of unrealized receivables as those amounts

4. A brief history lesson will be helpful in understanding current law. Section 751 was originally enacted to prevent taxpayers from using partnerships to convert ordinary income into capital gain or to shift ordinary income from one taxpayer to another. This goal was accomplished in § 751(a), which is triggered when a partnership interest is sold, and in § 751(b), which applies to certain partnership distributions (and is discussed in *Chapter Thirteen*). Prior to 1997, the reach of these sections to partnerships holding inventory was somewhat limited: they applied only if a partnership's inventory items had "appreciated substantially in value". This limitation had two significant consequences. First, because only appreciated inventory was reached by § 751, application of § 751 resulted only in ordinary gains, not losses. Second, not all inventory gains were reached by § 751, only those that represented "substantial" appreciation, which meant partnerships were able to manipulate this substantial appreciation requirement to avoid application of the section.

In 1997 Congress amended § 751(a) to extend its reach to all inventory items of the partnership. However, § 751(b) continues to apply only to substantially appreciated inventory. This change causes a certain amount of definitional confusion. Under prior law we used the terms "§ 751 property" and "hot assets" interchangeably to refer to the ordinary income assets reached by § 751, and Reg. § 1.751–1(e) continues to define "section 751 property" as including unrealized receivables and substantially appreciated inventory. We were hoping that Treasury would revise this definition when they promulgated regulations to reflect the 1997 changes. Unfortunately, the regulations retained the old definition of "section 751 property," even though it is perfectly clear they intend the term to encompass all inventory items. Hopefully, Treasury will eliminate this confusion at some point in the future. In the meantime, we propose to use the term "§ 751(a) property" to encompass unrealized receivables and inventory items, as defined in the statute, and to use the term "§ 751(b) property" or "hot assets" when referring to the property reached by § 751(b).

5. See §§ 724(a), 731(a)(2)(B), 732(c), 735(a), and 736(b)(2). The references to inventory items sometimes do and sometimes do not include the substantial appreciation requirement.

earned by a cash method taxpayer, but not yet received or reported as income. But the term is defined much more broadly in § 751(c) and includes three different types. The first two types include what the term "unrealized receivables" connotes: if the partnership holds rights to payments for either (i) goods delivered or to be delivered, or (ii) services rendered or to be rendered, and if the partnership has not yet included those amounts in income under its method of accounting, then the rights are categorized as "unrealized receivables." Notice that these rights are not limited to those for amounts that have already been earned; they also encompass rights to amounts for goods "to be delivered" and services "to be rendered." Therefore, the definition of unrealized receivables is broad enough to encompass the premium value of a long-term contract held by the partnership.[6]

The description of the third type of unrealized receivable has been aptly characterized as a " ... mini-history of the unending struggle between Congress and taxpayers on the capital gain front."[7] Since 1962, Congress has repeatedly carved out exceptions to the preferential treatment afforded capital gains. The third type of unrealized receivable essentially is a list of these exceptions ("recapture items"), the most significant being § 1245 recapture income. Essentially, for purposes of §§ 741 and 751,[8] § 751(c) includes as an unrealized receivable any amount that would be recaptured as ordinary income if the partnership had sold its property for its fair market value.

Inventory Items. The second category of § 751(a) property is a partnership's inventory items. As noted above, prior to 1997 § 751(a) applied only to inventory items which had substantially appreciated in value. Under current law however, all inventory items, including those which have an unrealized loss, are covered by the statute.

The definition of inventory items is also quite broad. Certainly included are those items listed in § 1221(1), i.e., classic inventory and other property held for sale to customers.[9] In addition, § 751(d) includes in the definition of inventory items *any* property which, if sold, would not be considered a capital asset or property described in § 1231.[10] Therefore, among other items, the term literally en-

---

6. See, e.g., *Ledoux v. Commissioner*, 77 T.C. 293 (1981), *aff'd per curiam* 695 F.2d 1320 (11th Cir. 1983). There is an obvious tension between treating the premium value of long-term contracts as ordinary income and treating amounts paid for goodwill as capital gains. For this reason, if a long-term contract can be cancelled by either party, the courts have been reluctant to characterize its premium value as an unrealized receivable.

7. McKee et al., para 16.03[1].

8. These recapture items are not unrealized receivables for purposes of § 736. See *Chapter Fourteen.*

9. § 751(d)(1).

10. § 751(d)(2). Inventory items also include property which, if held by the

compasses all unrealized receivables as defined in § 751(c), except recapture items.[11]

Section 751(a) Computation

If a partner in a partnership which holds § 751(a) property sells or exchanges her interest in the partnership, a portion of the gain will be taxed as ordinary income under § 751(a). The regulations[12] provide a mechanism for calculating that amount, which can be summarized as follows:

1. First, determine the total gain or loss realized by the selling partner from the sale of her partnership interest (i.e., the difference between her total amount realized and her outside basis);

2. Next, calculate the gain or loss from § 751(a) property which would be allocated to the selling partner if the partnership sold all of its assets for their fair market value immediately prior to the sale of the selling partner's interest (the "hypothetical transaction"). That amount of the seller's total gain or loss is characterized as ordinary by § 751(a).

3. Finally, subtract the amount characterized as ordinary under § 751(a) (#2), from the selling partner's total gain (#1). This is the amount of capital gain or loss determined under § 741.

Under current law, not all capital gains are taxed at the same rate. Under § 1(h) capital gains from collectibles are taxed at a maximum rate of 28%, section 1250 capital gain[13] at a maximum rate of 25%, while all other capital gains are taxed at a maximum rate of 15%. For this reason, the regulations created the so-called "look-through rule." This rule requires the seller of a partnership interest to determine if any part of her § 741 capital gain is allocable to either collectible gains or to section 1250 capital gain so that the appropriate rate can be applied. These two types of capital gains are referred to as "look-through capital gains."

selling or distributee partner, would be an inventory item in her hands. § 751(d)(3).

11. Although not entirely free from doubt, the reason that we believe a recapture item does not constitute an inventory item is that it is not "property;" rather it is merely a portion of the gain that would result from the sale of property.

12. Prop. Reg. § 1.751–1(a)(2).

13. § 1.1(h)(1)(b)(3). This type of gain is also referred to as unrecaptured 1250 gain. § 1(h)(6). Essentially it is the amount of gain on the sale of real property that is the result of depreciation deductions.

To illustrate the operation of § 751(a) and its interaction with § 741, consider the following:

Example #1: ABC is an equal partnership. On January 1 of the current year A sells her interest (in which she has an outside basis of $50) to X for $100 cash. On the date of the sale the partnership holds the following assets, and has no liabilities (the table also illustrates the partnership's unrealized gain or loss in each asset, and A's share of that gain or loss):

Asset	*Basis*	*FMV*	*Gain/Loss*	*A's share*
Inventory	$100	$130	$30	$10
Capital Asset	50	170	120	40

If the partnership held no § 751(a) property, then we could simply compute A's gain under § 741 by subtracting from her amount realized of $100 her outside basis of $50, resulting in long term capital gain of $50. But the partnership does contain an asset that will generate ordinary income, and A should not be able to convert her share of that income into capital gain by selling her interest in the partnership. Thus, § 751 is implicated, and we must determine what portion of her gain will be characterized under § 751(a). We must therefore identify the partnership's § 751(a) property and then determine the portion of A's gain attributable to that property. In this case the first determination is simple: only the inventory held by the partnership constitutes § 751(a) property.

Step #1: A's overall gain from the sale is $50 (amount realized from X of $100 less A's outside basis of $50).

Step #2: ABC has only one item of § 751(a) property, the inventory. If ABC had sold all of its property for its fair market value immediately prior to the sale of A's interest, A's share of the gain from the sale of the inventory would have been $10. Therefore, $10 of A's total gain from the sale of her partnership interest is characterized as ordinary under § 751(a).

Step #3: The difference between A's total gain ($50) and the amount characterized as ordinary under § 751(a) ($10) is $40. Thus, A will report $40 of long term capital gain, in addition to $10 of ordinary income.

Example #2: Same as *Example #1* except that on the date of sale ABC's assets had the following value and bases:

Asset	Basis	FMV	Gain/Loss	A's share
Inventory	$100	$40	($60)	($20)
Capital Asset	50	260	210	70

Again, because the partnership holds § 751(a) property (the inventory), we must analyze the transaction under § 751(a).

Step #1: Once again, A's overall gain on the sale is $50 (amount realized of $100 less outside basis of $50).

Step #2: The hypothetical sale would result in an allocation of a $20 ordinary loss from the inventory to A. Therefore, A will realize a $20 ordinary loss under § 751(a).

Step #3: The difference between A's total gain of $50 and the loss of $20 will be taxed under § 741. Thus, A will report a $20 ordinary loss and $70 capital gain.[14]

Now consider the following more complicated example:

Example #3: DEF is an equal three person partnership in which D, E and F each has an outside basis of $300. The partnership uses the accrual method of accounting. On January 1 of the current year, D sells her interest to X for $750. The partnership has the following assets and no liabilities:

Asset	Basis	FMV	Gain/Loss	D's share
Cash	$150	$150	n/a	$0
Stock	150	450	300	100
Machinery	75	150	75	25
Building	300	750	450	150
Inventory	120	210	90	30
Acc'ts Rec.	105	90	(15)	(5)
Goodwill	0	450	450	150
	$900	$2250	$1350	$450

Additional facts: The machinery was purchased for $150; therefore the entire $75 gain would be subject to recapture under § 1245. The building was purchased several years ago for $600; therefore $300 of the $450 gain would be section 1250 capital gain. Finally the stock was purchased by the partnership 10 months ago.

Step #1: D's overall gain from the sale of her partnership interest is $450, the difference between her amount realized of $750 and her outside basis of $300.

Step #2: The partnership has three items of § 751(a) property: the inherent recapture in the machinery is an unrealized receivable, and the inventory and the accounts receivable are inventory items.[15] If the partnership made a hypothetical sale of all of its assets, a net $50 gain would be allocated to D from the sale of these

14. $50 minus (20) equals $70. This result was not possible under pre 1997 law. Because only substantially appreciated inventory and unrealized receivables were reached by § 751(a), only ordinary income resulted from the application of that section. Now, however, a loss item can be § 751(a) property.

15. It is worth noting that the receivables are not "unrealized receivables" within the definition of the statute because they have been taken into

assets (total $55 gain less $5 loss). Thus, $50 of D's overall gain will be characterized as ordinary under § 751(a).

Step #3: The difference between D's total gain of $450 and the $50 taxed as ordinary under step #2 is $400, and that amount will be taxed as capital gain under § 741. Since D's share of the partnership's section 1250 capital gain (i.e. ⅓ of $300), under the look-through rule, $100 of this $400 gain is characterized as section 1250 capital gain.

Section 751(a) has become simpler to understand and apply since the 1997 amendments. The seller of a partnership interest must in all situations recognize her share of ordinary income or loss inherent in the partnership at the time of sale. Only thereafter will capital gain result. The results are quite similar in many respects to what they would have been if the selling partner had sold her undivided interest in each partnership asset: aggregate treatment in its purest form. But they are not identical. Note that if D had sold her one-third undivided interest in the stock she would have had a short term capital gain of $100. By selling her partnership interest, she has converted this gain into a long-term capital gain.

Installment Sales of Partnership Interests

Section 453 provides for installment method reporting of gains when at least one payment for the sale of property is received after the close of the year in which the sale takes place. This treatment is generally quite beneficial and allows a taxpayer to report her gain proportionately as she receives payments.[16] The gain from certain sales, such as those of inventory,[17] accounts receivable,[18] recapture,[19] and securities traded on an established exchange,[20] is not eligible for the installment method and must be reported in the year of sale.

The gain from sale of a partnership interest is generally eligible for the installment method, with one significant exception. The gain attributable to the seller's share of § 751(a) property which, if it had been sold directly, would not have been eligible for § 453

account for tax purposes, but they are inventory items because, if sold, any gain or loss would be ordinary. See §§ 1221(4) and 751(d)(2).

16. Under § 453(c), the seller must report that proportion of each payment received which gross profit bears to total contract price. § 453(d) permits a seller to elect out of the installment method of

reporting, and report all gain in the year of sale.

17. § 453(b)(2)(B).

18. We do not believe that the accounts receivable of a cash method taxpayer would constitute "property" for purposes of § 453.

19. § 453(i)(2).

20. § 453(k)(2).

treatment, must be reported immediately.[21] The rest of the gain is reported under the installment method.[22]

The Buyer

As we have already learned, ideally a partnership's aggregate inside basis should equal the sum of the partners' outside bases, and each partner's share of that inside basis should equal her outside basis. Nevertheless, the sale of a partnership interest will almost always result in a disparity between inside basis and outside basis. This disparity is caused by the fact that, even though the buying partner has an outside basis equal to her cost, the sale of an interest in the partnership generally has no effect on the partnership's inside basis in its assets.[23] The buying partner succeeds to the seller's share of inside basis, which does not reflect the gain or loss realized on the sale of the purchased interest. The result is that the buyer can be either over or under-taxed, at least temporarily. To illustrate, reconsider the facts of ***Example #1*** where X buys a one-third interest in a partnership with $30 of unrealized ordinary income in its inventory. When the partnership sells its inventory, it will recognize ordinary income of $30, one-third of which will be allocated to X. But A, the selling partner, was already taxed on her $10 share of that ordinary income under § 751(a), and X paid full value for her interest in those receivables!

There is one exception to these general rules. Under § 704(c)(1)(C), if a partner contributes property with a built-in loss to a partnership, only that partner is entitled to take the built-in loss into account.[24] For purposes of determining the amount of items related to that property (e.g., loss or depreciation) that is allocated to the other partners, the partnership is required to use as its basis the fair market value of the property when contributed. When a partner who has contributed built-in loss property sells her partnership interest, the buyer is not permitted to benefit from the built-in loss. In effect, the buyer's share of inside basis is equal to the seller's less any amount of § 704(c) loss inherent in the property at the time of purchase. To illustrate, consider the following example.

21. Rev. Rul. 89–108, 1989–2 C.B. 100.

22. Under § 453(k), Treasury has been authorized to promulgate regulations that could prohibit the use of the installment method to the extent that the gain from the sale of a partnership interest is attributable to marketable securities. To date, there are no such regulations. For an excellent discussion of how to interpret such lack of action, see **Phillip Gall**, *Phantom Tax Regulations: The Case of Spurned Delegations*, 56 Tax Law. 413 (2003).

23. § 743(a).

24. We introduced this rule in *Chapter Seven.*

Example #4: A, B and C form an equal general partnership to which A contributes land with a value of $100 in which A has a basis of $500. B and C each contribute $100 cash. The partnership's opening balance sheet is as follows:

	Assets		*Liabilities & Capital*
	Basis	*Book*	
Cash	$200	$200	
Land	500	100	
	$700	$300	

	Capital Accounts	
	Tax	*Book*
A	$500	$100
B	100	100
C	100	100
	$700	$300

A's outside basis and share of inside basis are initially both $500. After the land has appreciated in value to $250, A sells her interest to Z for $150. Prior to the enactment of § 704(c)(1)(C), Z would have simply stepped in the shoes of A, including the balances in both of her capital accounts. Under current law, however, Z is not entitled to benefit from A's built-in loss, and is treated just as though A contributed land with a basis of $100. If that had been the case, then the partnership's aggregate inside basis would be $300, and A's share $100. Therefore, Z's share of inside basis is also $100, an amount equal to A's actual share of inside basis ($500) less the built-in loss ($400). While regulations have yet to be proposed, we expect that they will provide that the balance in Z's capital account and the partnership's basis in the land will be reduced to $100.

It should be apparent that sales of partnership interests frequently result in a disparity between inside and outside basis. If a partnership makes a § 754 election or if it has a substantial built-in loss this disparity between inside and outside basis will be resolved, so that the buying partner will be treated as if she had purchased an undivided interest in each asset. A partnership making the election must make special basis adjustments whenever an interest in it is transferred (under the rules set forth in § 743) and following certain distributions (under the rules set forth is § 734). Once a partnership makes a § 754 election with respect to one transaction (either a transfer or distribution), the election remains in effect with respect to all future transactions, and it can be revoked only with the consent of the IRS.[25] Therefore, the partner-

---

25. § 1.754–1(c). This election should not be taken lightly. While in place, an electing partnership *must* make the required basis adjustments

ship in *Example #1* may have made a § 754 election in connection with a prior transfer or distribution, or it can make one following the purchase of A's interest. In either case, it will be required to adjust the basis of its assets in an amount determined under § 743(b).

Even in the absence of a § 754 election, if the partnership has a substantial built-in loss at the time of purchase, the partnership must make the adjustments prescribed by § 743(b). For this purpose, "substantial built-in loss" is defined as when the partnership's adjusted basis in its property exceeds the property's fair market value by more than $250,000.[26] In contrast with § 704(c) built-in loss discussed in the context of *Example #4*, a substantial built-in loss is typically one that is created after the partnership has been formed.[27]

The rules for making § 743(b) adjustments are discussed in detail below, and they can summarized as follows:

1. As discussed above, the adjustment is made only if the partnership makes or has previously made an election under § 754, or the partnership has a substantial built-in loss.

2. The amount of the adjustment is determined under § 743(b), and it is equal to the difference between the buyer's outside basis and her share of inside basis. The regulations under § 743 provide a means of calculating the buyer's share of inside basis.

3. Section 755 (and the regulations under that section) provide rules for allocating the adjustment among the partnership's assets. The goal of those rules is to essentially give the buying partner a cost basis in her share of each asset. This prevents her from being over or under taxed.

4. The basis adjustments made by the partnership apply *only with respect to the transferee partner,* so that they have no impact on future allocations of income, deduction, gain or loss to the other partners.

Calculating the § 743(b) Adjustment.

Examples #5, #6 and #7 illustrate the rules for calculating the amount of the special basis adjustment under § 743(b).

whenever an interest in the partnership is subsequently sold or transferred by reason of the death of a partner. This may not always be advantageous. Furthermore, as we shall see in *Chapter Twelve,* an electing partnership must also make the adjustments required under § 734(b) when a partnership distributes it assets.

26. § 743(d)(1).

27. Indeed, we do not believe that § 704(c) built-losses should be taken into account in determining whether the partnership has a substantial built-in loss.

Example #5: ABC is an equal partnership in which A, B and C each has an outside basis, capital account balance and share of inside basis of $100. On January 1 of this year, A sells her interest to X for $300. Immediately after the purchase, the partnership's balance sheet is as follows:

<table>
<tr><td colspan="3" align="center">***Assets***</td><td colspan="3" align="center">***Liabilities & Capital***</td></tr>
<tr><td></td><td align="center">*Basis/Book*</td><td align="center">*FMV*</td><td colspan="3"></td></tr>
<tr><td>Inventory</td><td align="center">$150</td><td align="center">$300</td><td colspan="3"></td></tr>
<tr><td>Land</td><td align="center">$150</td><td align="center">$600</td><td colspan="3"></td></tr>
<tr><td></td><td align="center">$300</td><td align="center">$900</td><td colspan="3"></td></tr>
<tr><td colspan="3"></td><td colspan="3" align="center">***Capital Accounts***</td></tr>
<tr><td colspan="3"></td><td></td><td align="center">*Tax/Book*[28]</td><td align="center">*FMV*</td></tr>
<tr><td colspan="3"></td><td>X</td><td align="center">$100</td><td align="center">$300</td></tr>
<tr><td colspan="3"></td><td>B</td><td align="center">$100</td><td align="center">$300</td></tr>
<tr><td colspan="3"></td><td>C</td><td align="center">$100</td><td align="center">$300</td></tr>
<tr><td colspan="3"></td><td></td><td align="center">$300</td><td align="center">$900</td></tr>
</table>

X paid $300 for her interest in this partnership. From an aggregate perspective, X has purchased a one-third interest in each of the partnership's assets, paying $100 for a one-third interest in the inventory and $200 for a one-third interest in the land. Nevertheless, in the absence of a § 754 election, X's purchase has no effect on the partnership's inside basis; it remains unchanged. X simply inherits A's capital account and share of inside basis, both $100. X's share of inside basis in the inventory is $50 (not the $100 X paid) and in the land is $50 (not the $200 X paid). In total, a $200 disparity has been created between the partnership's inside basis and the aggregate outside basis, and hence between X's share of inside basis and her outside basis.

This disparity could result in overtaxation of X, at least temporarily. To illustrate, if the partnership sold both assets for their fair market value shortly after the X's purchase, the partnership would have a $150 ordinary gain on the inventory and a $450 capital gain on the land, both of which would be shared equally by X, B and C. Although X has no economic gain, she still would have to report her share of these gains (a total of $200) on her income tax return, increasing her outside basis to $500.[29] After these sales the partnership's balance sheet would be as follows:

---

28. Note that book capital is no longer equal to outside basis. This is because § 1.704–1(b)(2)(iv)(*l*) requires that (absent a termination of the partnership) the seller's capital account must carry over to the purchaser.

29. § 705(a)(1)(A).

Assets			**Liabilities & Capital**

	Basis/Book	FMV
Cash	$900	$900

Capital Accounts

	Tax/Book	FMV
X	$300	$300
B	$300	$300
C	$300	$300
	$900	$900

As a result of these transactions, X has been currently overtaxed by $200. Since her outside basis is $200 higher than the value of her interest, she will eventually be entitled to an offsetting loss deduction, but not until she disposes of her partnership interest. This is undoubtedly not satisfactory from X's point of view: She must report income today, some of which is ordinary, in exchange for an offsetting capital loss sometime in the future. A taxpayer's nightmare.

If the partnership makes a § 754 election (or if there is one in place), it must adjust the basis in its assets whenever there is a transfer of a partnership interest[30] in an amount determined under § 743(b). This so-called "§ 743(b) adjustment" is then allocated among the partnership assets in accordance with the rules of § 755. The resulting "special basis adjustments" are then made to the partnership's assets, but only with respect to the transferee partner; the common basis of the partnership's assets remains unchanged.

The adjustment under § 743(b) is equal to the difference between the buyer's outside basis and her share of inside basis, and has the effect of equating these two amounts. If the buyer's outside basis is higher than her share of inside basis, the adjustment is positive; if the buyer's outside basis is less than her share of inside basis, the adjustment is negative. The buyer's outside basis is simply the amount she paid for her interest, i.e., her cost (including her share of liabilities, if any).[31] Determining the buyer's share of inside basis is more difficult. The regulations define a partner's share of inside basis as the sum of her share of "previously taxed capital" plus her share of liabilities.[32] A partner's share of "previously taxed capital" appears to be an entirely new term, which is defined in the proposed regulations in a fairly complex way. However, on closer examination, it appears that the regulations simply provide a new definition (and new name) for a concept we have

---

30. In this context, a transfer includes a sale, exchange, or a transfer at death; it does not normally include a transfer by gift. Transfers do not include either the admission of a new partner nor the liquidation of an old partner.

31. § 742.

32. § 1.743–1(d)

already used throughout this book: in most cases, a partner's share of previously taxed capital is simply the balance in her tax capital account. Although Treasury has used the concept of tax capital for many years (it is used extensively in the § 704(b) and § 704(c) regulations) it has never precisely defined the term. And although it is not done explicitly, the § 743 regulations now give a definition to tax capital through this new term "previously taxed capital". Under the regulations, determination of the buyer's share of previously taxed capital requires yet another "hypothetical transaction," in this case a cash sale by the partnership of all of its assets for their fair market value immediately *after* the transfer of the partnership interest. A partner's share of a partnership's "previously taxed capital" is equal to the sum of (i) the amount of cash the partner would receive on liquidation following this hypothetical transaction, plus (ii) the amount of any taxable loss allocated to the partner from the hypothetical transaction, less (iii) the amount of any taxable gain allocated to the partner as a result of the hypothetical transaction.

Applying these rules to the facts of *Example #5*, we have already seen that if the partnership sold all of its assets for fair market value, it would have $150 of ordinary income, and $450 of capital gain, one-third of which would be allocated to X. On liquidation, X would be entitled to $300 of cash. Thus, X's share of the partnership's previously taxed capital is $300 (cash distributable to X) plus 0 loss allocated to X, minus $200 gain allocated to X, for a total of $100. This amount, when added to X's share of liabilities (here zero) gives X a share of inside basis of $100. It is worth noting that X's share of previously taxed capital is precisely the amount in her tax capital account. We believe that this will be true in most cases.

Consider the following slightly more complicated example:

> *Example #6:* ABC is an equal three person partnership, formed some years ago when A contributed Blackacre (with a basis of $40 and a fair market value of $100) and B and C each contributed $100 cash. On January 1 of the current year, A sells her partnership interest to X for $350, resulting in a capital gain to her of $310. At the time of sale, the partnership's balance sheet (expanded to show fair market values) is as follows:

	Assets			**Liabilities & Capital**

	Basis	*Book*	*FMV*
Cash	$ 50	$ 50	$ 50
Blackacre	40	100	400
Whiteacre	150	150	600
	$240	$300	$1050

Capital Accounts

	Tax	*Book*	*FMV*
A(X)	$ 40	$100	$ 350
B	100	100	350
C	100	100	350
	$240	$300	$1050

X's outside basis is the amount she paid, $350. Using the rule advanced above, X's share of inside basis should be $40, the balance in the tax capital account inherited from A, plus her share of liabilities (here zero).[33] Thus, the § 743(b) adjustment should be $310, the difference between X's outside basis ($350) and share of inside basis ($40).

This result can be checked using the mechanism set forth in the regulations: assume that the partnership sells all of its assets for cash immediately following X's purchase of her interest. That sale would result in gain or loss in the partnership property as follows:

	Basis	*Book*	*FMV*	*gain/loss*	*X's share*
Cash	$50	$50	$50		
Blackacre	40	100	400	360	160
Whiteacre	150	150	600	450	150

On liquidation following the hypothetical sale, X would be entitled to $350 in cash (one-third of the total value). No loss would be allocated to her, but $310 of gain would be allocated to her. Thus, her share of the partnership's previously taxed capital is $350–310 or $40. This results in the § 743(b) adjustment of $310 which we found by using X's tax capital account as a short-cut.

The next example introduces the complication of liabilities:

Example #7: DEF is an equal partnership, formed some years ago when E contributed stock (with a basis of $50 and a fair market value of $100) and D and F each contributed $100 cash. The partnership has since acquired land subject to a recourse mortgage. On January 1 of the current year, E sells her partnership interest to Y for $200 cash. At the time of sale, the partnership's balance sheet (expanded to show fair market values) is as follows:

---

33. As discussed in *Chapter Seven*, because A had contributed Blackacre, her contribution to inside basis was less than the other two partners: it was limited to the $40 basis of Blackacre at the time of the contribution.

	Assets			Liabilities & Capital

	Basis	Book	FMV	
Cash	$ 50	$ 50	$ 50	Mortgage $300
Stock	50	100	250	
Land	450	450	600	
	$550	$600	$900	

Capital Accounts

	Tax	Book	FMV
D	$100	$100	$200
E(Y)	50	100	200
F	100	100	200
	$250	$300	$600

Y's outside basis is $300, the sum of the $200 cash she paid plus her $100 share of liabilities.[34] Her share of inside basis is the sum of her tax capital account ($50) plus her share of liabilities ($100) or a total of $150. Therefore, the appropriate amount of Y's § 743(b) adjustment is $150 ($300 less $150).

To check this under the "previously taxed capital" mechanism of the regulations, we can see that on liquidation the partnership would have $600 to distribute after paying off the mortgage. Y's share of that is $200. The hypothetical sale would result in gains and losses as follows:

	Basis	Book	FMV	gain/loss	Y's share
Cash	$50	$50	$50		
Stock	50	100	250	200	100
Land	450	450	600	150	50

Therefore, Y's share of previously taxed capital is $200 (cash distributable) less $150 (gain allocable to Y), or $50. Again, this is precisely the balance in her tax capital account! Her share of inside basis is the sum of her $50 share of previously taxed capital and her $100 share of liabilities, again $150, leading to the § 743(b) adjustment of $300 less $150, or $150.

Allocating the § 743(b) Adjustment Among the Partnership's Assets

The rules for allocating the § 743(b) adjustment among the partnership's assets are found in § 755 and the regulations thereunder. Those rules first divide the adjustment between two classes of assets, "ordinary income property" on the one hand, and "capital gain property" on the other.[35] The adjustment is then allocated among the assets in each class. The regulations treat the total

34. § 742.

35. These terms are defined at § 1.755–1(a). Capital gain property includes capital assets and § 1231(b) prop-erty, and all other property (including unrealized receivables and recapture items under § 751(c)) is ordinary income property.

amount of the § 743(b) adjustment as a *net* amount, which means that positive adjustments can be made with respect to some assets (or one class), and negative adjustments can be made with respect to others.

For purposes of calculating the amount to be allocated to each class, and to each asset within a class, the regulations employ the same "hypothetical transaction" approach that we have used throughout this chapter, first for calculating the seller's ordinary income under § 751(a), and later for purposes of calculating the buyer's share of previously taxed capital. In this case we calculate the buyer's allocable share of gain or loss from each asset if immediately after the transfer the partnership made a cash sale of all of its assets for fair market value.[36] This provides the template for allocating the adjustment, and the result will be that in many cases the adjustments will precisely offset the buyer's share of gain or loss inherent in each asset.[37]

To illustrate how the allocation rules work, recall the facts of **Example #6**, where we calculated a § 743(b) adjustment for X of $310. In arriving at that amount, we used the following chart which shows the amount of gain or loss allocable to X if each of the assets were sold for its fair market value on the date X purchased her interest:

	Basis	*Book*	*FMV*	*gain/loss*	*X's share*
Cash	$50	$50	$50		
Blackacre	40	100	400	360	160
Whiteacre	150	150	600	450	150

Under § 755(b), the entire § 743(b) adjustment is allocated to capital assets (because there are no ordinary income assets.) The adjustment is then divided between the capital assets (Blackacre and Whiteacre) based upon X's share of the appreciation in each asset, or $160 and $150, respectively.

When a partnership holds multiple assets, allocation of the § 743(b) adjustment becomes somewhat more complicated, but is essentially done in the same way. To illustrate reconsider **Example #3.** As you will recall, in that example, partner D sold her partnership interest to X for $750. At the time of the sale, the partnership

---

36. § 1.755–1(b)(1)(ii).

37. If the buyer pays a premium over asset value, under the residual approach of § 1060 the excess will be allocated to goodwill or other § 197 intangibles. If the buyer purchases at a discount below fair market value, the regulations first allocate the adjustment to ordinary income property to the extent possible, and then provide an extremely complicated mechanism for allocating the shortfall among the properties. The mechanism is based upon a combination of two factors: the unrealized appreciation in each asset and each asset's relative fair market value. See § 1.755–1(b)(3)(ii).

had the following assets (and no liabilities) with the following amounts of inherent appreciation:

Asset	Basis	FMV	Gain/Loss	D's share
Cash	$150	$150	n/a	$ 0
Stock	150	450	300	100
Machinery[38]	75	150	75	25
Building	300	750	450	150
Inventory	120	210	90	30
Acc'ts Rec.	105	90	(15)	(5)
Goodwill	0	450	450	150
	$900	$2250	$1350	$450

If there were a § 754 election in place, the § 743(b) adjustment would be +$450, determined as follows:

X's outside basis ($750) less X's share of inside basis ($300)[39] equals $450.

Under § 755(b), this $450 adjustment must first be allocated between capital assets and ordinary income property based on the income, gain or loss allocable to X following the hypothetical transaction. The ordinary income property in this partnership consists of the recapture on the equipment, the accounts receivable and the inventory. X's share of net ordinary income from these assets is $50. Her share of net gain from the capital assets is $400. Therefore, $50 of the § 743(b) adjustment is allocated to the ordinary income assets and $400 to the capital assets. These adjustments are then further allocated among the assets within each class, this time in accordance with the gain or loss potential in each asset. Of the $50 adjustment allocable to the ordinary income assets, $25 is allocated to the equipment, $30 is allocated to the inventory, and a negative $5 adjustment is allocated to the accounts receivable. These amounts constitute X's special basis adjustments with respect to these assets. Notice that these adjustments are precisely equal to X's share of income or loss in these assets on the date of purchase.

Similarly, the $400 allocated to the capital assets is divided as follows: $100 to the stock, $150 to the building, and $150 to the goodwill. Again the adjustments precisely equal X's share of gain or loss from the hypothetical transaction.

Effect of the Adjustment

Having calculated the adjustment, and allocated it among the various partnership assets, the obvious question remaining is what

38. Remember that the machinery was purchased for $150 so that the entire $75 gain is subject to recapture under § 1245.

39. X's share of inside basis is calculated by adjusting the amount of her share of cash distributable after the hypothetical transaction ($750) by the net gain or loss allocable to her after that transaction (–450) or $300.

to do with it! As a threshold matter, the adjustment is not reflected in capital accounts,[40] nor does it enter into the common basis of the partnership's assets.[41] The partnership making the adjustment will compute its taxable income, gain, loss and deduction without regard to the adjustment, and then allocate those amounts among all of the partners under the principles of § 704(b). Only then does the adjustment come into play. The partnership will adjust the transferee partner's distributive share of income, gain, loss and deduction to reflect the adjustment. That means that if the partnership has sold an asset with respect to which a partner has a special basis adjustment, the amount of that adjustment will reduce (or increase, if the adjustment is negative) the transferee partner's distributive share of the gain or loss from the sale of the asset.[42] If a positive adjustment is made with respect to property that is subject to amortization or depreciation, then the adjustment will increase the transferee's share of depreciation or amortization from that property. In effect, she is treated as if she purchased new property of the same type for a price equal to the adjustment.[43]

To illustrate, recall **_Example #7_**, where we determined that D had a special basis adjustment of $100 with respect to the partnership's stock. If the partnership were to sell that stock for $450, it would have a gain on the sale of $300, which it would allocate equally among B, C and D. But D's share of the gain would be reduced by the $100 special basis adjustment, and she would report zero gain from the sale. Similarly, if the stock were sold for $750, D's $200 share of the gain would be offset by the $100 adjustment, and she would report a gain of $100. Finally, if the stock were sold for $300, D's $50 share of the gain would be offset by the adjustment, and she would report a loss on the sale of ($50).

In that example D also had a special basis adjustment of $25 allocable to the machinery. Under the regulations, D is treated as though she purchased a new piece of machinery for $25, and she will recover that amount under whatever recovery period and method is appropriate for that type of machinery under § 168. So, for example, if the machinery was 5 year property, and D elected to use the straight-line method, then (ignoring conventions) D's share of depreciation on the machinery will be increased each year by $5. This will be in addition to his one-third share of the partnership's common cost recovery deduction. Similar principles would apply to D's share of depreciation on the building and amortization of the goodwill.

40. § 1.704–1(b)(2)(iv)(m).

41. § 1.743–1(j)(1). There is a limited exception in the case of certain distributions to a transferee partner. See § 1.734–2(b)(1).

42. § 1.743–1(j)(3).

43. § 1.743–1(j)(4).

Related Matters—§§ 706(c) & (d)

Although the major focus of this chapter is the tax consequences of a sale of a partnership interest, there are two related issues that arise whenever there is a change, or shift, in the ownership of a partnership. A shift in partnership interest can be created by a variety of transactions, including the withdrawal of an old partner, the admission of a new one, or the sale of all or a portion of an interest in the partnership. First, under § 706(c) the shift in interest may close the partnership's taxable year with respect to one or more partners; and second, under § 706(d), the partnership must allocate its income, gain and loss for the year of change to take into account the varying interests of the partners.

Closing a Partnership's Taxable Year

As we saw in *Chapter Three*, under § 706(a) a partner includes her share of partnership income or loss in her tax return for the year during which the last day of the partnership year occurs.[44] If for some reason the partnership year was to close early, for example if the partnership liquidated midyear, that could shift the partner's share of income for that year into an earlier year of the partner. Thus, for example, assume a calendar year partner owns a 30% interest in a partnership with a fiscal year ending June 30. That partner will include her share of the partnership's income for the period beginning July 1, 2009 and ending June 30, 2010 in her calendar year 2010 return, because the partnership year ends within the 2010 calendar year. If the partnership were to liquidate on November 15, 2009, however, the partnership year would close on that date, and income for the partial year ending November 15 would now be included in our partner's 2009 return.

The question is in what contexts, other than a liquidation of a partnership, will the partnership's year close early, and result in potential acceleration of income to a partner? Under § 706(c)(2) there are two situations in which the partnership's year will close prematurely.

1.   The first is in the event of a partnership "termination," which is defined in § 708(b)(1). A termination will occur if the partnership ceases to do business (which would encompass our liquidation example), or if within a 12 month period there is a sale or exchange of 50% or more of the total interests in partnership capital and profits (§ 708(b)(1)(B)). In that case,

---

44. Recall the language of § 706(a), which provides a partner must take into account items of partnership income, etc. for any partnership taxable year "ending within or with the taxable year of the partner."

the partnership's year terminates with respect to all of its partners.

2.   The second event triggering a premature closing of the partnership's taxable year is the sale, exchange or liquidation of a partner's entire interest in the partnership, or the death of a partner.[45] In that event, the partnership's year will close SOLELY with respect to the terminated partner, who will be required to include her share of income for the year (calculated as discussed below) in her current taxable year. Transfer or liquidation of less than a partner's entire interest does NOT trigger a premature closing of the partnership's taxable year unless, of course, the transfer would otherwise trigger a "termination" under § 708.[46]

To illustrate, if our calendar year partner described above transferred her entire 30% interest in the partnership on December 28, 2009, then the partnership's year with respect to her would close on that date, and her share of income for the short period beginning July 1, 2009 and ending December 28, 2009 would be included in her 2009 return. If, on the other hand, she doesn't sell her interest until January 2, 2010 then the partnership year will close with respect to her on that date, and her year of inclusion would remain 2010, i.e., the income would not be accelerated into her 2009 return. This provides obvious planning opportunities.

Allocation of Income for the Year of Change

Whether or not a transfer of a partner's interest terminates the partnership's year, which may affect the *timing* of inclusions, whenever ownership interests in a partnership vary during the year it is necessary to compute the *amount* of each partner's appropriate share of the income for the year. As a general proposition, under § 706(d)(1), Congress mandates that the partners' relative shares of income, gain, loss, deduction or credit be determined taking into account their varying interests. When it enacted § 706(d)(1) in 1976 Congress left it to the Treasury to develop the necessary rules for implementing the mandate, although the legislative history provided some guidance. Proposed regulations were not issued until 2009.

Congress enacted § 706(d)(1) during the heyday of the tax shelter industry of the 1970s. One of the techniques employed by tax shelters was to admit a limited partner to a partnership at the end of the partnership's taxable year, and allocate to the new partner a full year's share of the venture's deductions and losses.

---

45. See § 706(c)(2)(A).   **46.** See § 706(c)(2)(B).

Section 706(d)(1) was designed to eliminate these "retroactive allocations." It applies, however, in a far wider range of situations.

Under the proposed regulations, if one or more partners' interests in a partnership varies during a year, either because of a sale or a liquidation of a partner's interest (in whole or in part), the death of a partner, or any other transaction having that effect,[47] the partnership must take into account these variations in determining it partners' shares of partnership items for the year. The proposed regulations prescribe two methods for accomplishing this, the "interim closing method," and the "proration method." The default method is the interim closing method, which will apply unless the partners agree to use the proration method. For any given taxable year, the partnership can only use one method, and whichever method is chosen, it must be used consistently by all partners and the partnership.[48]

Both methods envision dividing the partnership year into "segments" representing periods of time during which the partners' interests in the partnership remain constant.[49] When a partner's interest changes, whether by sale, liquidation, or death, a segment ends and a new segment begins on the following day. To determine the end of a segment under the interim closing method,[50] the partnership has the choice of two conventions, either the "calendar day" convention,[51] under which a segment would end on the actual date that the partner's interest changes, or the "semi-monthly" convention,[52] under which the date the segment ends is basically rounded back to the last day of the prior month or the 15th day of the current month. Under the semi-monthly convention, if the variation in interest occurs on the 1st through the 15th day of any calendar month, the segment ends as of the last day of the previous month. If the variation occurs on the 16th or later in the month, the segment ends on the 15th of that month. Whatever date that is prescribed under these conventions is the date that the partnership must close its books. The calendar day convention is required for the proration method.

Because the interim closing method might be burdensome and costly, the regulations permit partners to agree to use the proration method.[53] Under this method, the partnership simply waits until the end of the taxable year and prorates its annual income on a

47. Prop. Reg. § 1.706–4(a)(1). Other transactions include the admission of a new partner and the contribution of capital by an existing partner. The proposed regulations do not explicitly deal with the admission of a new partner.

48. Id.

49. Prop. Reg. § 1.706–4(a)(2)(i).

50. Prop. Reg. § 1.706–4(c).

51. Prop. Reg. § 1.706–4(e)(1).

52. Prop. Reg. § 1.706–4(e)(2).

53. Prop. Reg. § 1.706–4(d).

daily basis between or among the segments.[54] Under this method, extraordinary items cannot be prorated; these items must be taken into account in proportion to each partner's interest in the partnership at the beginning of the day that the items are taken into account.[55] The regulations list several extraordinary items, including gains and losses from the sale or other disposition of all capital assets and § 1231(b) property.[56]

You can imagine the complexity and expense involved in applying these rules, and the proposed regulations do carve out several exceptions where they need not apply.[57] The first is for "[p]ermissible changes among contemporary partners." This exception makes it clear that the varying interest rules are not meant to restrict the existing partners' ability to reallocate items among themselves during the course of a year as long as the allocations would otherwise be respected. This exception applies provided that the change in allocation is not attributable to a contribution to, a distribution from, the partnership. The second exception is for service partnerships. Service partnerships are allowed to take into account varying interests using "any reasonable method" provided that the partnership's allocations are respected under § 704(b).[58] Finally, a safe harbor is carved out for publicly traded partnerships.

The proposed regulations have been the subject of extensive public comments. The focus of much of the commentary has been that final regulations should allow for more flexibility to partnerships in choosing reasonable methods of accounting for variations. Nevertheless, we expect that much of the heart of the proposed rules, including the two basic methods and the conventions, will survive. We will therefore provide an illustration of how we expect they will apply in the context of the sale of a partnership interest. Consider the following:

> ***Example #8***: PRS is an equal partnership that has a fiscal year ending on June 30. P, R, and S are individual, calendar year taxpayers. On November 27, 2011, P sells her one-third partnership interest to Q. For its fiscal year ending June 30, 2012, PRS has $366,000 of bottom-line income, $90,000 of which was earned prior to November 16, 2011. In addition, on April 15, 2012, the partnership (now QRS) sells stock it held

---

54. Under the proration method, the partnership must use the calendar day convention.

55. Prop. Reg. § 1.706–4(d)(1).

56. Prop. Reg. § 1.706–4(d)(3). The regulations list nine extraordinary items.

57. Prop. Reg. § 1.706–4(b).

58. Prop. Reg. § 1.706–4(b)(2). For this purpose, service partnerships are those in which substantially all the activities involve the performance of services in the fields of health, law, engineering architecture, accounting, and actuarial science or consulting.

for an investment for a capital loss of $30,000. Note that 2012 is a leap year.

For the partnership's taxable year, the one-third interest sold by P to Q is entitled to 1/3 of the bottom-line income (i.e., $122,000) and 1/3 of the capital loss (i.e., $10,000). The principal issue raised in this example is how these items should be shared by P and Q. Under the proposed regulations, since P's and Q's interests in the partnership have varied during the year, the partnership must account for this variation under either the interim closing method or the proration method. Whichever method is chosen, the partnership year will close with respect to P, who is terminating her interest in the partnership. This means that P must report her share of the partnership income on her 2011 return.

If the partnership uses the interim closing method and adopts the semi-monthly convention, then the partnership will close its books as of November 15, 2011. Thus, the partnership's taxable year is divided into two segments, the first from July 1, 2011 until November 15, 2011, and the second from November 16, 2011 until June 30, 2012. During the first segment while P owns the 1/3 interest, the partnership has $90,000 of bottom-line income, $30,000 of which is allocated to P. Since P sold her entire interest in the partnership, the partnership's taxable year closes with respect to P and P must include the $30,000 in income for 2011. During the second segment while Q owns the 1/3 interest, the partnership has $276,000 of bottom-line income and a $30,000 capital loss of which Q is allocated 1/3 (i.e., $92,000 of bottom-line income and $10,000 capital loss).[59]

If, on the other hand, the partnership were to use the proration method, the partnership's taxable year would once again be divided into two segments. The first segment would begin on July 1, 2011 and end on the date of the sale, November 27, 2011, for a total of 150 days. Note that the semi-monthly convention is not available under the proration method.[60] The second segment runs from November 28, 2011 to June 30, 2012 for a total of 216 days. Under the proration method, the partnership waits until year end and then allocates its income for the year ratably on a daily basis. Extraordinary items, such as the capital loss, are not prorated but must be allocated to the partners on the day that they are accounted for. On these facts, that means that the partnership is deemed to have earned $1000 a day throughout its taxable year. Therefore, $150,000 is attributable to the first segment, $50,000 of which is allocated to P, and $216,000 attributable to the second segment,

59. Note that if the partnership elected the calendar day convention, then the partnership would close its books on November 27, 2011.

60. Prop. Reg. 1.706–4(d)(2).

$72,000 of is allocated to Q. Because the capital loss was realized while Q owned the partnership interest, Q would be allocated the $10,000 capital loss.

At first blush, these results seem widely disparate: Under the interim closing method, P reports income of $30,000 and under the proration method she reports $50,000. The difference, however, may not be as great as it first seems. Note that whichever method is used, P's outside basis will be increased by her share of income for the year. So while she includes more under the proration method, she will have a correspondingly greater adjustment to her outside basis, which will reduce the gain and or increase the loss on the sale. So to the extent that games may be played with these rules, they will revolve mostly about the character of income and gain that P must report, rather than the amounts.

Chapter Eleven

DISTRIBUTIONS—THE BASICS

Introduction

Sections 731 through 737 prescribe the general rules for partnership distributions. In combination with the provisions governing contributions, these rules reflect a Congressional policy of deferring recognition of gain or loss by partners and partnerships whenever possible—a policy of maximum nonrecognition. The basic objective is to remove tax disincentives to the movement of property into and out of partnerships; that movement, to the greatest extent possible, should be prompted by business, not tax, considerations. The distribution rules further this objective by permitting partners to withdraw their previously taxed profits without further tax consequences. Thus, the general rule is that neither the partnership nor the partner recognizes gain or loss on a distribution of cash or property. It is only when deferral is impracticable or when it would result in a change of character that gain or loss is recognized upon a distribution.

We have divided our discussion of distributions into four chapters. This chapter deals with the basic rules for both current and liquidating distributions, and it is limited to distributions that are respected as such and are not recharacterized by the Code.[1] A "current distribution" is one made to a partner whose interest in the partnership continues after the distribution, although perhaps (but not necessarily) at a reduced share. A "liquidating distribution" refers to one or more distributions that terminate a partner's

---

1. Several provisions of Subchapter K recharacterize what might otherwise appear to be a "distribution" and we take them up in succeeding chapters. These are: (i) §§ 704(c)(1)(B) and 737 (gain or loss recognized by a partner who contributed property to a partnership); (ii) § 707(a)(2)(B)(contribution and related distribution treated as a disguised sale); (iii) § 736 (part of a distribution treated as a guaranteed payment); and (iv) § 751(b)(disproportionate distribution recharacterized as a sale or exchange).

interest in the partnership (and which may, as well, terminate the partnership if all partners' interests are liquidated).[2] As we shall see, although the basic rules are not very difficult to apply, they can create disparities between inside and outside basis (similar to those we examined in the context of the sale of a partnership interest),[3] which may result in either a windfall or a hardship to the continuing partners. To reduce or eliminate these disparities, § 734(b) provides a basis adjustment for those partnerships with a § 754 election in effect. This adjustment, and its allocation, is the subject of *Chapter Twelve*. *Chapter Thirteen* deals with disproportionate distributions,[4] which are governed by rules that are among the most complex in the Internal Revenue Code. Finally, *Chapter Fourteen* examines the tax consequences of payments made to a retiring partner.

The two principal issues addressed in this chapter are the recognition of gain or loss by the distributee, and the determination of her basis in the distributed property. Resolution of these issues depends in part on whether the distribution is a current or liquidating distribution. First, however, several preliminary matters that are common to all distributions must be considered.

Preliminary Issues

Sections 706(c) & (d)

In the last chapter, we saw that a sale of a partnership interest may close the taxable year of the partnership with respect to the selling partner and require the partnership to take into account the varying interests of the partners for the year of sale. These same rules generally apply to any distribution that has the effect of changing the relative interests of the partners (i.e., a partial or complete liquidation).[5]

---

2. § 1.731–1(a)(2).

3. See *Chapter Ten*.

4. Disproportionate distributions are those that change the partners' relative ownership of § 751 property (commonly referred to as "hot assets," i.e., unrealized receivables and substantially appreciated inventory). § 751(b). Deferral of gain upon a disproportionate distribution through the normal basis mechanism would permit conversion of the ordinary income potential of the assets into capital gain.

5. There are exceptions. For example, although a sale of 50% or more of the total capital and profits interests in a partnership within a 12–month period results in the termination of a partnership (and therefore a closing of the partnership's taxable year as to all partners under § 706(c)(1)), the liquidation of a partner's interest, no matter how large, does not. § 708(b).

Capital Accounting Rules

Under the capital accounting rules,[6] whenever property is distributed by a partnership, the partnership must recognize any gain or loss inherent in the distributed property for *book* (not tax) purposes.[7] This is accomplished by first adjusting all partners' capital accounts to reflect the way in which the partners have agreed to share in the inherent book gain or loss in the distributed property. Then the balance of the distributee's capital account must be reduced by the net fair market value of the distributed property.[8]

As you will recall from *Chapter Four*, a partial or complete liquidation of a partner's interest is one of the circumstances in which the capital accounting rules permit the partnership to revalue all of its assets and restate capital accounts to reflect that revaluation.[9]

Character and Holding Period of Distributed Property

Section 735(a) provides special rules regarding the character of certain types of distributed property. These rules are very similar in design and purpose to § 724, which we examined in connection with the contribution of property to a partnership.[10] The principal purpose of § 735(a) is to prevent conversion of partnership ordinary income into partner capital gain simply by distributing property to a partner.

Under § 735(a), a distributee partner will realize ordinary income if she sells or exchanges certain property previously distributed to her by a partnership. The ordinary income taint applies to previously distributed "inventory items" (as defined in § 751(d)) which are sold or exchanged within 5 years of the distribution, and to "unrealized receivables" (as defined in § 751(c)), regardless of when they are sold.[11]

---

6. § 1.704–1(b)(2)(iv).

7. § 1.704–1(b)(2)(iv)(e)(1).

8. *Id.*

9. § 1.704–1(b)(2)(iv)(f).

10. See *Chapter Two*.

11. To illustrate, suppose partnership P, a dealer in real estate, distributes one lot to each of its partners. Even if the lot would otherwise be a capital asset in the hands of a partner, any gain or loss on disposition will be ordinary if the lot is disposed of within 5 years of the distribution. Unlike § 704(c), which limits the allocation of built-in gain or loss to the difference between tax basis and fair market value at the time of contribution, neither § 724 (as to con-

tributed property) nor § 735 (as to distributed property) has any such limit. Moreover, both sections apply to inventory items as defined in § 751(d)—that is, regardless of appreciation. Assume that P in the example distributes to partner B a lot with a value of $10 and an inside basis of $30 which, in B's hands, takes a basis of $30. If B sells the lot for $50 within 5 years after the distribution, B recognizes $20 of ordinary income even though he received loss property. In effect, both § 724 and § 735 treat the transferee as succeeding, for 5 years, to the transferor's purpose in holding primarily for sale to customers in the ordinary course, regardless of the transferee's actual purpose in holding the property.

Section 735(b) provides that when property is distributed by a partnership, the distributee's holding period in the property includes the period during which the partnership held the property. This "tacking" of holding periods ensures that long term capital gain property distributed by a partnership retains its character as such in the distributee partner's hands. The rule does not apply in determining how long the distributee has held the property for purposes of the five year rule of § 735(a)(2).

Basis of Partnership's Undistributed Property

Section 734(a) provides that, unless a § 754 election is in effect or there is a substantial basis reduction,[12] the partnership's basis in its property is unaffected by a distribution. If a § 754 election is in effect or there is a substantial basis reduction, however, the basis of partnership property must be adjusted (in the manner prescribed in § 755) by the amount determined under § 734(b). This is the subject of *Chapter Twelve*. For purposes of the remainder of this chapter, we shall assume that no § 754 election is in effect.

Recognition of Gain or Loss

Section 731 generally provides for nonrecognition of gain or loss to all parties when partnership property or money is distributed. Unless the distribution is recharacterized, the partnership never recognizes gain or loss,[13] and the distributee partner will recognize gain only under very narrow circumstances. Normally, in the case of a cash distribution, the distributee simply reduces her outside basis by the amount of money received,[14] preserving any inherent gain or loss in her partnership interest. In the case of a property distribution, the distributee's outside basis is allocated among both the properties received and her continuing interest in the partnership (if any).[15] In this way, any predistribution inherent gain or loss in the distributee's partnership interest is preserved either in the property received or in her continuing interest in the partnership.

Only when deferral is impracticable or would change the character of income or loss, must gain or loss be recognized. The gain or loss generally is treated as though it arose from the sale or exchange of the partnership interest, i.e., capital gain or loss.[16]

---

12. A substantial basis reduction is defined as one that would require the partnership to reduce the basis it has in its property by more than $250,000. § 734(d)(1). This rule was added by Congress in 2004 and is discussed more fully in *Chapter Twelve*.

13. § 731(b).

14. § 733.

15. §§ 732 & 733.

16. §§ 731(a)(2) & 741.

Recognition of Gain. Distributions trigger gain to the distributee only under one circumstance: if a partner receives a distribution of money in excess of her outside basis, § 731(a)(1) requires her to recognize that excess as a gain. When a partnership distributes property to a partner, the inherent gain or loss in the partner's interest can be preserved by adjusting the basis of the distributed property under the basis mechanism noted below. But when a partner receives cash in excess of her outside basis, whether in a current or liquidating distribution, the gain represented by the excess cannot be deferred by adjusting the basis of the asset received, i.e., the cash. Therefore, the gain *must* be recognized upon receipt of the cash.

When analyzing distributions, it is essential to remember that a reduction in a partner's share of partnership liabilities is treated as a distribution of money.[17] As a result, if a distribution reduces or eliminates a partner's share in the partnership, and hence her share of partnership liabilities, the resulting constructive cash distribution under § 752(b) must be added to the actual cash distribution in calculating the amount of gain or loss. To illustrate, suppose a partner, whose outside basis is $100, receives a $75 cash distribution that liquidates her partnership interest. Suppose also that because of the liquidation, her $50 share of partnership liabilities is reduced to zero. Although the actual cash distributed does not exceed her basis, because the partner is treated as receiving a total of $125 in cash, she will have a $25 capital gain under § 731(a)(1).

Section 731(c)[18] contains a special rule applicable to distributions of marketable securities by partnerships, other than investment partnerships. Distributed marketable securities are treated as cash to the extent of their fair market value, reduced by the distributee's share of net appreciation in those securities.[19] The basis of the securities in the hands of the distributee is the basis determined under the normal rules of § 732, plus any gain recognized by the distributee.[20] Both the distributee's outside basis and the partnership's basis in its remaining assets are determined as if no gain were recognized.[21] This provision is quite detailed and has several exceptions and limitations that are beyond the scope of this book. To see how it applies in a simple case, however, consider:

> ***Example #1***: AB is an equal partnership in which A has an outside basis of $50. AB makes a current distribution to A of

---

17. § 752(b).

18. This provision was added in 1994 in response to the so-called "mixing bowl" transactions discussed in *Chapter Fifteen*.

19. § 731(c)(3)(B).

20. § 731(c)(4).

21. § 731(c)(5).

its only marketable securities (with a fair market value of $100, and a basis to the partnership of $40).

As a result of the distribution of the securities, A is treated as though she received $70 in cash: the fair market value of the securities, $100, less A's share of the appreciation in those securities, $30.[22] Since her outside basis is only $50, she must recognize $20 of gain.[23] Her basis in the securities is equal to $60, the $40 basis she would have taken normally under § 732(a) plus the $20 gain recognized. After the distribution A's outside basis is reduced to $10, determined without regard to the gain recognized.[24]

Recognition of Loss. A partner recognizes a loss *only* in a liquidating distribution, and then only under narrow circumstances. *A loss is never recognized in a current (non-liquidating) distribution.* When a liquidating distribution consists of only cash, unrealized receivables[25] and inventory,[26] if the distributee's outside basis exceeds the sum of money distributed plus the partnership's basis in the distributed property, she must recognize a capital loss.[27] In this case, current loss recognition is necessary because the partner receives no capital asset in which to defer the loss. The basis of the cash received cannot be adjusted to defer the loss, and adjusting the basis of the ordinary income assets to postpone the loss until they are sold will result in conversion of the capital loss inherent in the partnership interest into an ordinary loss.

To illustrate this latter point, suppose partner X has an outside basis of $125. In a liquidating distribution, X receives $50 cash and accounts receivable with a basis and value of $50 (assume this is a pro-rata distribution). X clearly has sustained a $25 loss on her investment in the partnership. This loss cannot be deferred in the cash, but could be deferred by giving X a basis in the accounts receivable of $75. This would produce a $25 ordinary loss when the receivables are collected. To prevent X from converting her capital loss into an ordinary loss, § 732(c)(1) limits X's basis in the receivables to their $50 inside basis to the partnership, and § 731(a)(2) requires X to recognize the capital loss at the time of the distribution.

Basis of Distributed Property

Sections 732 and 733 work in tandem to determine both the basis of distributed property in the hands of a distributee as well as

22. §§ 731(c)(1) & (c)(3)(B).

23. § 731(a)(1).

24. § 731(c)(5). In the absence of § 731(c), A would have taken a $40 basis under § 732(a)(1), leaving $10 as her outside basis under § 733. Note also that because of § 731(c)(5), the partnership would not be entitled to a § 734(b) adjustment.

25. As defined in § 751(c).

26. As defined in § 751(d).

27. § 731(a)(2).

the appropriate adjustments to her outside basis. Section 732 provides different rules, depending on whether the distribution is a current or a liquidating distribution.

Current Distributions

In a current distribution, the principal task is to allocate the distributee's outside basis among the properties she holds after the distribution, including any money or other property distributed and her continuing interest in the partnership. The rules for accomplishing this task are found in §§ 732(a) and 733. Under the general rule of § 732(a), the distributee takes a transferred basis in the distributed property,[28] and, correspondingly, § 733 requires the distributee to reduce her outside basis by any money received plus the basis she takes in distributed property. Implicitly, the statute allocates her outside basis first to any money received, next to any other distributed property in an amount equal to the partnership's basis in that property, and finally, the balance, if any, to her continuing interest in the partnership.

Section 732(a)(2) imposes a limit on the distributee's basis in property received in a current distribution: the basis cannot exceed the distributee's outside basis, reduced by any cash distributed (including liability relief) in the same transaction (for ease of reference we will refer to this amount as "reduced outside basis" or "ROB"). Whenever a partner is subject to the § 732(a)(2) limitation, she will take a basis in the distributed property equal to her reduced outside basis, and her continuing outside basis will be zero.[29] If she receives more than one property, her reduced outside basis must be allocated among the distributed properties. The rules for making this allocation are contained in § 732(c), which is discussed in detail below.

The procedure for analyzing a current distribution can be summarized as follows:

1. Begin with the distributee's outside basis, and reduce that amount by any cash distributed, *including liability relief*, to determine her ROB. If, the distributee receives cash in excess of her outside basis, she will recognize gain in the amount of the excess. Otherwise, no gain or loss will be recognized by either the partnership or the distributee.

2. As long as the distributee's ROB equals or exceeds the partnership's basis in the distributed property, she simply

---

28. That is, the property has the same basis in her hands as it did in the partnership's.

29. § 733.

takes a transferred basis in that property. The balance of the ROB, if any, becomes her continuing outside basis.

3.   If the distributee's ROB is insufficient to give her a transferred basis in the distributed property, then the distributee must divide her ROB among the distributed properties under the rules of § 732(c) (discussed below). The distributee's continuing outside basis will be zero.

To illustrate these rules, consider:

Example #2: *Ratable Distribution.* ABC is an equal partnership that holds only capital assets worth $1,200 and has no liabilities. A has an outside basis of $100. Consider the tax consequences to A of the following alternative distributions:

(a) ABC distributes $20 cash to each of its partners.

> Since the cash distribution of $20 is less than her outside basis, A recognizes no gain on the distribution,[30] and her continuing outside basis is reduced to $80.[31]

b) ABC distributes $20 cash to B and C and property to A worth $20 in which ABC has a basis of $15.

> A receives no cash so she does not recognize any gain.[32] Since A's outside basis of $100 is greater than the partnership's basis in the property distributed, A takes a transferred basis in the property of $15,[33] and her continuing outside basis is reduced to $85.[34]

Example #3: *Partial Liquidation.* Same as ***Example #2***, except ABC distributes $200 of money and/or property to A to reduce her interest in the partnership from 33 1/3% to 20%. In the alternative,

a) ABC distributes $200 cash.

> Since A receives a cash distribution of $200, an amount in excess of her outside basis of $100, she must recognize $100 as capital gain.[35] Her continuing outside basis is reduced to zero.

b) ABC distributes a capital asset with a fair market value of $200 in which ABC has a basis of $40.

> A receives no cash so she does not recognize any gain.[36] Since her outside basis is greater than the partnership's basis in the distributed property, she takes a transferred

---

30. § 731(a).

31. § 733(1). See also § 705(a)(2). Distributions, even if made during the middle of the taxable year, are generally treated as advances against each of the partner's distributive share of income and are not taken into account until the last day of the taxable year. § 1.731–1(a)(1)(ii). See *Chapter Three.*

32. § 731(a).

33. § 732(a)(1).

34. § 733(2).

35. § 731(a).

36. § 731(a).

basis in the capital asset of $40,[37] and reduces her continuing outside basis to $60.[38]

c) Same as (b) except that ABC's basis in the asset is $225.

This variation raises the limitation described in § 732(a)(2). Since A's outside basis ($100) is less than the partnership's basis in the property distributed ($225), A's basis in the distributed properties is limited to $100. As she only received a single asset, the entire $100 is allocated to the capital asset,[39] and her continuing outside basis is reduced to zero.[40]

d) ABC distributes $40 in cash and a capital asset with a FMV of $160 in which ABC has a basis of $100.

Since A did not receive cash in excess of her outside basis, A recognizes no gain.[41] A's ROB is $60, an amount less than the basis that the partnership had in the property distributed ($100). Under § 732(a)(2), A's basis in the capital asset is limited to $60 and her continuing outside basis is again reduced to zero.[42]

Example #4: *Liabilities.* Same facts as ***Example #3***, except that prior to the distribution, ABC borrows $600 and acquires $600 worth of additional assets. Under § 752(a), A's outside basis is increased by her share of that liability ($200) to $300. ABC distributes $200 of cash to A to reduce her interest in the partnership from 33 1/3% to 20%.

The analysis of this example is identical to that of ***Example #3(a)***, except we must take into account the reduction in A's share of the liability from $200 (i.e., 33 1/3% of $600) to $120 (i.e., 20% of $600). This reduction of $80 is treated as a cash distribution to A. Therefore, A is treated as having received a total $280 cash distribution. Since her outside basis is $300 before the distribution, she recognizes no gain or loss.[43] Her outside basis is reduced to $20.[44] Compare this result to the one described in ***Example #3(a)***.

Example #5: *Liabilities.* Same as ***Example #3***, except that prior to the distribution, ABC purchases a capital asset with a value of $275 for $200 cash plus a purchase money mortgage of $75. ABC then distributes this asset to A who assumes the

---

37. § 732(a)(1).

38. § 733(a)(2).

39. § 732(c)(1)(B). Notice that $125 of partnership basis disappears; it is no longer reflected in either inside basis or the basis of the property distributed. This raises the specter of § 734(b), which is the subject of *Chapter 12.*

40. § 733.

41. § 731(a).

42. Again, $40 of partnership basis disappears.

43. § 731(a).

44. § 733.

mortgage, reducing A's interest in the partnership from 33 1/3% to 20%.

Initially, ABC has a cost basis of $275 in the asset. When ABC incurs the purchase money mortgage of $75, § 752(a) treats each partner as having contributed $25 in cash to the partnership. Thus, A's outside basis prior to the distribution is $125.

As a result of the distribution of the encumbered property, we first must look at the effects of the mortgage, then the effects of the distribution of the property. First, with respect to A's assumption of the mortgage,[45] A is considered to have made a net contribution of cash to the partnership of $50, increasing her outside basis to $175.[46] A has no gain or loss on the distribution. Since her outside basis of $175 is less than the partnership's $275 basis in the property, she takes a $175 basis in the asset and her outside basis is reduced to zero.[47]

Liquidating Distributions

The rules for determining the basis of distributed property are necessarily different for liquidating distributions because the distributee is closing out her investment in the partnership; she will not have a continuing outside basis after the distribution. The object therefore is to allocate the distributee's reduced outside basis among the distributed properties. The starting point for making this allocation is to assign to each asset distributed a basis equal to that which the partnership had in the asset. Since the sum of these bases will invariably be more or less than the distributee's reduced outside basis, the bases must be adjusted. In some cases, the bases must be increased, and in others they must be decreased. Under § 732(c), Congress created special rules for making these adjustments to accomplish the ultimate goal of having the sum of the bases in the distributed properties precisely equal the distributee's reduced outside basis. For purposes of the following discussion, ignore the potential application of § 736(a).

45. Whether or not, as a matter of local law, A in fact assumes the mortgage or simply takes the property subject to it, § 752(c) treats A as having assumed the mortgage in applying § 752.

46. Although A is assuming a partnership liability of $75, simultaneously her share of partnership liabilities is being reduced by $25. This makes sense in that A was already given credit for $25

of the liability before the distribution. When she assumes the full liability, she is given credit for the balance. The outside bases of B and C were increased by $25 each under § 752(a) when the partnership borrowed and the distribution now washes out their initial increases under § 752(b).

47. Try and anticipate the appropriate § 734(b) adjustment on these facts.

Allocation of outside basis among distributed properties.

When a partner receives property in a liquidating distribution, or in a current distribution to which the limitation of § 732(a)(2) applies, the rules of § 732(c) allocate the reduced outside basis among the distributed properties. Under these rules, the reduced outside basis is first allocated to any distributed § 751(a) property (i.e., unrealized receivables and inventory) in an amount equal to (but not more than) the partnership's bases in these assets.[48] The remaining balance, if any, is then allocated among all other distributed properties.[49]

Section 751(a) Property. The § 732(c) rules are easiest to apply in the context of distributed § 751(a) property: in most cases the distributee simply takes a transferred basis in the property (i.e., the basis the partnership had in the distributed property). The only exception applies when the distributee's reduced outside basis is *less than* the sum of bases of the distributed § 751(a) property.[50] In that case, it is necessary to reduce the bases the distributee would otherwise take so that the sum equals the distributee's reduced outside basis. The rules for accomplishing this reduction are described below. It is important to note that the transferred basis in § 751(a) property will never be *increased* if the distributee's reduced outside basis is greater than the transferred basis. The excess will either be allocated to other property received in the distribution, if any, or treated as a capital loss under the rules of § 731(a)(2), discussed earlier in this chapter.

Other Property. The determination of the basis that a distributee takes in distributed non–§ 751(a) property ("other property") is necessarily more complicated. As a starting point, the distributee takes a transferred basis in the other property.[51] The complication is that the distributee's remaining reduced outside basis (after reduction for any § 751(a) property distributed in the same transaction) will invariably be more or less than the sum of the partnership's bases in the distributed properties. If the remaining balance is less than the sum, then it is necessary to decrease the basis of the distributed property by that amount, and if the remaining balance exceeds the sum, then the basis of the distributed property must be increased to include that excess.[52] The rules for making these increases and decreases are described immediately below.

Decrease. A decrease in the basis of distributed property is required anytime the distributee's reduced outside basis is less than the sum of the transferred bases of the distributed properties. This can occur in the context of a current or a liquidating distribution

---

48. § 732(c)(1)(A)(i).

49. § 732(c)(1)(B).

50. § 732(c)(1)(A)(ii).

51. § 732(c)(1)(B)(i).

52. § 732(c)(1)(B)(ii).

and can apply to § 751(a) property or to other property. Under § 732(c)(3), the decrease is first allocated (proportionately) to those properties that have unrealized depreciation (to the extent thereof).[53] In this way, the required decrease is first used to reduce or eliminate any inherent losses that may be present. If a further decrease is required, then, it is allocated among all properties in proportion to their respective bases (after reduction for any unrealized depreciation).[54] To illustrate, consider the following:

> ***Example #6:*** A is an equal partner in the ABC partnership which holds only capital assets and has no liabilities. On January 1 of this year, A receives Blackacre and Whiteacre in complete liquidation of her interest. Immediately before the distribution, A's outside basis is $900 and ABC holds the following assets:

Assets	*Basis*	*FMV*
Blackacre	$ 500	$1,000
Whiteacre	1,200	1,000
Other Assets	1,000	4,000
	$2,700	$6,000

Under § 731(a) A recognizes no gain or loss on the distribution. The principal issue is what basis A will take in the distributed properties. Since A received no cash or § 751(a) property, A's $900 outside basis must be allocated between Blackacre and Whiteacre. As a starting point, each property is assigned its respective transferred basis: $500 to Blackacre and $1,200 to Whiteacre.[55] Since the sum of these bases ($1,700) exceeds A's reduced outside basis ($900) by $800, A must decrease her basis in Blackacre and Whiteacre by that excess.[56] Since Whiteacre has $200 of unrealized depreciation, the first $200 of the decrease is allocated to Whiteacre, reducing its basis to $1,000.[57] The remaining $600 decrease is allocated between the properties in proportion to their respective adjusted bases.[58] Since Blackacre's basis is $500 and Whiteacre's is $1,000, 1/3 of the $600 decrease ($500/$1,500), or $200, is allocated to Blackacre, reducing its basis to $300. The remaining 2/3 of the decrease ($1,000/$1,500), or $400, is allocated to Whiteacre, reducing its basis to $600. In sum, A's outside basis of $900 is allocated $300 to Blackacre and $600 to Whiteacre.

Increase. An increase in the basis of distributed property will only occur in the context of a liquidating distribution, and then only in the case where the distributee receives at least one item of other property AND her reduced outside basis is greater than the

53. § 732(c)(3)(A).
54. § 732(c)(3)(B).
55. § 732(c)(1)(B)(i).
56. § 732(c)(1)(B)(ii).
57. § 732(c)(3)(A).
58. § 732(c)(3)(B).

sum of the transferred bases of the distributed properties. In order to preserve that excess amount of basis, the basis of the other property must be increased. Only the basis of other property can be increased; the basis in § 751(a) property is never increased, because if the distributee receives cash and/or § 751(a) property and still has unrecovered basis, she will recognize a loss under § 731(a).[59] Under the rules of § 732(c)(2), the basis increase is first allocated (proportionately) to those properties that have unrealized appreciation (to the extent thereof).[60] In this way, the required increase is used first to reduce or eliminate any inherent gain that may be present. If a further increase is required, then it is allocated among all other property in proportion to their fair market values.[61] To illustrate, consider the following:

> *Example #7:* Same as *Example #6* except that A's outside basis at the time of the distribution is $2,800.

Once again, A recognizes no gain or loss on the distribution. Since she only receives capital assets, the real issue is how to allocate her outside basis between Blackacre and Whiteacre. As in *Example #6*, Blackacre and Whiteacre are tentatively assigned their respective transferred bases.[62] In this case, however, the sum of these bases, $1,700, is less than A's reduced outside basis of $2,800. Because A is not allowed a current capital loss, the bases of Blackacre and Whiteacre must be increased by the excess of $1,100.[63] Since Blackacre has unrealized appreciation of $500, under § 732(c)(2)(A), the first $500 of the increase must be allocated to Blackacre. Under § 732(c)(2)(B), the balance of $600 is allocated between the properties in proportion to their relative fair market values. Since the properties are both worth $1,000 each, this latter amount is split equally, resulting in A taking a basis in Blackacre of $1,300 and a basis in Whiteacre of $1,500.

One might ask, why is it that, after eliminating inherent gains and losses in the distributed property, the statute uses basis to allocate decreases and fair market value to allocate increases.[64]

---

59. Recall that if the distributee receives only cash and § 751 property, any remaining reduced outside basis will be allowed as a current loss under § 731(a)(2).

60. § 732(c)(2)(A).

61. § 732(c)(2)(B).

62. § 732(c)(1)(B)(i).

63. § 732(c)(1)(B)(ii).

64. Actually, prior to 1997 the statute did not eliminate inherent gains or losses and used basis for both adjustments. This allowed taxpayers to artificially inflate the basis of depreciable property To illustrate the abuse, suppose a partnership distributes two properties to a partner in complete liquidation of her interest: land with a value of $1,000 and a basis of $100, and a new computer with a value and basis of $100. The distributee has an outside basis prior to the distribution of $500. Under old § 732(c)(2), the partner would take each property with a basis of $250. This rule was very hard to justify, and was the subject of two examples under the partnership general anti-abuse rules. See § 1.701–2(d) Exs. 10 & 11. These anti-

First of all, allocating decreases in accordance with fair market value just would not work in all cases because there might not be enough basis to reduce. For example, A receives a distribution in complete liquidation of her interest in the partnership consisting of Land #1 with a fair market value of $1000 in which the partnership has a basis of $900, and Land #2 with a fair market value of $1000 and in which the partnership has a basis of $100. Immediately before the distribution, A's (reduced) outside basis is $600. Since A's outside basis is $400 less than the the basis the partnership had in the distributed properties, A must decrease her basis in the properties received by that amount. If the allocation of this decrease were based on their relative fair market values, she would be required to reduce her basis in each by $200. But this is not possible for Land #2 since the partnership only has a basis in that property of $100. For this reason, Congress chose to use relative basis to allocate decreases in the basis of distributed property. On these facts, the basis in Land #1 would be decreased by $360 to $540, and the basis in Land #2 would be decreased by $40 to $60.

Increases in basis do not present this problem and Congress decided that it was more appropriate to allocate increases in proportion to fair market value rather than basis. Once inherent gains have been eliminated, further increases in basis necessarily create (or increase) losses. By using fair market value for this purpose, the statute allocates these losses in proportion to their value in the hands of the distributee. Congress found this more appropriate than using basis, which would allocate these losses disproportionately to properties that already have large inherent losses. To illustrate, consider the following:

> A receives a distribution in complete liquidation of her interest in the partnership consisting of Land #1 with a fair market value of $1,000 in which the partnership has a basis of $1,000, and Land #2 with a fair market value of $1,000 and in which the partnership has a basis of $9,000. Immediately before the distribution, A's (reduced) outside basis was $12,000. Since A's outside basis ($12,000) is greater than the partnership's basis in the two properties distributed ($10,000), A must increase her basis in these properties by the difference ($2,000). Under § 732(c)(2), this increase is allocated to each property in proportion to there relative fair market values. Therefore, under § 732(c)(2), A is required to increase her basis in each of the two properties by $1,000. This has the effect of creating a loss in Land #1 of $1,000, and increasing the loss in Land #2 by $1,000.

abuse rules are the subject of *Chapter Sixteen*.

On the other hand, if Congress had used basis to allocate these increases, then Land #2 would have been allocated $1,800 of the increase and Land #1 only $200. This has the effect of increasing the loss in Land #1 by $1,800 and creating a loss in Land #1 of $200. These latter results were viewed by Congress as unnecessarily arbitrary.

The procedure for analyzing a liquidating distribution can be summarized as follows:

1.   As with current distributions, begin with the distributee's outside basis, and reduce that amount by any cash distributed, *including liability relief*, to determine her ROB. If the distributee receives cash in excess of her outside basis, she will recognize gain in the amount of the excess. If not, then the distributee must allocate her ROB among the properties she received in the distribution in accordance with § 732(c).

2.   Under § 732(c), the ROB is first allocated to any § 751(a) property distributed in an amount equal to the partnership's basis in that property. The balance, if any, must be allocated to "other property" (i.e., non-§ 751(a) property). If there is a balance and the partner received no other property, then she recognizes a capital loss in the amount of her balance. § 731(a)(2).

3.   If the partner receives other property in the distribution, then the remaining ROB must be divided among those assets. As a starting point, these assets are assigned a transferred basis, which is then adjusted under §§ 732(c)(2) & (3) so that in the aggregate their bases will equal the partner's remaining ROB.

Additional Illustrations:

Below are three additional examples. In each of the three, assume that the distributions are not disproportionate and that § 736(a) does not apply.[65]

> **Example #8**: X is a partner in the XYZ partnership. X receives a distribution in complete liquidation of her interest, consisting of accounts receivable (value of $50, basis to the partnership of $60), and inventory (value of $100, basis to the partnership of $75). X's outside basis immediately before the distribution is $200.

Under § 732(c)(1)(A), X takes a transferred basis of $60 in the accounts receivable and $75 in the inventory, both of which consti-

---

65. A disproportionate distribution is when a distributee receives more or less than certain so-called "hot assets." These distributions are the subject of *Chapter Thirteen*.

tute § 751(a) property. Since she did not receive any other property, she must recognize a capital loss of $65, the amount by which her outside basis of $200 exceeds the sum of the bases she took in the § 751(a) property of $135.[66]

> *Example #9*: Same as in *Example #8*, except X's outside basis immediately before the distribution is $100.

Once again, X only receives § 751(a) property. This time, however, the sum of the bases she tentatively takes in the accounts receivable and the inventory of $135 exceeds her reduced outside basis of $100. Therefore she must decrease the bases she takes in the distributed property by $35. Because the accounts receivable have unrealized depreciation of $10, the first $10 of the decrease is allocated to them (bringing the basis down to $50). The remaining decrease of $25 is allocated between the two properties in proportion to their respective bases.[67] Therefore, $15 of the balance (75/125 of 25) is allocated to the inventory, reducing its basis to $60, and $10 (50/125 of 25) to the accounts receivable, reducing their basis to $40.

> *Example #10*: Same as *Example #8*, except X receives, in addition to the accounts receivable and the inventory, land (value of $200, basis to the partnership of $150). Furthermore, X is relieved of her $30 share of partnership liabilities.

First, X must reduce her outside basis by her share of the partnership's liabilities ($30) to $170. Next, the accounts receivable and the inventory are each assigned a transferred basis of $60 and $75 respectively. Finally, the $35 balance of her reduced outside basis is allocated to the land.[68]

Special Rule under § 732(d)

We noted above that a purchasing partner's § 743(b) special basis adjustments are taken into account in determining the basis of property distributed to her. You will recall from *Chapter Ten*, however, that if a partnership does not make a § 754 election, the purchaser of a partnership interest is not entitled to a special basis adjustment in the partnership's assets. As illustrated below, this may result in an unintended windfall or hardship to a partner who receives a property distribution after purchasing her partnership interest. For this reason, § 732(d) provides two special rules. First, if a partner acquired her interest by transfer (i.e., by purchase or by

66. § 731(a)(2).

67. § 732(c)(3)(B).

68. As discussed above, technically the land is first assigned a transferred basis of $150, but because X's reduced outside basis is only $35, that basis must be decreased by the excess. Since there is only one piece of other property, the entire decrease is allocated to the land.

reason of the death of a partner) during the two years prior to a distribution, that partner may elect to be treated as if there had been a § 754 election in place at the time of the transfer. Second, no matter when the distribution occurs, and even if the purchasing partner makes no § 732(d) election, under certain circumstances the regulations make the application of § 732(d) mandatory.[69] This latter rule is designed to prevent the shifting of basis from nondepreciable to depreciable assets. Prior to the 1997 amendments to § 732(c) discussed above, this type of basis shifting could readily occur and was thought to be source of potential abuse. The 1997 amendments, however, eliminated most of the circumstances where the abuse could occur, so that it would be the rare case indeed where the Service will invoke this mandatory rule.

The following example illustrates the potential benefits of making an election under § 732(d) if the distributee is eligible to do so.

> *Example #11.* ABC is an equal partnership in which each partner has an outside basis and a balance in her capital account of $1,000. The partnership has not made a § 754 election. The partnership owns the following two assets and has no liabilities:

Assets	*Basis*	*FMV*
Land #1	$1,000	$ 4,000
Land #2	2,000	17,000
	$3,000	$21,000

A sells her interest in ABC to D for $7,000, resulting in a $6,000 gain. D's outside basis is $7,000. If there had been a § 754 election in place, D's § 743(b) adjustment would have been $6,000, and D would have had a special basis adjustment of $1,000 in Land #1 and $5,000 in Land #2.[70] Since there is no § 754 election, however, D is not entitled to a special basis adjustment for either asset. Shortly after D's purchase, BCD distributes an undivided ⅓ interest in Land #1 to each partner.

Absent a § 732(d) election, D would take a basis of $333 in her undivided ⅓ interest. If D makes an election under § 732(d), however, D would take a basis of $1,333 in her ⅓ interest, the sum of her share of the common basis of $333 plus the amount of her "special basis adjustment" of $1,000. Notice that, if D were to sell her undivided ⅓ interest in the land for its fair market value

---

69. § 1.732–2(d)(4).

70. D's adjustment determined under § 743(b) is $6,000—D's outside basis ($7,000) less her share of inside basis ($1,000). Under § 755, since there are no ordinary assets, the entire adjust-

ment would be allocated between Land #1 and Land #2 on the basis of their relative appreciation, i.e., ⅙ of $6,000 to Land #1 and ⅚ of $6,000 to Land #2. See *Chapter Ten.*

($1,333), she would have no gain or loss. This is correct, for D, in effect, paid fair market value for her undivided ⅓ interest in the land when she bought her partnership interest. Section 732(d) enables D to step-up her basis in the distributed property, even though the partnership, for whatever reasons, is unwilling to make a § 754 election.

Partnership Termination

Section 708(b) provides that a partnership will terminate if it ceases to do business, or if there is a sale or exchange of 50 percent or more of the total interests in partnership capital and profits within a twelve month period.[71] This latter rule was enacted in 1954 in order to curb the practice of selling partnerships with favorable taxable years. With the advent of the restrictive rules for choosing taxable years under § 706(b), the termination rule of § 708(b) is probably no longer necessary. For this reason, in 1997 Treasury amended the regulations under § 708 to minimize the tax consequences of a termination. Under the current regulations, if a partnership terminates by reason of a sale or exchange of a partnership interest, the partnership is deemed to contribute all of its assets and its liabilities to a new partnership in exchange for an interest in the new partnership. The terminated partnership then makes a liquidating distribution of partnership interests in the new partnership to its partners (including the purchasing partner) in proportion to their respective interests.[72] The taxable year closes for the terminated partnership.

To eliminate as many of the tax consequences of terminations as possible, the following special rules apply:

1. The capital accounts of the terminated partnership carry-over to the new partnership; the purchasing partner assumes the capital accounts of the selling partner.[73]

2. No § 704(c) property will be created by the termination. The only § 704(c) property of the new partnership will be that held by the terminated partnership.[74]

3. If the terminated partnership had a § 754 election in effect for the year of termination, this election applies to the new

71. This rule does *not* apply to contributions or liquidations, even though the composition of the partnership may change dramatically. For example, neither the contribution of property to a partnership for a 90% interest in capital and profits, nor the liquidation of the interest of a 90% partner causes a termination.

72. § 1.708–1(b)(iv).

73. § 1.704–1(b)(2)(iv)(*l*).

74. § 1.704–3(a)(3)(i).

partnership. Therefore, the purchaser would be entitled to a § 743 adjustment.[75]

When all the dust settles, it appears the main tax consequence of a termination is the closing of the taxable year.

75.   § 1.708–1(b)(5).

Chapter Twelve

OPTIONAL BASIS ADJUSTMENT— § 734(b)

Introduction

Partnership distributions may create disparities between inside and outside basis. As illustrated below, a disparity arises whenever the distributee recognizes gain or loss on a distribution or takes a basis in the distributed property different from that of the partnership. These disparities artificially increase or decrease potential income (or loss) at the partnership level, and can be corrected only by adjusting the partnership's basis in its assets.

Section 734(b) authorizes just such an adjustment, and § 755 provides the rules for allocating it, but there is an important qualification: in the absence of a "substantial basis reduction," the § 734(b) adjustment is elective. It applies *only* if a § 754 election is, or has been, made by the partnership. Under many circumstances, it will be advantageous for a partnership not to make the adjustment. Indeed, the elective nature of § 734(b) has been extensively used in partnership tax planning. In addition to its elective nature, historically §§ 734 and 755 and the regulations thereunder have been plagued with technical problems that have both frustrated the purpose of § 734(b) and generated much criticism.[1] Fortunately, Treasury has finalized regulations under § 755 that resolve many of these issues in a reasonable way.

The § 734(b) adjustment was entirely elective until recently. In 2004, Congress determined that if there is a "substantial basis

---

1. See William D. Andrews, *Inside Basis Adjustments and Hot Asset Exchanges in Partnership Distributions*, 47 Tax L. Rev. 3, 3–40 (1991) and Noël B. Cunningham, *Needed Reform: Tending the Sick Rose*, 47 Tax L. Rev. 77, 77–88 (1991).

reduction," the partnership is required to adjust the basis of its property under § 734, even though it had not made an election under § 754. For this purpose, there is a substantial basis reduction if the negative adjustments under § 734(b) exceed $250,000. This new rule is illustrated and discussed below in ***Example #4.***

In this chapter we first examine in detail the rules for adjusting inside basis under §§ 734(b) and 755. We then explore the remaining shortcomings of the rules and some proposals for change.

Determination of the Amount of the Adjustment—Section 734(b)

The determination of the amount of the § 734(b) adjustment is relatively straightforward. Conceptually, the adjustment is triggered any time a distributee partner receives more (and, in the case of a liquidating distribution, less) than her share of inside basis in the partnership property. As a statutory matter, the adjustment is determined as follows:

1.   If a distributee partner recognizes gain on a distribution, the § 734(b) adjustment *increases* the basis of partnership assets by the amount of that gain;

2.   If a distributee partner recognizes a loss on a liquidating distribution,[2] the § 734(b) adjustment *decreases* the basis of partnership assets by the amount of that loss;

3.   If a distributee takes a basis in distributed property that is lower than that which the partnership had in the property immediately before the distribution, the § 734(b) adjustment *increases* the basis of the remaining partnership property by the difference;[3] and

4.   If a distributee takes a basis in distributed property that is higher than that which the partnership had in the property immediately before the distribution, § 734(b) *decreases* the basis of the remaining partnership property by the amount of the difference.

Thus, a distribution triggers a possible § 734(b) adjustment *whenever* the distributee recognizes either gain or loss, or takes a basis in the distributed property different from that which the partnership had in the property.[4] You should also note that a

---

2.   As you will recall, no loss can be recognized as a result of a current distribution. § 731(a)(2).

3.   This can occur either because of the limitation of § 731(a)(2) in the case of a current distribution, or that of

§ 732(b) in the case of a liquidating distribution.

4.   We say "possible" adjustment because the adjustment is only made if the partnership has a § 754 election in effect or if there is a substantial basis adjustment.

negative § 734(b) adjustment, i.e., a reduction in the inside basis of partnership assets, can be triggered only by a liquidating distribution.

Although the amount of the adjustment is simple to determine (it is the sum of the gain or loss recognized by the distributee and the increase or decrease in the basis of partnership assets caused by the distribution), one complicating factor must be noted: in determining the amount of the adjustment, special basis adjustments made under §§ 743(b) and 732(d) must be taken into account.[5]

Allocating the Adjustment Among Partnership Assets— Section 755

If a partnership has a § 754 election in effect, or if there is a substantial basis reduction, the partnership allocates its § 734(b) adjustment among its remaining assets under rules provided by § 755. Unlike § 743(b) adjustments, which are partner-specific, adjustments under § 734(b) affect the common basis of partnership property.[6] We have previously discussed the § 755 allocation rules in the context of § 743(b),[7] and the same general approach is used when applied to § 734(b).

Just as was the case for § 743(b) adjustments, the § 755 regulations allocate the § 734(b) adjustment among the remaining partnership properties in a two step process: First the adjustment is divided between two classes of the partnership's assets: (i) "ordinary income property," and (ii) "capital gain property."[8] Next the portion of the adjustment allocated to each class of assets is then further divided among the assets in each class. The mechanism for making the allocation, however, is different from that for § 743(b) adjustments.

In contrast with the "hypothetical sale" approach used for § 743(b) adjustments, the § 755 regulations allocate a § 734(b) adjustment based specifically on the event that triggers the adjustment. If the adjustment is triggered by the recognition of gain or loss by the distributee, the § 734(b) adjustment is assigned exclusively to capital gain property.[9] If the adjustment is triggered by a change in basis of an asset within a particular class, the adjustment must be assigned only to assets in the same class.[10] If the partner-

---

5. §§ 1.734–1(b)(1)(ii) and 1.734–1(b)(2)(ii).

6. Compare the § 743(b) adjustment, which creates a special basis adjustment solely for the transferee partner.

7. See *Chapter Ten*.

8. § 1.755–1(a).

9. § 1.755–1(c)(1)(ii).

10. § 1.755–1(c)(1)(i).

ship has no assets in the appropriate class, the adjustment is held in abeyance until the partnership acquires one.[11]

To illustrate, if the distributee takes a basis in distributed property that is $10 less than the partnership's basis in that property, the partnership is entitled to a positive § 734(b) adjustment of $10.[12] If the distributed property is capital gain property, the adjustment can only be made to the basis of other capital gain property; if it is ordinary income property (e.g., inventory), the adjustment can only be made to the basis of other ordinary income property.

Once the adjustment has been assigned to a particular class of assets, the regulations provide rules for allocating it among assets within that class. These rules are strikingly similar to those under § 732(c) which we examined in *Chapter Eleven*. Positive adjustments (i.e., increases in basis) are first allocated to assets with unrealized appreciation, and if multiple properties have unrealized appreciation, the increase is divided among them in proportion to their relative appreciation. This has the effect of reducing or eliminating any inherent gain in the assets. Once all of the unrealized appreciation has been eliminated, then the remaining amount of the adjustment is divided among the properties of the class in proportion to their relative *fair market values*.[13] Negative adjustments (i.e., decreases in basis) are allocated first to assets within the relevant class which have unrealized depreciation, and if there are multiple properties the adjustment is allocated in proportion to their relative unrealized depreciation. This has the effect of reducing any inherent loss in the assets. Once all of the unrealized depreciation has been eliminated, then the adjustment is allocated among all assets in the class in proportion to their *adjusted bases*.[14] The basis of property cannot be reduced below zero.[15]

Examples

The following four examples illustrate various situations that can give rise to a § 734(b) adjustment, and the rules for allocating the adjustment. The fourth example also illustrates the new mandatory adjustment when there is a substantial basis reduction. For purposes of these examples, assume three zeroes (000s) have been omitted from all amounts.

> ***Example #1:*** *Recognition of Gain.* ABC is an equal partnership in which each partner's outside basis, share of inside basis and capital account balance are $1,000. The partnership has the following balance sheet:

---

11. § 1.755–1(c)(4).
12. § 734(b)(1)(B).
13. § 1.755–1(c)(2)(i).

14. § 1.755–1(c)(2)(ii).
15. § 1.755–1(c)(3).

	Assets		**Liabilities & Capital**
	Basis/Book	*FMV*	
Cash	$2,000	$2,000	
Capital Asset #1	800	800	
Capital Asset #2	200	3,200	
	$3,000	$6,000	

Capital Accounts

	Tax/Book	*FMV*
A	$1,000	$2,000
B	1,000	2,000
C	1,000	2,000
	$3,000	$6,000

ABC distributes $2,000 cash to A in complete liquidation of her interest. Since A's outside basis is only $1,000, A must recognize $1,000 capital gain as a result of this distribution.[16]

This example clearly illustrates the need for § 734(b) or a similar provision. Without a basis adjustment, if ABC booked-up its assets,[17] its balance sheet after the distribution would appear as follows:

	Assets		**Liabilities & Capital**
	Basis	*Book*	
Capital Asset #1	800	800	
Capital Asset #2	200	3,200	
	$1,000	$4,000	

Capital Accounts

	Tax	*Book*
B	1,000	2,000
C	1,000	2,000
	$2,000	$4,000

While before the distribution each partner's share of inside basis was $1,000, after the distribution the partnership has only $1,000 of inside basis to be shared by B and C. This creates a disparity between these partners' outside bases (still $1,000 each), and their shares of inside basis (now $500 each). This disparity stems from the distribution to A of partnership property with an inside basis of $2,000 even though A's share of inside basis was only $1,000, and it artificially increases the unrealized gain at the partnership level by $1,000.

To illustrate, before the distribution to A, the partnership had a total of $3,000 of net unrealized gain in its assets, and each

---

16. § 731(a)(1).

17. As you will recall from *Chapter Four*, the liquidation of a partner's in-
terest is one of the occurrences that enables a partnership to revalue its assets. § 1.704–1(b)(2)(iv)(f)(5)(ii).

partner's share of that unrealized gain was $1,000. Upon the distribution, A is required to recognize her $1,000 share of the gain; yet after the distribution the partnership continues to have $3,000 of net unrealized gain. This may mean that B and C may be overtaxed, at least temporarily, for if BC sold the remaining assets, B and C would each be required to report $1,500 of gain, $500 more than either has economically. This excess gain eventually would be offset when B and C dispose of their interests in the partnership because the gain would be reflected in their outside bases.[18]

This result is precisely the one that § 734(b) was intended to counteract. If ABC makes a § 754 election, the partnership must increase the basis in its remaining assets by $1,000, the amount of gain that A recognized.[19] Because A's gain recognition triggered the § 734(b)(1)(A) adjustment, it must be reflected in the basis of capital gain property.[20] After the distribution to A, the partnership holds two capital assets, Capital Asset #1 with a basis equal to its value, and Capital Asset #2, which has $3,000 of unrealized appreciation. Under the regulations, the adjustment will be allocated first to assets with unrealized appreciation, up to the amount of that appreciation. Therefore, the entire $1,000 adjustment is allocated to Capital Asset #2, increasing its basis to $1,200. This adjustment entirely eliminates the disparity created by the distribution and restores the identity between inside and outside basis.

Example #2: *Recognition of Loss.* XYZ is an equal partnership in which each partner's outside basis, share of inside basis, and balance in her capital account are $300. The partnership has the following balance sheet:

	Assets		***Liabilities & Capital***
	Basis/Book	*FMV*	
Cash	$200	$200	
Capital Asset #1	100	200	
Capital Asset #2	600	200	
	$900	$600	

Capital Accounts

	Tax/Book	*FMV*
X	$300	$200
Y	300	200
Z	300	200
	$900	$600

---

18. If each partner had to report $1,500, her basis would increase to $2,500. Since she would receive only $2,000 on liquidation, she would have a $500 capital loss. It should be pointed out that, although capital gains are always taxable, capital losses are not always currently deductible. See §§ 165(f) and 1211.

19. § 734(b)(1)(A).

20. § 1.755–1(c)(1)(ii).

XYZ distributes $200 cash to X in complete liquidation of her interest in the partnership. Under § 731(a)(2), X recognizes a $100 capital loss.

Absent a § 754 election, if XYZ booked up its assets after the distribution, the partnership's balance sheet would appear as follows:

	Assets		**Liabilities & Capital**
	Basis	*Book*	
Capital Asset #1	100	200	
Capital Asset #2	600	200	
	$700	$400	

Capital Accounts

	Tax	*Book*
Y	$300	$200
Z	300	200
	$600	$400

Although the distribution has no effect on either Y's or Z's outside basis, each remaining at $300, each partner's share of inside basis increases from $300 to $350. This disparity between inside and outside basis may result in undertaxation of B and C, at least temporarily. For example, if the partnership sells its remaining assets, it will have a net loss of $300, which X and Y would share equally, $150 each. Yet the partnership would still be worth $400, and X and Y have each lost only $100 at this point (their outside basis of $300 less their share of partnership capital of $200). The $50 excess loss deduction will eventually be offset if and when the partners dispose of their partnership interests.[21]

If a § 754 election were in place, a negative § 734(b)(1)(B) adjustment of $100 (the amount of X's recognized loss) would, under § 755, reduce the partnership's adjusted basis in its capital assets.[22] The regulations require that the negative adjustment be first allocated to assets with unrealized depreciation. Because only Capital Asset #2 has unrealized depreciation, the entire adjustment would be allocated to it, reducing its basis to $500. The adjustment eliminates the artificial loss created by the distribution and preserves the identity of inside and outside basis.

Reconsider **Examples #1 and #2**. Assume that, at the time of the distribution, neither partnership has made a § 754 election. In

---

21. The $150 recognized loss will have reduced each partner's basis to $150, and a liquidating distribution of their $200 capital account balances would give each a $50 capital gain.

22. Note that there is not a substantial basis reduction present in this example because the adjustment under § 734(b)(2)(A) is only (adding 000) $100,000.

which case do you think the partnership would make the election? From a policy point of view, do you think the adjustments under § 734(b) should be elective?

Example #3: *Distribution of Property.* ABC is an equal partnership in which each partner's outside basis, share of inside basis and capital account balance are $2,000. The partnership has the following balance sheet:

Assets			Liabilities & Capital
	Basis/Book	*FMV*	
Inventory[23]	$1,800	$2,000	
Capital Asset #1	3,000	2,000	
Capital Asset #2	1,200	2,000	
	$6,000	$6,000	

			Capital Accounts		
				Tax/Book	*FMV*
			A	$2,000	$2,000
			B	2,000	2,000
			C	2,000	2,000
				$6,000	$6,000

ABC distributes Capital Asset #1 to A in complete liquidation of her interest in the partnership. A recognizes no gain or loss as a result of the distribution, and takes a basis in Capital Asset #1 of $2,000 under § 732(b) and (c), an amount which is $1,000 less than the asset's basis in the partnership's hands.

If ABC books up its assets following the distribution its balance sheet would appear as follows:

Assets			Liabilities & Capital
	Basis	*Book*	
Inventory	$1,800	$2,000	
Capital Asset #2	1,200	2,000	
	$3,000	$4,000	

			Capital Accounts		
				Tax	*Book*
			B	$2,000	$2,000
			C	2,000	2,000
				$4,000	$4,000

As you can see, after the distribution each partner has an outside basis of $2,000, but a share of inside basis of $1,500. Prior to the distribution if the partnership had sold all of its assets, it

---

23. Note that the inventory is not a hot asset for purposes of § 751(b) be-   cause it is not substantially appreciated.

would have realized a net capital loss of $200 and an ordinary gain of $200. Now there is $800 of capital gain and $200 of ordinary income inherent in the partnership, which must be recognized by B and C: on a net basis this is $1000 more capital gain than existed prior to the distribution. While this excess gain would eventually be balanced by a capital loss upon liquidation of the partnership or sale of an interest, this may be insufficient to comfort B and C. The clear solution is to make a § 754 election, which would result in a positive $1,000 § 734(b) adjustment. Because the adjustment is triggered by a decrease in basis of capital gain property, the § 755 regulations require that it be allocated only to capital gain property in the partnership. The result will be to increase the basis of Capital Asset #2 by $1,000, the amount by which the basis of Capital Asset #1 was reduced upon distribution to A.

> **Example #4:** *Distribution of Property.* Same as **Example #3** except Capital Asset #2 is distributed to A in liquidation of her interest. A recognizes no gain or loss, and takes a basis of $2,000 in Capital Asset #2, i.e., an amount $800 higher than the partnership's basis. The balance sheet after the distribution clearly displays the disparity created by the distribution:

	Assets		**Liabilities & Capital**
	Basis	*Book*	
Inventory	$1,800	$2,000	
Capital Asset #1	3,000	2,000	
	$4,800	$4,000	

	Capital Accounts	
	Tax	*Book*
B	$2,000	$2,000
C	2,000	2,000
	$4,000	$4,000

Prior to 2004, distributions similar to the one described in **Example #4** were quite common. Notice that A takes a basis $800 higher than the partnership had in Capital Asset #1. This results in the partnership having an inside basis of $800 more than the sum of the outside bases of the partners. In the absence of a § 734(b) adjustment, the partners would essentially be able to defer taxation on $800 of gain until they disposed of their partnership interests. In 2004, Congress amended § 734(b) to change this result: If a distribution would trigger a "substantial basis reduction," that is a negative basis adjustment of more than $250,000, then the § 734(b) adjustment is mandatory. On these facts, since there is a substantial basis reduction of $800 (000 omitted), even in th absence of a § 754 election, the § 734(b) adjustment is mandatory. Therefore, the partnership's basis in Capital Asset #1 would be reduced by $800 to $2,200.

Final Thoughts

At the time of the first edition of this book, there were many serious problems with how § 734(b) adjustments were determined and how they were allocated. Since then, Treasury has significantly improved the § 755 regulations, solving many of the problems that previously existed. Nevertheless, problems remain. For example, there is a potential problem anytime the distributee's share of inside basis does not equal her outside basis.[24] Read literally, § 734(b) produces an absurd adjustment.

Under current law the adjustment under § 734(b) is determined by comparing the partnership's basis in the distributed property (including cash) with the distributee's outside basis. The idea is that, if the partnership distributes property with more (or, in the case of a liquidating distribution, less) basis than the distributee's outside basis, the partnership's basis in its remaining assets will be less (more) than the aggregate outside basis of the continuing partners, and should be adjusted accordingly.

In most cases, § 734(b) gives this result. If, however, the distributee acquired her interest in the partnership by purchase, exchange or by reason of death at a time when the partnership had not yet made a § 754 election, the adjustment determined under § 734(b) will invariably be wrong! The reason is that there will not be any relationship—except pure chance—between the exiting partner's outside basis and her share of inside basis. To illustrate, consider:

> **Example #5:** Several years ago, A, B and C formed an equal partnership to invest in land and contributed equal amounts of cash. The partnership has bought and sold various parcels of land and generally has been quite successful. The partnership has not made a § 754 election. Before the various transactions described below, its balance sheet is as follows:

	Assets		*Liabilities & Capital*
	Basis/Book	*FMV*	
Land #1	$400	$600	
Land #2	100	500	
Land #3	400	400	
	$900	$1,500	

		Capital Accounts	
		Tax/Book	*FMV*
	A	$300	$ 500
	B	300	500
	C	300	500
		$900	$1,500

---

24. For an excellent analysis of these issues, see Leigh Osofsky, "Solving Section 734(b)," 60 *Tax Lawyer* 473 (2007).

Each partner's outside basis, share of inside basis, and capital account balance are $300. A sells her interest to X for $500.

In the absence of a § 754 election, X is not entitled to a special basis adjustment under § 743. This creates a discrepancy between X's outside basis of $500 and her share of inside basis of $300.[25] Three years later X receives Land #2 in complete liquidation of her interest in the partnership, which has made a § 754 election. For simplicity, assume that the values and bases of the partnership's assets have not changed since X's purchase. Assuming that the partnership books up its assets, its balance sheet after the distribution is as follows:

	Assets		**Liabilities & Capital**
	Basis	*Book*	
Land #1	$400	$ 600	
Land #3	400	400	
	$800	$1,000	

		Capital Accounts	
		Tax	*Book*
B		$300	$500
C		300	500
		$600	$1,000

The balance sheet makes it quite apparent that the appropriate § 734(b) adjustment would force the partnership to reduce its basis in its remaining assets by $200. On these facts, however, the § 734(b) adjustment is a reduction of $400—the difference between X's outside basis ($500) and the partnership's basis in the property distributed ($100).[26] It has been correctly suggested that if the amount of the adjustment were determined with reference to the exiting partner's share of inside basis (rather than outside basis), this glitch would disappear.[27] This modification of the rule would, on these facts, give the correct downward adjustment of $200, regardless of whether there had been a § 754 election in place (i.e.,

25. Upon purchasing A's interest, X steps into A shoes in respect to the entity-level attributes of A's partnership interest. X, therefore, succeeds to A's book and tax capital accounts, A's share of partnership liabilities, and A's share of inside basis.

26. Sections 732(b) and (c) assign X's entire $500 outside basis to Land #2. This represents a $400 increase from the partnership's $100 basis in the land. Since X recognized no gain or loss on the distribution, § 734(b) calls for an equal inverse adjustment, a decrease of $400, to the inside bases of the partnership's capital assets (Land #2 came from the capital asset class).

27. See, e.g., McKee et al., ¶ 25.01[3] and William D. Andrews, *Inside Basis Adjustments and Hot Asset Exchanges in Partnership Distributions, supra* note 1.

the difference between X's share of inside basis, $300, and the basis of the property distributed, $100).

Another continuing problem with § 734(b) adjustments is that they are elective, rather than mandatory. This problem has been alleviated significantly by the new rule mandating the adjustment for substantial basis reductions. Nevertheless, it remains elective under most circumstances. From the continuing partners' point of view, a distribution of property to a partner is a nonrecognition event and § 734 supplies the appropriate basis adjustments. No other nonrecognition provision tolerates elective basis adjustments.[28] Although it may have once seemed unduly burdensome to require partnerships to make the adjustments, today the elective nature of § 734(b) is very difficult to justify.

28. For a more complete discussion of these issues see William D. Andrews, *Inside Basis Adjustments and Hot Asset Exchanges in Partnership Distributions*, *supra* note 1, and Noël B. Cunningham, *Needed Reform: Tending the Sick Rose*, *supra* note 1.

Chapter Thirteen

DISPROPORTIONATE DISTRIBUTIONS

Introduction

In *Chapter Eleven* we noted that, in some cases, what might otherwise appear to be a partnership distribution will be recharacterized as a sale or exchange between the partnership and the "distributee" partner. We now turn to those rules, which are found in § 751(b). In brief, § 751(b) will treat part of a distribution as a sale or exchange whenever a partnership holding certain ordinary income assets ("hot assets") makes a "disproportionate" or non-pro rata distribution of its assets.

As we saw in *Chapter Ten*, § 751(a) acts to prevent the shifting ordinary income among partners by taxing a selling partner on his share of ordinary income from the partnership's "§ 751(a) property," which includes unrealized receivables and inventory items. Section 751(b) serves a similar role in distributions, but its reach is somewhat different; while it does apply to unrealized receivables, it does not apply to inventory items unless they are *substantially appreciated.*[1] Inventory will not be considered substantially appreciated unless, in the aggregate, its fair market value exceeds 120% of its basis.[2] In our discussion we refer to the property covered by § 751(b) either as "§ 751(b) property," or "hot assets," and items of non-§ 751(b) property are generally referred to as "cold assets."

Section 751(b) applies when a partnership that holds hot assets makes a "non-pro rata" distribution to a partner. The distributions that we have seen in prior chapters did not trigger § 751(b) because

---

1. § 751(b)(1)(A)(ii).
2. § 751(b)(3). For example, if a partnership has a basis in all of its inventory items of $1000, then their fair market value must be greater than $1200 or they will not be considered hot assets.

they were pro rata, i.e., each partner's share of hot and cold assets was unchanged by the distribution. In contrast, if a distribution has the effect of changing the partners' shares of hot and cold assets, then it is "disproportionate," or non-pro rata, and § 751(b) will recharacterize part of the distribution as a taxable exchange between the partnership and the distributee partner. As we will see, numerous tax consequences can result.

Section 751(b): The "Evil" and The "Cure"

Section 751(b) is one of the many complex sections in the Internal Revenue Code that are required solely because of the preferential treatment given to capital gains. Its purpose is to prevent taxpayers from using the liberal distribution rules of Subchapter K to convert ordinary income into capital gain by ensuring that each partner report her share of the partnership's ordinary income.[3] To illustrate the "evil" that § 751(b) was designed to stem, and the Congressional "cure," let us consider the simplest example possible, one in which the partnership has only two assets, one hot and one cold:

Example #1: ABC is an equal partnership in which each of the partners has an outside basis and capital account balance of $1,000. ABC's balance sheet (expanded to show fair market values) appears as follows:

Assets			*Liabilities & Capital*
	Basis/Book	*FMV*	
Inventory	$2,400	$3,000	
Capital Asset	600	1,500	
	3,000	4,500	

		Capital Accounts	
		Tax/Book	*FMV*
	A	$1,000	$1,500
	B	1,000	1,500
	C	1,000	1,500
		3,000	4,500

The value of the inventory exceeds its basis by more than 120%, so the inventory is substantially appreciated and is therefore a hot asset.[4] ABC distributes the capital asset to A in complete liquidation of her one-third interest in the partnership.

---

3. As you will recall from our discussion in *Chapter Ten*, the purpose of § 751(a) was to prevent partners from converting ordinary income into capital gains by selling their partnership interests. Section 751(b) (or a similar provi-sion) is necessary to prevent partners from accomplishing the proscribed conversion simply by making a distribution.

4. § 751(b)(3).

The "Evil"

Prior to the distribution, A had an undivided one-third interest in ABC, and therefore, indirectly, a one-third interest in both the inventory and the capital asset. If ABC had sold both of these assets it would have realized $600 of ordinary income and $900 of capital gain, and one-third of each would have been allocated to A. As you learned in *Chapter Ten*, if A had sold her interest in ABC to an outsider, § 751(a) would have required that she report $200 of her gain as ordinary income. Absent a special rule, the normal distribution rules would allow A to avoid her share of the partnership's ordinary income by taking a capital asset in the distribution. To illustrate, if the above distribution were subject to the normal distribution rules, the tax consequences would be as follows: A would have no gain or loss on the distribution[5] and would take a $1,000 basis in the capital asset.[6] If and when A sold the capital asset, all gain on the sale would be capital gain; she would never have any ordinary income. A's share of ordinary income would be shifted to the remaining partners, B and C, who would have to report it when the partnership sold the inventory.[7]

The "Cure"—§ 751(b)

In an effort to prevent partners from shifting the character of income among themselves in this way, Congress enacted § 751(b). Section 751(b) is triggered whenever the *value* of a distributee's interest in hot or cold assets changes as a result of a distribution. All the statute tells us is that if a distributee receives hot assets in exchange for her interest in cold assets (or cold in exchange for hot) the distribution will be treated as a sale or exchange. The regulations provide the mechanism for accomplishing the sale or exchange: they first assume a distribution to the distributee of the type of property in which the distributee's interest is ultimately decreased, they then treat the distributee as using that distributed property to purchase her non-pro rata share of the property she ultimately receives. When the dust has settled, the distributee is treated as acquiring her non-pro rata share of the distributed property by purchase, and her pro rata share by distribution. Using this line of reasoning, the regulations treat all disproportionate distributions as if they consisted of three distinct transactions:

    1. *Hypothetical Distribution.* First, the distributee is deemed to receive a current distribution of the type of asset in which,

---

5. § 731(a).

6. § 732(b).

7. Conversely, B could shift a portion of their shares of ABC's ordinary income

if the partnership distributed to A a disproportionate share of the inventory.

and in the amount by which, her interest decreases as a result of the disproportionate distribution.

2.   *Section 751(b) Exchange.* She then is deemed to sell (or exchange) the property she received in the hypothetical distribution to the partnership (as constituted after the distribution) for an equal amount of the type of asset in which her interest increases.

3.   *Non–§ 751(b) Distribution.* Finally, the balance of the distribution, i.e., the portion that represents the distributee's pro rata share of the distributed assets, is treated under the normal distribution rules.

It may not always be obvious whether there has been a disproportionate distribution, and if there has been, exactly which assets were involved in each one of these three transactions. An extremely useful tool for analyzing disproportionate distributions is the "Partnership Exchange Table."[8] This table identifies, by value, the distributee's interest in each partnership asset, both before and after the distribution, and quantifies any change. Once constructed, it helps establish whether a distribution is in fact disproportionate, and, if it is, what assets are involved in each of the three deemed transactions. We recommend that you always use a Partnership Exchange Table as the first step in your analysis when dealing with a disproportionate distribution, even the simplest ones.

Our suggested four step analysis is therefore:

Step #1: Construct Partnership Exchange Table

Step #2: Analyze the hypothetical distribution

Step #3: Analyze the § 751(b) exchange

Step #4: Analyze the non–§ 751(b) distribution

To summarize the results of these transactions, you may find it useful to reconstruct the partnership's balance sheet after the distribution is completed.

Applying this four-step analysis to ***Example #1***:

Step #1: Construct Partnership Exchange Table

The Partnership Exchange Table for A would be constructed as follows:

---

8.   McKee et al., at ¶ 21.03[3].

Partnership Exchange Table[9]

	1 *A's Post–* *Distribution* *Interest In* *Pship Assets*	+	*2* *A's* *Actual* *Distribution* *(Incl. § 752(b))*	–	*3* *A's Pre–* *Distribution* *Interest In* *Pship Assets*	=	*4* *A's* *Change* *In* *Interest*
"Hot" Assets:							
Inventory	0	+	0	–	$1,000	=	($1,000)
"Cold" Assets:							
Capital Asset	0	+	$1,500	–	$500	=	$1,000

With the aid of this table it is easy to see that this is a disproportionate distribution: A's interest in hot assets has decreased by $1,000 while her interest in cold assets has increased by $1,000. Therefore, since there is only one hot asset (the inventory) and one cold asset (the capital asset), the three transactions that are deemed to occur under § 751(b) are as follows:[10]

1. *Hypothetical distribution*: A is deemed to receive $1,000 of inventory as a current distribution;

2. *Section 751(b) exchange*: A is deemed to transfer the hypothetically distributed inventory to ABC in exchange for $1,000 worth of the capital asset; and finally

3. *Non–§ 751(b) distribution*: A is deemed to receive a liquidating distribution of the remaining $500 worth (i.e., her pro rata share) of the capital asset.

Each of these transactions must be analyzed separately.

Step #2: Analyze Hypothetical Distribution

The tax consequences of the hypothetical distribution to A of $1,000 of inventory (basis of $800)[11] are:

To A: A has no gain or loss and takes a transferred basis in the inventory of $800.[12] Under § 733(2), her outside basis is reduced from $1,000 to $200.

To ABC: ABC has no gain or loss.[13] Its basis in the remaining $2,000 worth of inventory is $1,600.

Step #3: Analyze § 751(b) Exchange

Under § 751(b), A is treated as if she transferred the hypothetically distributed inventory to ABC in exchange for $1,000 in value

---

9. All values on this chart equal fair market value of the underlying assets, undiminished by any liabilities. If the distributee's share of partnership liabilities is reduced as a result of the distribution, this reduction is treated as a cash distribution.

10. If the partnership had more than one type of hot asset, in the absence of an agreement to the contrary, the distributee would be deemed to have sold a proportionate amount of each asset in which her interest declined. Obviously the arithmetic involved could become enormously complex.

11. The partnership's basis in the distributed portion of the inventory is determined proportionately by value. Since ABC distributed ⅓ of its inventory ($1,000/$3,000), the basis in the distributed portion is ⅓ of its basis immediately before the distribution (i.e., ⅓ of $2,400).

12. § 732(a)(1).

13. § 731(b).

of the capital asset (basis of $400).[14] The tax consequences of this exchange are:

> *To A:* A has an ordinary gain of $200[15] and takes a cost basis of $1,000 (and a new holding period) in this portion of the capital asset.

> *To ABC:* ABC has received $1,000 worth of inventory in exchange for the capital asset, in which it had a basis of $400. ABC therefore recognizes capital gain of $600 that will be shared equally by B and C.[16] ABC's basis in the inventory acquired in the exchange is a cost basis of $1,000. Its total basis in all of its inventory is $2,600.[17]

Step #4: Analyze Non–§ 751(b) Distribution

Finally, the partnership distributes the balance of the capital asset, which represents A's pro rata share of that asset, to A in complete liquidation of her partnership interest. The consequences of the distribution are:

> *To A:* Under § 731, A has no gain or loss and takes a basis in this portion of the capital asset equal to her outside basis of $200.[18] Her total basis in the capital asset is therefore $1,200 [$1,000 + $200].

> *To ABC:* On these facts, there are no tax consequences to ABC. ABC has no gain or loss on the distribution, and, even if there were a § 754 election in place, there would be no § 734(b) adjustment because A took a basis in the portion of the capital asset distributed precisely equal to that which ABC had in that asset, i.e., $200.

To summarize, A has $200 of ordinary income and a basis of $1,200 in the capital asset; BC, the partnership, has $600 of capital gain that is allocated equally between B and C; BC's basis in the inventory is $2,600. It may be instructive to look at how these transactions are reflected in the capital accounts of the partners. For this purpose, we shall assume that the partnership booked up

---

14. Again the basis of that portion of the capital asset involved in the exchange is determined proportionately based on value, i.e., $1,000/$1,500 x $600 = $400.

15. Her amount realized is the $1,000 of capital asset and her basis in the inventory is $800. The ordinary character is mandated by § 735(a).

16. Since the exchange is deemed to occur between the distributee and the partnership "(as constituted after the distribution)," the gain must be allocat-

ed between B and C. As we shall see, even in the case of a current distribution, if the partnership has a gain or loss as a result of the § 751 exchange, none of that gain or loss can be allocated to the distributee. § 1.751–1(b)(3)(ii).

17. ABC's basis in that portion of the inventory not involved in the exchange is $1,600.

18. A must reduce her original $1,000 basis by the hypothetical distribution of inventory.

its assets just before the distribution. The required capital account adjustments are as follows:

	A		B		C	
	Tax	*Book*	*Tax*	*Book*	*Tax*	*Book*
Initial Balances	$1,000	$1,000	$1,000	$1,000	$1,000	$1,000
Book up[19]		500		500		500
	1,000	1,500	1,000	1,500	1,000	1,500
Hypothetical distribution of inventory	(800)	(1,000)				
	200	500	1,000	1,500	1,000	1,500
Gain on deemed exchange of land for inventory[20]			300		300	
Actual distribution of land	(200)	(500)				
Final Balances[21]	0	0	$1,300	$1,500	$1,300	$1,500

As should be apparent from this simple example, disproportionate distributions are enormously complex. It is for this reason that we recommend a very mechanical approach to analyzing such problems, using the four step process outlined above.

Scope

You should consider the possible application of § 751(b) any time a partnership with hot assets makes a distribution, including a deemed cash distribution under § 752(b). In Revenue Ruling 84–102,[22] the Service held that the admission of a new partner to a law firm triggered § 751(b). The law firm had both unrealized receivables and liabilities. Each new partner became entitled to share in the unrealized receivables and also became liable for a portion of the partnership's liabilities. Correspondingly, each old partner's share of liabilities was reduced, as was her share of receivables. Since a reduction in a partner's share of partnership's liabilities is treated as a cash distribution under § 752(b), the ruling held that the old partners exchanged a portion of their interest in the unrealized receivables for cash, resulting in a § 751(b) exchange.

19. § 1.704–1(b)(2)(iv)(f).

20. Note that no book gain arises on the exchange, because all unrealized appreciation was already reflected on the partnership's books when its property was restated at fair market value.

21. The $200 book/tax discrepancies of B and C reflect the remaining unrealized appreciation of the inventory. Remember that the inventory has a $3,000 fair market value, and a basis in the partnership's hands of $2,600 ($1,000 cost of inventory deemed purchased

from A, plus $1,600 basis in the $2,000 balance). If the BC partnership sells all its inventory for $3,000, it will recognize a $400 tax gain (but no further book gain) that will be allocated equally to B and C. Their tax and book accounts will be equalized at $1,500, and if the partnership were liquidated at that time, the partnership's $3,000 of cash from the inventory sale would be just enough to return B's and C's capital.

22. 1984–2 C.B. 119.

Additional Examples

Because of the complexity of § 751(b) transactions, we have included several additional examples for the reader. In contrast with our "simple" example, most partnerships have more than one asset in each of the two categories of hot and cold, and most have liabilities. As you tackle the following examples you should keep in mind two important rules. First, § 751(b) is concerned with the effect of a distribution on the distributee partner's interest in hot and cold assets as a class: if the net result of a distribution leaves her interest in total hot assets unchanged, § 751(b) will not apply, even though she may have received (or given up) a disproportionate share of a particular hot asset. Second, you will recall that a reduction in a partner's share of liabilities is treated under § 752 as a cash distribution. These deemed distributions of cash must be taken into account in your analysis.

Example #2: ABC is an equal partnership in which each of the partners has an outside basis of $1,500 and a capital account of $1,000. ABC's balance sheet (expanded to show fair market values) is as follows:

Assets			**Liabilities & Capital**	
	Basis/Book	*FMV*	Loan	$1,500
Cash	$3,000	$3,000		
Inventory	900	1,500		
Capital Asset	600	1,500		
	$4,500	$6,000		

	Capital Accounts	
	Tax/Book	*FMV*
A	$1,000	$1,500
B	1,000	1,500
C	1,000	1,500
	$3,000	$4,500

The inventory is substantially appreciated and therefore constitutes a hot asset. In complete liquidation of her interest in the partnership, ABC distributes $1,500 cash to A.

Step #1: Construct a Partnership Exchange Table

In constructing this table, remember that to the extent A is relieved of a partnership liability, she is treated as receiving a cash distribution.[23] Hence, on these facts, she is treated though she received a total cash distribution of $2,000.

---

23. In determining a partner's pre-distribution interest in partnership assets, liabilities *per se* are ignored. The reason for this is that the asset side of the balance sheet already takes liabilities into account (i.e., when you borrow $1,000, your assets go up by $1,000). Nevertheless, if a partner's share of

Partnership Exchange Table

	1 A's Post–Distribution Interest In Pship Assets	+	2 A's Actual Distribution (Incl. § 752(b))	–	3 A's Pre–Distribution Interest In Pship Assets	=	4 A's Change In Interest
"Hot" Assets:							
Inventory	0	+	0	–	$500	=	($500)
"Cold" Assets:							
Cash	0	+	$2,000	–	$1,000	=	$1,000
Capital Asset	0	+	0	–	$500	=	(500)
							$500

This is clearly a disproportionate distribution: A's interest in hot assets, i.e., the inventory, decreased by $500, while her interest in cold assets increased by $500. This example illustrates an important point: Section 751(b) is concerned with whether a partner's interest in a *class* of assets (viz., hot or cold) has changed as a result of a distribution, not whether the partner's interest in the individual assets within each class has changed. Therefore, in this example, the fact that A's interest in the capital asset decreased is of no consequence because her interest in cold assets overall increased. The three deemed transactions that we must analyze are:

1. *Hypothetical distribution*: ABC makes a current distribution of $500 inventory to A.

2. *Section § 751 exchange*: A is deemed to exchange the distributed inventory for $500 of cash.

3. *Non–§ 751 distribution*: ABC makes a distribution of $1,500 cash to A in complete liquidation of her interest in the partnership.

Step #2: Analyze the Hypothetical Distribution

The tax consequences of the hypothetical distribution to A of $500 of inventory (basis of $300) are:

To A: A has no gain or loss on this distribution, takes a $300 transferred basis in the inventory,[24] and reduces her outside basis from $1,500 to $1,200.[25]

To ABC: ABC has no gain or loss on the distribution.[26] Its remaining basis in its inventory is $600.

partnership liabilities is decreased, she is treated as receiving a cash distribution.

24. § 732(a)(1) (⅓ of $900).

25. § 733(2).

26. § 731(b).

Step #3: Analyze the § 751(b) Exchange

In the § 751(b) exchange in which A is treated as having sold the hypothetically distributed inventory to the partnership for $500 cash, the tax consequences are:

> *To A:* A has an ordinary gain of $200 on the sale of the inventory to the partnership for $500 cash.[27]

> *To ABC:* ABC takes a cost basis of $500 in the inventory purchased. Its total basis in its inventory is now $1,100 (i.e., $500 + $600).

Step #4: Analyze the Non–§ 751(b) Distribution

Finally, the tax consequences to A as a result of the liquidating distribution in which she receives $1,500 cash ($1,000 actual and $500 under § 752(b)) are:

> *To A:* Since the distribution of $1,500 cash to A is in excess of her $1,200 outside basis, A has a capital gain of $300.[28]

> *To ABC (now BC):* BC has no gain or loss on the distribution.[29] If there is a § 754 election in place, BC will have a positive § 734(b) adjustment of $300 which will increase BC's basis in the capital asset to $900.

To summarize, A has ordinary income of $200 and capital gain of $300. BC recognizes no gain or loss and its basis in the inventory is $1,100. BC's basis in the capital asset depends on whether there is a § 754 election in place. If there is one in place, BC's basis is $900; if not it remains $600.

> **Example #3**: Assume the same facts as in **Example #2** except that ABC distributes the capital asset to A in complete liquidation of her interest in the partnership.

Step #1: Construct a Partnership Exchange Table

Partnership Exchange Table

	1 *A's Post–* *Distribution* *Interest In* *Pship Assets*	*+*	*2* *A's* *Actual* *Distribution* *(Incl. § 752(b))*	*–*	*3* *A's Pre–* *Distribution* *Interest In* *Pship Assets*	*=*	*4* *A's* *Change* *In* *Interest*
"Hot" Assets:							
Inventory	0	+	0	–	$500	=	($500)
"Cold" Assets:							
Cash	0	+	$500	–	$1,000	=	($500)
Capital Asset	0	+	$1,500	–	$500	=	$1,000
							$500

The analysis of **Example #3** is quite similar to that of **Example #2**: Once again, A's interest in the inventory has decreased, while

---

27. Note the character of this gain is assured by § 735(a)(2).

28. § 731(a).

29. § 731(b).

her interest in the cold assets has increased. The three transactions that we must analyze are as follows:

    1. *Hypothetical distribution*: ABC distributes to A $500 of inventory (basis = $300) in a current distribution;

    2. *Section 751(b) exchange*: A is deemed to exchange this inventory with ABC for $500 of the Capital Asset.

    3. *Non–§ 751(b) distribution*: Finally, ABC makes a distribution to A of $500 cash and $1,000 worth of the Capital Asset (basis of $400).

Step #2: Analyze the Hypothetical Distribution

    In the hypothetical distribution in which A receives $500 of inventory in which the partnership had a basis of $300, the tax consequences are:

    To A: A has no gain or loss on this distribution. A takes a $300 basis in the inventory[30] and reduces her outside basis from $1,500 to $1,200.[31]

    To ABC: ABC has no gain or loss on the distribution;[32] its remaining basis in its inventory is $600.

Step #3: Analyze the § 751(b) exchange:

    In the § 751(b) exchange in which A is treated as transferring the hypothetically distributed inventory to ABC in exchange for $500 worth of the capital asset (basis of $200) the tax consequences are:

    To A: A has an ordinary gain of $200 on the exchange of the inventory to the partnership for $500 of the capital asset. A takes a new holding period and a $500 cost basis in this portion of the capital asset.

    To ABC: ABC has a capital gain of $300 on the exchange. This gain must be allocated to B and C equally. ABC takes a cost basis of $500 in the inventory it receives from A. Its total basis in its inventory is now $1,100 ($500 + $600).

Step #4: Analyze the Non–§ 751(b) Distribution

    Finally, as a result of the liquidating distribution in which A receives $1,000 worth of the capital asset (basis of $400) and is deemed to receive $500 cash under § 752(b), the tax consequences are:

    To A: A has no gain or loss on the distribution. Her outside basis of $1,200 is first reduced by the $500 cash distribution. The remaining $700 becomes her basis in the $1,000 of capital

30. § 731(a)(1).   **32.** § 731(c).
31. § 733(2).

asset she receives. A's total basis in the capital asset is $1,200 ($500 + $700).

To ABC (now BC): BC has no gain or loss on the distribution. If there is a § 754 election in place, BC would have a negative $300 § 734(b) adjustment. However, since BC has no other capital assets, under § 755 no adjustment is currently possible.[33]

To summarize, A has ordinary income of $200, and takes a $1,200 basis in the capital asset. BC has a $300 capital gain which must be allocated equally between B and C, and has a $1,100 basis in its inventory. If BC has a § 754 election in place, it will carryover a negative $300 § 734(b) adjustment to future years.

> *Example #4*: Same facts as *Example #2*, except that A receives the inventory in complete liquidation of her interest in the partnership.

Step #1: Construct a Partnership Exchange Table

Partnership Exchange Table

	1 *A's Post–* *Distribution* *Interest In* *Pship Assets*	*+*	*2* *A's* *Actual* *Distribution* *(Incl. § 752(b))*	*–*	*3* *A's Pre–* *Distribution* *Interest In* *Pship Assets*	*=*	*4* *A's* *Change* *In* *Interest*
"Hot" Assets:							
Inventory	0	+	$1,500	–	$500	=	$1,000
"Cold" Assets:							
Cash	0	+	$500	–	$1,000	=	($500)
Capital Asset	0	+	0	–	$500	=	($500)
							($1,000)

From the table, it is clear that A has increased her interest in hot assets by $1,000, while her interest in cold assets has decreased by $1,000. Therefore, the three transactions that we must analyze are:

1. *Hypothetical distribution*: To engage in the § 751(b) exchange, ABC must make a hypothetical distribution to A of $1,000 of cold assets, but which one(s)? The exchange table provides the answer: we can see that the distribution had the effect of reducing A's interest in the cash by $500 and in the capital asset by $500 as well. Thus, in the hypothetical distribution A is deemed to receive $500 of each.

2. *Section 751(b) exchange:* A is deemed to transfer the cash and the capital asset to ABC in exchange for $1,000 of inventory (basis of $600).

---

33. The adjustment carries over until BC acquires a capital asset. § 1.751–   1(c)(4).

3. *Non–§ 751(b) distribution:* Finally, ABC makes a liquidating distribution to A consisting of $500 of inventory (basis of $300) and, as a result of the decrease in her share of partnership liabilities, $500 in cash.[34]

Step #2: Analyze the Hypothetical Distribution

In the hypothetical distribution in which ABC distributes to A $500 cash and $500 of the capital asset (basis of $200), the tax consequences are as follows:

> *To A:* A has no gain or loss on this distribution. She takes a basis in the capital asset distributed of $200,[35] and reduces her outside basis by the cash received ($500) and basis taken in the capital asset ($200) to $800.[36]

> *To ABC:* ABC has no gain or loss on the distribution.[37] Its basis in that portion of the capital asset retained is $400.[38]

Step #3: Analyze the § 751(b) Exchange

In the § 751(b) exchange in which A is deemed to transfer the hypothetically distributed cash and capital asset to ABC in exchange for $1,000 worth of inventory (basis of $600), the tax consequences are:

> *To A:* A has a capital gain of $300[39] on the exchange and takes a new holding period[40] and a $1,000 cost basis in this portion of the inventory.

> *To ABC:* ABC has an ordinary gain of $400 on the exchange. This gain must be allocated to B and C equally. ABC takes a new holding period and a basis of $500 in this portion of the capital asset. Its total basis in the capital asset is now $900 ($400 + $500).

Step #4: Analyze the Non–§ 751(b) Distribution

Finally, in the liquidating distribution in which A received $500 of inventory (basis of $300) and $500 in cash under § 752(b), the tax consequences are as follows:

> *To A:* A has no gain or loss on the distribution. Under § 732(b), A first reduces her outside basis by the $500 deemed cash distribution, leaving $300 which, under § 732(c), is allocated entirely to the inventory.

---

34. § 752(b).

35. § 732(a)(1).

36. § 733.

37. § 731(c).

38. The basis before the distribution, $600, less the portion distributed, $200.

39. $500 worth of inventory was exchanged for the capital asset in which A had a $200 basis.

40. This may be relevant if the inventory is a capital asset in A's hands. Since she acquired the inventory in a taxable transaction and not a distribution, § 735(a)(2) is not applicable.

To ABC (now BC): BC has no gain or loss on the distribution.[41]

To summarize, A has a capital gain of $300, and takes a basis in the inventory of $1,300.[42] BC has $400 in ordinary income that must be allocated equally between B and C. BC has a basis of $900 in the capital asset.[43]

The analysis of disproportionate distributions is necessarily more complex when the transaction is a partial liquidation, because the distributee continues to have an interest in the partnership after the distribution.

Example #5: X owns 50% of the XYZ partnership. The remaining 50% is owned equally by Y and Z. Prior to any distributions, X's outside basis is $650 and the balance in her capital account is $200. At that time, XYZ's balance sheet (expanded to show fair market values) is as follows:

Assets			Liabilities & Capital	
	Basis/Book	*FMV*		
Inventory	$120	$240	Mortgage	$900
Land	80	200		
Building	1,100	1,260		
	$1,300	$1,700		

	Capital Accounts	
	Tax/Book	*FMV*
X	$200	$400
Y	100	200
Z	100	200
	$400	$800

The mortgage is secured by the building and is fully recourse. XYZ distributes Land to X to reduce X's interest in the partnership from 50% to 33%.

Step #1: Construct a Partnership Exchange Table

The analysis of this distribution is identical to those above, except you must take into account that after the distribution X stills holds a ⅓ interest in the partnership. Also, you must remember to take into account that as a result of the partial liquidation of X's interest in XYZ, her share of partnership liabilities is reduced from $450 to $300, a reduction of $150. X's Partnership Exchange Table is as follows:

41. § 731(b).

42. $1,000 in the portion received in the § 751(b) exchange and $300 in the portion received in the liquidating distribution.

43. BC has a $400 basis in the portion of the capital asset retained, and a $500 cost basis in the portion received in the § 751(b) exchange.

Partnership Exchange Table

	1 X's Post-Distribution Interest In Pship Assets	+	2 X's Actual Distribution (Incl. § 752(b))	–	3 X's Pre-Distribution Interest In Pship Assets	=	4 X's Change In Interest
"Hot" Assets:							
Inventory	$80	+	0	–	$120	=	($40)
"Cold" Assets:							
Cash	0	+	$150	–	0	=	150
Land	0	+	$200	–	$100	=	100
Building	$420	+	0	–	$630	=	(210)
							$40

From this table, it is clear that X's interest in cold assets has increased by $40, while her interest in hot assets has decreased correspondingly by $40. The three transactions that we must analyze are:

1. *Hypothetical distribution*: XYZ distributes $40 of inventory (basis of $20) to X in a current distribution.

2. *Section 751(b) exchange*: X is deemed to transfer this inventory to XYZ in exchange for $40 of the land (basis of $16).

3. *Non-§ 751(b) distribution*: Finally, XYZ distributes the remaining $160 of land (basis of $64) to X and X's share of partnership liabilities decreases, resulting in a deemed cash distribution of $150.

Step #2: Analyze the Hypothetical Distribution

In the hypothetical distribution in which X receives $40 of inventory (basis of $20), the tax consequences are:

To X: X has no gain or loss on this distribution.[44] X takes a basis in the inventory of $20[45] and reduces her outside basis to $630.[46]

To XYZ: XYZ has no gain or loss on the distribution;[47] XYZ's basis in that portion of the inventory retained is $100.

Step #3: Analyze the § 751(b) Exchange

In the § 751(b) exchange in which X transfers the hypothetically distributed inventory to XYZ in exchange for $40 worth of the land (basis of $16), the tax consequences are:

To X: X has ordinary income of $20 and takes a $40 cost basis (and new holding period) in the portion of the land received.

To XYZ: XYZ has a capital gain of $24 on the exchange which must be allocated equally between Y and Z. XYZ takes a cost

---

44. § 731(a).

45. § 732(a)(1).

46. § 733(2).

47. § 731(b).

basis of $40 in that portion of the inventory received. Its total basis in its inventory is now $140 ($100 + $40).

Step #4: Analyze the Non–§ 751(b) Distribution

Finally, in the current distribution in which X actually receives $160 worth of land (basis of $64) and is deemed to receive cash of $150,[48] the tax consequences are:

To X: X has no gain or loss on the distribution[49] and takes a $64 basis in the distributed portion of the land. X's aggregate basis in the land is $104 ($40 + $64). X's outside basis is reduced from $630 to $416.[50]

To XYZ: XYZ has no gain or loss on the distribution.[51] Even if there is a § 754 election in place, there is no § 734(b) adjustment.

In summary, X has $20 of ordinary income and takes a basis of $104 in the land. Her outside basis in her remaining ⅓ interest in the partnership is $416. XYZ has $24 of capital gain which must be allocated equally between Y and Z. XYZ's aggregate basis in the inventory is $140. Even if there is a § 754 election in place, there is no § 734(b) adjustment.

Final Observation

As you can see from these very simple examples, § 751(b) exchanges can be extraordinarily complex. Indeed, they are so complex that many tax professionals consciously ignore their application, not to avoid taxes, but to avoid the unmanageable complexity. This begs the question of whether the "cure" is worse than the disease. Several commentators have argued that § 751(b) should be repealed.[52] There is a middle ground that should be considered. That is, is there any way that § 751(b) could be simplified without sacrificing its underlying policy? This is the position of Professor William D. Andrews who argues persuasively that this is not only possible, but important to do.[53] He demonstrates that if two basic changes were made, § 751(b) would be far more manageable. First, the focal point of § 751(b) should be changed from each partner's share of the *value* of hot assets to each partner's share of the

---

48. § 752(b).

49. § 731(a).

50. Under § 733, her outside basis is reduced by both the cash ($150) distributed and the basis she takes in the land distributed ($64).

51. § 731(b).

52. Two distinguished panels have called for its repeal. Revised Report on

Partners and Partnerships, Advisory Group on Subchapter K 40 (1957) and ALI Federal Income Tax Project, Subchapter K (1984).

53. William D. Andrews, *Inside Basis Adjustments and Hot Asset Exchanges in Partnership Distributions*, 47 Tax L.Rev. 3 (1991).

appreciation in those assets. This would avoid the problem of determining whether inventory is substantially appreciated, and assure that each partner would report her appropriate amount of ordinary income. Second, and more importantly, Andrews' would change the basic operation of § 751(b) from an exchange to simply a sale by the partner(s) who reduced their interest in hot asset appreciation. Therefore, there would never be any capital gain recognized. Although Andrews' proposals are far from simple, they would be a vast improvement over current law and should be seriously considered.

Chapter Fourteen

RETIREMENT AND DEATH OF A PARTNER

Retirements—Overview

Payments made in liquidation of the interest of a retiring or deceased partner are governed by § 736.[1] Prior to the enactment of this provision in 1954, there was some confusion as to how such payments should be treated. The confusion resulted from the fact that often a retiring partner continues as a partner under local law during the payout period. For this reason, it was not clear whether payments received during this period should be treated as made in liquidation of the partner's interest in the partnership, or simply as distributions of her distributive share of partnership income. Section 736 originally was quite generous in resolving this issue; it gave partnerships great flexibility in structuring liquidating payments. Probably the most beneficial aspect of the § 736 regime, and the one most exploited, was a rule that permitted the partnership to expense amounts paid to the retiring partner for goodwill. In 1993, Congress severely restricted the benefits of § 736, which are now available in their original form only when a *general* partner retires from a partnership in which capital is not a material income producing factor (i.e., a "service partnership").

Section 736 performs a channeling function. It sends liquidating payments down one of two routes: either they are treated as distributions or, alternatively, as distributive shares (or guaranteed payments). Unfortunately, the statute is quite awkwardly drafted. Section 736(a) states that, except as provided in § 736(b), payments

---

1. Section 736 only applies to one or a series of payments made by the partnership to a retiring partner or to a deceased partner's successor in interest in complete termination of a partner's interest. It does not apply to distributions to a continuing partner or to current distributions during the course of the liquidation of a partner's interest.

217

in liquidation of a retiring partner or a deceased partner's interest shall be treated as part of the recipient's distributive share, or as a guaranteed payment, and not as in exchange for that interest. Section 736(b), however, is actually the general rule. It provides that to the extent liquidating payments are in exchange for the retiring partner's interest in partnership property, they will be treated as distributions, and not under § 736(a), with only two exceptions. Therefore, only payments described in one of these two exceptions can fall under § 736(a). The two exceptions are for amounts paid to a retiring general partner of a service partnership[2] for:

(i) unrealized receivables, as defined in § 751(c),[3] or

(ii) goodwill of the partnership (unless the partnership agreement provides for a payment with respect to goodwill).

In sum, all payments to a retiring partner of a capital-intensive partnership will be governed by § 736(b). Section 736(a) applies only to service partnerships, and then only to the extent that the liquidating payments are being made to a retiring general partner for her share of traditional unrealized receivables and certain unstated goodwill.[4]

Prior to the 1993 changes, the common wisdom was to divide liquidating payments between § 736(a) and (b) by first identifying all amounts paid for a retiring partner's interest in property other than unrealized receivables and unstated goodwill. These amounts would be treated under § 736(b). Only the excess, if any, would be treated under § 736(a). With the advent of § 1060, which requires use of the residual method to value goodwill, and the narrowed scope of § 736(a), in our view, this approach remains the appropriate method only in the case of a retiring general partner of a service partnership. In all other cases, liquidating payments should simply be analyzed under § 736(b).

Section 736(b)—Deferred Liquidation Payments

The general rule under § 736(b) is that liquidating payments to retiring partners are taxed under the normal distribution rules, including § 751(b). Although we have already examined these rules

---

2. § 736(b)(3). Since, under local law, the members of a limited liability company normally are not personally responsible for claims against the company, either in contract or tort, payments made by the company in complete termination of a member's interest generally will be governed exclusively by § 736(b), whether or not the LLC is engaged in a capital-intensive business.

3. For this purpose, unrealized receivables are narrowly defined to exclude recapture items.

4. This is a slight overgeneralization. It is possible to have a liquidating payment that is not for partnership property, such as mutual insurance, or perhaps compensation for past services. Such amounts are technically within § 736(a), whether or not the partnership is a service partnership and whether the interest being liquidated is a general or limited interest. See § 1.736–1(a)(2).

in detail, we have not considered the effect of deferral. Deferred payment arrangements are quite common, in part for financing reasons, and in part because of the especially favorable treatment partners receive under the § 736 regulations as compared with the rules for installment sales.

Installment sale contracts are required to state a minimum rate of interest, or one will be imputed under § 483 or § 1274. Since partnership distributions are not sales or exchanges, they are not subject to these rules. In addition, basis recovery is generally pro rata under the installment method, while under the distribution rules a partner is permitted to recover her basis first. Further, sales of certain assets cannot be reported under § 453; no such limitation applies to distributions. Finally, under the installment sale rules, sellers generally must treat the relief from liabilities as a payment in the year of sale; under the distribution rules, since the retiree remains a partner until receipt of her last payment, she may be able to defer at least a portion of her § 752(b) distribution until that time.

To illustrate the operation of § 736, consider:

Example #1 : ABC is an equal capital-intensive partnership. A, whose outside basis is $250, is retiring. On January 1, 2010, the partnership agrees to make four payments to A, totalling $370, in complete liquidation of her interest: The partnership will pay her $100 on January 1 of 2010, 2011, and 2012, and a final payment of $70 on January 1, 2013. A will remain ultimately liable for 1/3 of the partnership liabilities until receipt of the last payment.[5] At the time of the agreement, ABC's balance sheet (expanded to show fair market values) is as follows:

Assets			*Liabilities & Capital*
	Basis/Book	*FMV*	
Cash	$150	$150	Mortgage = $390
Acc'ts Rec.	300	300	
Building	240	330	
Land	60	420	
Goodwill	0	300	
	$750	$1,500	

	Capital Accounts	
	Tax/Book	*FMV*
A	$120	$370
B	120	370
C	120	370
	$360	$1,110

5. A's share of a partnership recourse obligation for purposes of § 752 depends on the extent to which she bears the ultimate risk of loss with respect to the liability. Even if A ceases to be a partner as a local law matter when she and ABC sign the withdrawal agreement, A may contractually assume a continuing responsibility for a share of partnership debts outstanding at that date. There appears to be no reason why her contractual commitment should not forestall application of § 752(b), even though her underlying liability as a partner under local law may have terminated.

The partnership has no hot assets. No principal payments are due on the mortgage until the year 2020.

Since this is a capital-intensive partnership, all payments are described in § 736(b) and are governed by the distribution rules. A will receive a total of $500, $370 in cash and a $130 decrease in her share of partnership liabilities. This decrease in liabilities will be treated as a cash distribution to her in 2013 when she receives her last payment. Since the partnership has no hot assets, § 751(b) is inapplicable. Under § 731(a)(1), A may recover her entire basis before reporting any gain. Therefore, the tax consequences of this series of distributions are:

January 1, 2010:	No gain or loss; A's outside basis is reduced from $250 to $150.
January 1, 2011:	No gain or loss; A's outside basis is reduced from $150 to $50.
January 1, 2012:	Since the $100 payment exceeds A's remaining outside basis, A recognizes a $50 capital gain. If a § 754 election is in place, the partnership will have a positive § 734 adjustment of $50.
January 1, 2013:	A receives a $200 distribution, $70 in actual cash and $130 under § 752(b). Since A's basis is zero, the entire amount is a capital gain. Again, if a § 754 election is in place, the partnership will have a positive § 734(b) adjustment of $200.

Section 736(a) Payments

Since, as a practical matter, § 736(a) only applies to liquidating payments of a service partnership, it is crucial to know how that term is defined. A service partnership is one in which "capital is not a material income-producing factor."[6] Although there are no regulations to date, the legislative history accompanying the enactment of § 736(b)(3) states that one looks for guidance to other Code provisions that use similar terminology.[7] In general, capital will not

---

6. § 736(b)(3)(A).

7. See e.g., §§ 401(c)(2), 911(d)(2) and former 1348(b)(1)(A), all of which

define "earned income," as opposed to income from capital.

be a material income-producing factor if most of the partnership's revenue is generated by the services of individuals (fees, commissions, etc.). The partnership can have a substantial investment in capital that is merely incidental to those services. It appears highly likely that most professional partnerships will be considered service partnerships.[8]

Payments described in § 736(a) are treated either as part of the retiring partner's distributive share, if the amount is determined with respect to the income of the partnership, or as a guaranteed payment described in § 707(c) if it is not. A retiring partner's distributive share, of course, is excluded from the determination of the other partners' income; this is the economic equivalent of a deduction. Under this regime, the character of partnership income flows through to the recipient. A liquidating payment treated as a guaranteed payment is ordinary income to the recipient in all events. Although guaranteed payments often are subject to § 263, the common understanding is that guaranteed payments under § 736(a)(2) are deductible in all events.[9]

The most taxpayer-friendly aspect of § 736(a) is the ability to treat amounts paid for goodwill as a deductible expense. This was particularly beneficial from 1986 through 1993 when there was no (or only a nominal) differential between the tax rates on ordinary income and capital gains, and goodwill was a nondepreciable capital asset. During those years, most retiring partners suffered no tax disadvantage from shifting the allocation of retirement payments from § 736(b) to § 736(a), but the continuing partners received an immediate deduction for amounts attributable to unstated goodwill that otherwise would not have even been depreciable. Needless to say, amounts attributable to goodwill were invariably unstated. Today, the retiring partner would have to give up the more favorable capital gains tax rate (15% versus 35%) to confer an immediate deduction on the continuing partners.

Prior to 1993, there was an even more beneficial aspect to § 736(a): Amounts paid to retiring partners for § 1245 and similar recapture items were considered "unrealized receivables" for this purpose. As with goodwill, this had the effect of enabling a partnership to deduct an item that, economically, is a capital expenditure. In 1993 this rule was changed and various recapture items (e.g.,

---

8. But cf. Rev. Rul. 78–306, 1978–2 C.B.218, (holding, under § 1348, that capital was a material income-producing factor for an investment banking firm). On the other hand, capital should not be a material income producing factor with respect to a stock broker that does not act as a dealer or engage in firm-commitment underwriting.

9. Section 1.736–1(a)(4) flatly states that they are deductible under § 162(a) without referring to the possibility of capitalization. See also § 1.707–1(c). But see *Cagle v. Commissioner*, 63 T.C. 86 (1974), (identifying and reserving judgment on the issue).

§ 1245)[10] are no longer considered unrealized receivables for purposes of § 736. All liquidating payments for recapture items are treated under § 736(b) no matter what the nature of the partnership.[11]

To illustrate how § 736 applies to a service partnership, consider:

> **Example #2**: ABC is an equal general partnership in which capital is not a material income-producing factor. A is planning to retire when ABC's balance sheet (expanded to show fair market values) is as follows:

	Assets		**Liabilities & Capital**
	Basis/Book	*FMV*	
Cash	$375	$375	Mortgage = $390
Acc'ts Rec.	0	300	
Equipment	75	75	
Building	240	330	
Land	60	120	
Goodwill	0	300	
	$750	$1,500	

	Capital Accounts	
	Tax/Book	*FMV*
A	$120	$370
B	120	370
C	120	370
	$360	$1,110

> A's outside basis is $250. There is no provision in the partnership agreement for goodwill. The partnership has agreed to make a lump sum distribution to A of $370 in cash in complete liquidation of her interest.

As a result of this distribution, A is considered to have received a $500 payment: $370 in cash and $130 under § 752(b) as a result of the decrease in her share of the partnership's liabilities. Since ABC is a service partnership and A is a general partner, this payment must be divided between § 736(a) and § 736(b). The $200 paid for the unrealized receivables ($100) and the goodwill ($100) is treated under (a), and the balance of $300 is treated under (b).

Since the $200 payment under § 736(a) is not determined with respect to the income of the partnership, it is treated as a guaranteed payment under § 707(c) and, as such, is ordinary income to A and deductible by the partnership under § 162(a). This is an excellent outcome for B and C as to the $100 representing goodwill. If they had purchased this goodwill from A, they would have been

---

10. § 751(c) (flush language).

11. This significantly increases the chances that liquidating payments will be brought under § 751(b) as disproportionate distributions.

required to recover their cost over a 15–year period.[12] Under the § 736(a) regime, the partnership can deduct the full amount in the year of payment.

The $300 payment under § 736(b) is treated as a distribution. The accounts receivables are the only hot assets of the partnership and were already accounted for under § 736(a). Therefore, they are not taken into account under § 736(b), avoiding the complexity of § 751(b).[13] Since the distribution is $50 greater than her outside basis, A has a $50 capital gain under § 731(a)(1).[14] If the partnership makes, or has in place, a § 754 election, it would be entitled to a positive $50 basis adjustment under § 734(b).

The analysis of a deferred-payment liquidation on these facts is more complicated because each payment must be divided between § 736(a) and § 736(b). In the absence of an agreement to the contrary, the regulations divide fixed payments proportionately, and allocate contingent payments first to § 736(b) amounts.[15] To illustrate, consider:

> *Example #3*. Same facts as in *Example #2*, except the partnership agrees to pay A the $370 in four annual installments, the first three in the amount of $100, and the final payment of $70. A agrees to remain liable for one-third of the mortgage until she receives her last payment.

As in *Example #2*, A eventually will receive $500, $200 of which will be a guaranteed payment under § 736(a) and $300 of which will be for her interest in partnership property under § 736(b). Since A will remain liable for ⅓ of the liability until the final payment, her share of partnership liabilities will not decrease until then. She will therefore receive three payments of $100 and a final payment of $200 (i.e., $70 + $130). Since these payments are fixed, in the absence of an agreement to the contrary, ⅖ of each payment will be characterized as a guaranteed payment, and ⅗ as a distribution under § 731. Therefore, for each of the first three years, $40 of each annual payment is treated a guaranteed payment, includible by A as ordinary income and deductible in full by the partnership, and $60 of each annual payment is treated as a distribution under § 731. Since A's initial outside basis is $250, these latter amounts simply reduce her basis by $180 (3 x $60) to $70.

12. § 197.

13. Notice that this analysis can become considerably more complex in the presence of either substantially appreciated inventory or recapture. In either event, the distribution under § 736(b) would be disproportionate, implicating § 751(b).

14. The $300 distribution exceeds A's outside basis of $250 by $50.

15. § 1.736–1(b)(5)(i) & (ii).

224   **RETIREMENT & DEATH OF PARTNER**   **Ch. 14**

In the fourth year, A is deemed to receive $200, $80 of which is treated as a guaranteed payment and $120 under § 731. Of the $120, $50 is taxable as a capital gain. If the partnership has a § 754 election in effect, it will have a positive § 734(b) adjustment of $50.

The Relationship between § 736 and § 751(b)

The normal rules of § 751(b) apply to all liquidating payments described in § 736(b). They do not, however, apply to payments described in § 736(a).[16] If § 736(a) applies to some (but not all) of the liquidating payments, § 736(b) applies to the balance. In such a case, since traditional unrealized receivables are accounted for under § 736(a), the only assets that can trigger a § 751(b) exchange are substantially appreciated inventory and recapture items. For example, if in *Example #2* there had been appreciation in the equipment that would have been characterized as § 1245 recapture, the distribution would have been disproportionate.

Death of a Partner

As we noted in *Chapter Ten,* the death of a partner terminates the partnership's taxable year with respect to that partner.[17] As a result, the deceased partner's distributive share of partnership income or loss for the year of death must be reported on the decedent's final return.[18] In addition, there are certain special rules that apply to the decedent's estate and other successors in interest, most importantly, §§ 1014 and 691. In this section, we summarize these rules and illustrate how they intersect with Subchapter K.[19]

Property acquired from a decedent[20] receives under § 1014 a basis equal to its fair market value at the date of death ("stepped-up basis").[21] Under this rule, a person who acquires a partnership

---

16. § 751(b)(2)(b).

17. § 706(c)(2).

18. See § 1.706–1(c)(2)(ii) for possible methods for determining the decedent's distributive shares. See also the discussion of § 706(d) in *Chapter Ten.*

19. It should be noted that as we are preparing this edition in mid–2010, § 1014 is not operative. For the calendar year 2010, those who inherit property will take a carryover basis (with some adjustments) under § 1022. Section 1014, however, is slated to become the law again as of January 1, 2011. Since this edition is not scheduled to be available until then, the text is written as if § 1014 is in effect.

20. The broadest prescription of an acquisition by death is found in § 1014(b)(9), whereby property is deemed to have been acquired from a decedent if it is includible in the decedent's gross estate for federal estate tax purposes (whether or not the estate is required to file a federal estate tax return). Thus, many assets not actually owned by the decedent may nevertheless take a § 1014(a) death-value basis.

21. Since the basis of property under § 1014 is measured by value on the date of death, in some cases the beneficiary will actually take a "stepped-down" basis.

interest from a decedent takes as her outside basis an amount equal to the interest's full fair market value,[22] including her share of any liabilities. For reasons described immediately below, this basis must be reduced by any items of income in respect of a decedent in the partnership. The death of a partner is treated as a "transfer" for purposes of § 743(b); if there is a § 754 election in place, or if there is a substantial built-in loss, the partnership adjusts the bases of its assets under § 743(b) and § 755.

Section 1014 does not apply to a right to income in respect of a decedent (IRD),[23] even though the value of that right is includible in the decedent's estate. An item of IRD is any right to gross income that was never properly includible by the decedent under her method of accounting during her lifetime.[24] For example, accounts receivable of a cash method decedent, or an installment note held by a decedent reporting her gain under § 453 would both be items of IRD. Due to § 1014(c), items of IRD do not change their basis at death, and, under § 691(a), are generally includible in the income of the recipient in the year received.[25] In the partnership context, this means that the decedent's successor in interest must reduce her § 1014 outside basis by any items of IRD attributable to the partnership interest and report those items when received.

In Subchapter K, two types of IRD stand out. The first type is statutory: under § 753, all payments made to the deceased partner's successor in interest under § 736(a) are considered IRD. As discussed earlier in this chapter, since 1993 this rule only applies to a deceased general partner of a service partnership. Although goodwill is not usually an item of IRD, it can be in this context. Treating goodwill as a § 736(a) payment to a decedent's successor is not nearly as advantageous a rule as it is in the case of a retirement. Upon retirement, amounts received for goodwill are taxable in all events; the only question is character. Upon the liquidation of a decedent's interest, the issue is not merely one of

---

22. Under § 1.742–1, technically, a successor's outside basis is equal to the net value of the partnership interest, plus her share of liabilities, less any items of income in respect of a decedent.

23. § 1014(c).

24. The "right" in question need not be a legally enforceable right. The general contours of the IRD concept have been fleshed out by 50–odd years of persistent litigation and lie beyond the scope of this book. Ferguson, Freeland and Ascher, *Federal Income Taxation of Estates, Trusts, and Beneficiaries*, ch. 3 (2d Ed. Little, Brown 1993). As a generally reliable rule of thumb (not rule of law), however, we have observed a close correlation between anticipatory assignment of income doctrine and IRD. That is, if an item of potential gross income transferred by lifetime gift is so mature that it would, upon recognition, be taxed to the donor rather than the donee under anticipatory assignment of income principles, it is a virtually sure bet that the same item when transferred at death is income in respect of a decedent under § 691. Section 1014(c) will deny the item a basis change despite inclusion in the gross estate for federal estate tax purposes.

25. The recipient may be entitled to deduct a portion of the estate tax paid. § 691(c).

character, but of whether amounts received for goodwill are taxable at all. This is illustrated in ***Example #4.***

The second type of IRD is judicial: if a partnership holds any right to income that would have been an item of IRD if held by the deceased partner individually, the courts have been willing to pierce the "partnership veil" and find IRD.[26] Common examples of this type are accounts receivable of a cash method partnership, or an installment sales contract.

Once the items of IRD have been identified at the partnership level, the decedent's successor's outside basis is determined by subtracting the value of these items from the fair market value of the entire partnership interest as of the date of death.[27] To illustrate, consider:

> ***Example #4:*** DEF is an equal general partnership in which capital is not a material income producing factor. On January 1, 2005, D died, triggering the partnership's buy/sell agreement. According to the agreement, the partnership is to pay D's successor in interest, B, $300 cash in liquidation of her interest in the partnership. The partnership agreement says nothing about goodwill. On the date of death, DEF's balance sheet was as follows:

Assets	Basis/Book	FMV	**Liabilities & Capital**
Cash	$360	$360	Liabilities = $300
Acc'ts Receivables	0	150	
Various Capital Assets	90	450	
Goodwill	0	240	
	$450	$1,200	

Capital Accounts	Tax/Book	FMV
D	$50	$300
E	50	300
F	50	300
	$150	$900

Under this agreement, B is deemed to receive $400, $300 cash and $100 under § 752(b). Section 736 governs this payment. Since the partnership agreement says nothing about goodwill, that portion of the $400 allocable to the accounts receivable ($50) and goodwill ($80), or $130, is treated under § 736(a)(2) as a guaranteed payment. This amount is also an item of IRD. The balance of the liquidating payment, $270, is treated as a distribution under

26. See e.g., *Quick's Trust v. Commissioner*, 54 T.C. 1336 (1970), *aff'd per curiam* 444 F.2d 90 (8th Cir. 1971), and *Woodhall v. Commissioner*, 454 F.2d 226 (9th Cir. 1972).

27. Again, under § 1.742–1, technically, the successor's basis is equal to the net value of the interest, plus her share of partnership liabilities, less any items of IRD.

§ 736(b). In determining the tax consequences of this distribution, B's outside basis is the value of D's interest on the date of death, $400, less all items of IRD ($130), or $270. Assuming that the distribution is not disproportionate, it will prompt no further tax consequences. B merely recovers her $270 basis.

Contrast the results under a partnership agreement that explicitly allocates $80 of the liquidating payment to goodwill. In this case, only the $50 allocable to the unrealized receivables falls within § 736(a); the $350 balance is a § 736(b) payment. Under this scenario, the only items of IRD are the receivables; therefore, B's outside basis is $350.

Notice the dramatically different tax consequences to B with respect to the payment for goodwill depending on whether it is subject to § 736(a). As a § 736(a) payment, it generates $80 of ordinary income; as § 736(b) payment, it generates no income whatsoever.

Example #5: Same facts as in **Example #4**, except that there is no buy/sell agreement and B, D's successor in interest, plans to become a partner in D's place.

In this case, § 736 has no application. Nevertheless, D's share of the accounts receivable ($50) is an item of IRD. Therefore, B's initial outside basis is $350 ($400–$50). If there were a § 754 election in place, a $200 § 743(b) adjustment would arise:

	B's outside basis =	$350
LESS	B's share of inside basis =	$150
		$200

This adjustment would be allocated among the various capital assets and the goodwill; the basis of the receivables would not be adjusted. Therefore, as the receivables are collected, they would be fully taxable to B.

Chapter Fifteen

DISGUISED SALES AND EXCHANGES

Background

In the interest of ensuring that property can freely flow into and out of partnerships without the impediment of taxation, the provisions of Subchapter K have historically permitted partners to contribute property to, and receive distributions from, a partnership without the recognition of gain.[1] The result was the most powerful nonrecognition regime in the Internal Revenue Code. Pushed to its extreme limits, this regime (arguably) permitted taxpayers to use partnerships to exchange one type of property for another, or even to sell property for cash, without recognizing any gain. Concerned about this unintended use of Subchapter K, Congress enacted a panoply of statutes designed to stem the abuse: §§ 707(a)(2)(B), 704(c)(1)(B), and 737.

Before reviewing these provisions in detail, it may be useful to consider the types of transactions at which they were aimed: contributions of (usually appreciated) property to a partnership, followed by either (i) a cash distribution to the contributing partner, (ii) a distribution of different property to the contributing partner, or (iii) a distribution of the contributed property to another partner. Each of these transactions attempted to avoid the recognition of the gain on the contributed property by the contributor.

A related but somewhat more complicated transaction was also addressed by Congress in § 707(a)(2)(B): the disguised sale of a partnership interest (not the underlying property). In 2004, Treasury proposed regulations dealing with this transaction, but they

---

1. §§ 721 & 731.

were withdrawn in 2009. These disguised sales are discussed briefly at the end of this chapter.

An example of a case in which a taxpayer successfully received cash without recognizing gain was *Otey v. Commissioner*.[2] In *Otey* the taxpayer contributed property with a value of $65,000 and a basis of $18,000 to a partnership in exchange for a 50% partnership interest. The other 50% partner contributed no capital. Shortly after formation, the partnership took out a recourse loan for $870,000 to develop the property, increasing each partner's outside basis by $435,000.[3] As contemplated at the time of formation, the partnership immediately distributed $65,000 of the loan proceeds to T. The government argued that the contribution and distribution, considered together, constituted a sale, but the court, applying §§ 731 and 733, disagreed and held that T recognized no gain.

Another type of transaction, the so-called "mixing bowl transaction," arguably permitted taxpayers to exchange non-like kind properties without recognition of gain. To illustrate, suppose A and B form a partnership to which A contributes Blackacre and B contributes nonmarketable securities.[4] Both properties have appreciated and are of equal value. Sometime thereafter, the partnership liquidates, distributing Blackacre to B and securities to A. If the formation and liquidation of this partnership were independently respected then A and B would have effectively swapped properties without recognizing gain.

A partnership interest could effectively be exchanged without recognition of gain under the following scenario: AB partnership holds appreciated real property. C is admitted to the partnership in exchange for a contribution of stock. Shortly thereafter, A receives the stock in complete liquidation of his partnership interest. A's gain will be deferred, even though he has essentially exchanged his partnership interest for stock.

In 1984 Congress began its attack on these transactions by enacting § 707(a)(2)(B). Specifically disapproving of the result in *Otey*, Congress directed Treasury to identify by regulation the circumstances under which a contribution and related distribution should be characterized as a sale or exchange of property. The § 707(a)(2)(B) regulations are discussed immediately below. Congress subsequently also enacted §§ 704(c)(1)(B) and 737 as backstops to § 707(a)(2)(B). These two provisions apply only to the extent that § 707(a)(2)(B) does not, and were targeted at the basic mixing bowl transaction described above, and variations on that

---

2. 634 F.2d 1046 (6th Cir.1980). The result in *Otey* was specifically disapproved in the committee reports accompanying the enactment of § 707(a)(2)(B).

3. § 752(a).

4. Prior to the enactment of § 731(c), mixing bowl transactions typically involved marketable securities.

theme. They are discussed immediately after § 707(a)(2)(B). Finally, we end with a few words on the disguised sales of partnership interests.

Disguised Sales of Property

The Regulations Under § 707(a)(2)(B)

Since almost any contribution of property to a partnership followed by a distribution to the same partner *could* be viewed as a sale of the property,[5] Treasury's task in drafting regulations under § 707(a)(2)(B) was to identify when two transfers are sufficiently related that they are more "properly characterized as a sale or exchange of property."[6] Treasury ultimately determined that a contribution and a related distribution will be characterized as a sale only if, based on all of the facts and circumstances, two conditions are met:

1. The partnership would not have transferred money or property to the partner BUT FOR the transfer of the property by the partner to the partnership; and

2. In the case of transfers that are not simultaneous, the subsequent transfer is not dependent on the entrepreneurial risks of the partnership's operations.[7]

The first condition is relatively straightforward and requires the contribution and distribution to be reciprocal transfers, each in consideration of the other. In the case of a simultaneous transfer, this is the only condition that must be met. All simultaneous transfers are automatically highly suspect, and most will be recharacterized as sales.[8]

The second condition, which must be met whenever the transfers are not simultaneous, requires that the subsequent transfer (usually the distribution) be independent of the entrepreneurial risks of the partnership. The underlying thought is that if the contributing partner's capital is at risk in the venture for a sufficient time, then she should be entitled to the nonrecognition afforded to partners, even in the case of reciprocal transfers. On the other hand, if the subsequent transfer occurs shortly after the first, or is secured by other assets or guarantees, or otherwise insulated from the risks of the venture, then the two transfers are more properly viewed as a sale.

---

5. The regulations define the term sale to include exchange. § 1.707–3(a)(2).

6. § 707(a)(2)(B)(iii).

7. § 1.707–3(b)(1).

8. For this reason, the regulations create special rules for liabilities (§ 1.707–5) and do not treat terminations under § 708(b)(1)(B) as transfers. § 1.707–3(a)(4).

In the event that two transfers are recharacterized as a sale (in whole or in part), the transaction is treated as a sale or exchange for all purposes of the Internal Revenue Code, including §§ 453, 1001, 1012, 1031, and 1274.[9] The sale is deemed to occur on the date that the partnership becomes the owner of the property for Federal income tax purposes, i.e., on the date of the contribution.[10] If the transfers are not simultaneous, the parties are treated as though the contributing partner exchanged the contributed property for the partnership's obligation (i.e., an installment obligation) to make the subsequent transfer of money or other property.[11]

Analytically, the determination of whether a given contribution and related distribution constitute a disguised sale of property ultimately depends on all of the attendant facts and circumstances. To aid in this determination, the regulations create two important presumptions, list 10 of the most important facts and circumstances, and create an exception for normal distributions. They also create special rules for liabilities. Each of these is discussed below.

Two-Year Presumptions

The regulations create two alternative presumptions that will determine the fate of most related transfers:

1.   Transfers that occur within two years of one another are presumed to constitute a sale.[12]

2.   Transfers separated by more than two years are presumed not to constitute a sale.[13]

The thrust of these presumptions is quite clear. If the taxpayer's capital has been at the risk of the venture for more than two years, the transfers normally will not be recharacterized as a sale. These presumptions may be rebutted, but only if the relevant facts and circumstances "clearly establish" the contrary. In this context, Treasury lists 10 of the most important facts and circumstances that tend to prove the existence of a sale.[14] These are:

1.   The certainty of the timing and amount of the second transfer;

2.   The second transfer is legally enforceable;

3.   The second transfer is secured in any way;

4.   A third party is obligated to make a contribution to the partnership to enable it to make the second transfer;

9. § 1.707–3(a)(2).
10. Id.
11. Id.
12. § 1.707–3(c).

13. § 1.707–3(d).
14. § 1.707–3(b)(2).

5. A third party is obligated to make a loan to the partnership to enable it to make the second transfer;

6. The partnership has incurred, or is obligated to incur, debt to enable it to make the second transfer;

7. The partnership has excess liquid assets that are expected to be available for the second transfer;

8. The partnership distributions, allocations, or control of operations are designed to effect an exchange of the benefits and burdens of the ownership of contributed property;

9. The amount of the distribution to a partner is disproportionately large in relation to his general and continuing interest in partnership profits; and

10. The partner has no obligation (or one with a relatively small present value) to return distributions to the partnership.

Note that all 10 of these factors tend to prove the existence of a sale; none tends to disprove its existence. On their face, at least, these factors may only be used by the government to rebut a presumption that a sale did not occur. The regulations indicate, however, that the absence of these factors may be used by a taxpayer to rebut the presumption that a sale did occur.[15] Nevertheless, one is left with the clear impression that it will be easier for the government to successfully argue that a sale has occurred even though the transfers were more than two years apart than it will be for the taxpayer to argue that a sale has not occurred even though both transfers occurred within two years. Also note that the first seven factors all go to the same issue: The extent to which the contributing partner's capital is subject to the entrepreneurial risk of the venture.

Normal Distributions

Absent a special rule, all partnership distributions to a partner who had contributed money or property within the prior two years would be presumed to be part of a sale of property. Most partnerships, however, make periodic distributions to their partners, including distributions of operating cash flow (typically matched by income allocations) and guaranteed payments and preferred returns, which are intended to compensate partners for the *use* of their capital rather than to buy out the partner's interest in contributed capital (the essence of a disguised sale). To prevent tainting normal distributions, the regulations provide exceptions for distributions out of operating cash flow[16] and "reasonable"

---

15. § 1.707–3(f) Ex. 3.

16. § 1.707–4(b) contains a complicated set of rules designed to identify a distribution from operating cash flow.

guaranteed payments and preferred returns.[17] In essence, these exceptions allow a partnership to make normal distributions to its partners without raising the specter of § 707(a)(2)(B).

Examples

To illustrate how the disguised sale rules operate in the absence of liabilities, consider the following three examples. Assume in each case that at all relevant times the Applicable Federal Rate is 10%, compounded annually.

> *Example #1:* A, B, and C form an equal partnership to which A contributes Blackacre with a basis of $300 and a value of $1,000, and B and C each contribute $750 in cash. To equalize their capital accounts, A receives an immediate cash distribution of $250.

The principal issue raised by these facts is whether the contribution of Blackacre by A and the distribution of $250 to A should be characterized as a sale of a portion of Blackacre. Since the transfers are simultaneous, the transaction will be a characterized as a sale if the partnership would not have made the $250 distribution to A in the absence of A's contribution of Blackacre to the partnership. On these facts, this condition is clearly met: The only reason for the $250 distribution was the contribution of Blackacre. The desire to equalize the partners' capital accounts is not a sufficient independent justification for the distribution. Therefore, A is treated as having sold 25% of Blackacre[18] and as having contributed the balance.

At this point we can divide the transaction into its two separate components: a sale of 25% of Blackacre, and a contribution of the remaining 75%. We will allocate A's basis in Blackacre in the same proportions[19] in order to analyze the two transactions.

	Sale Portion **(25%)**	**Contribution Portion** **(75%)**
Value	$250	$750
Basis	75	225

The chart gives us the information we need to analyze both the sale and the contribution components of the transaction.

> *The Sale.* A has an amount realized for 25% of Blackacre of $250, and has a resulting gain from the sale of $175. ABC will

---

17. The rules for guaranteed payments and preferred returns are in § 1.707–4(a). Reasonableness is determined by reference to return on invested capital at a safe harbor interest rate equal to 150% of the highest applicable federal rate. § 1.707–4(a)(3)(ii).

18. 150/900= ⅙. See § 1.707–3(f) Ex. 1.

19. § 1.707–3(f) Ex. 1.

take a cost basis of $250 and a new holding period in that portion of Blackacre.

The Contribution. A has contributed the remaining 75% of Blackacre to ABC. This portion of the property is worth $750 and has a basis of $225. A takes an initial outside basis of $225,[20] and ABC will take a transferred basis in the contributed portion of Blackacre equal to $225.[21] A will receive credit in her capital account for the $750 value of the contributed property.

Immediately after formation, the partnership's balance sheet would be:

	Assets		**Liabilities & Capital**
	Basis	*Book*	
Cash	$1,250	$1,250	
Blackacre[22]	475	1,000	
	$1,725	$2,250	

Capital Accounts

	Tax	*Book*
A	$225	$750
B	750	750
C	750	750
	$1,725	$2,250

Example #2: Same as ***Example #1*** except that instead of receiving a $250 distribution upon formation, ABC distributes $275 to A (and only A) one year later.

Since the transfers are not simultaneous, both conditions of the regulations must be met: The transfers must be reciprocal and the subsequent distribution must not depend on the entrepreneurial risks of the venture. Because the distribution occurred within two years of the contribution, a presumption is created that both conditions are met and that a sale has occurred, unless the facts and circumstances clearly establish the contrary. On these facts, there is little doubt that A would not have received the distribution but for her contribution of Blackacre. If A can show that there existed a significant risk that ABC would be unable to make the distribution, she might be able to rebut the presumption that it was not dependent on the entrepreneurial risks of the partnership. If she cannot, then she is deemed to have sold a portion of Blackacre to the partnership on the date of the contribution in exchange for the partnership's installment obligation with a stated principal amount of $275, and an imputed principal amount (under § 1274) of $250.[23]

20. § 722.

21. § 723.

22. Note that A still has $525 of § 704(c) gain that must be taken into account.

23. The imputed principal amount (which is the selling price for § 453 purposes) is determined under § 1274 by discounting the stated principal amount of $275 by 10% for one year, or $150. A

Example #3: Same as *Example #1* except that instead of receiving a $250 distribution upon formation, A receives $302.50 two years and one day after the formation of the partnership. At all times since its formation, the ABC partnership had liquid assets in excess of $300.

Once again, since the transfers are not simultaneous, both conditions must be met: The transfers must be reciprocal and the subsequent distribution must not be dependent on the entrepreneurial risks of the venture. Since the distribution does not occur until more than two years after the contribution, a presumption is created that the two conditions are not met and there is no sale. The government can rebut this presumption by clearly establishing the contrary. Since ABC apparently has had excessive liquid assets on hand since its formation, the government might be able to successfully argue that the timing and amount of the distribution was never in serious doubt and that a sale has occurred.[21] From these limited facts, the answer is unclear.

Liabilities

As we already know, when encumbered property is contributed to a partnership, the contributor is deemed to receive a cash distribution to the extent of her net liability relief.[25] One of the key issues faced by Treasury in drafting the disguised sale rules was how to treat these deemed distributions. Should distributions triggered by § 752 be treated as actual distributions for purposes of the disguised sale rules, or should an exception be made? To illustrate, consider:

Example #4: A owns Blackacre which has a fair market value of $1,000 but is subject to a recourse mortgage of $800. A's basis is $400. A contributes Blackacre to the AB partnership in exchange for a 50% partnership interest. B contributes cash of $200 in exchange for the remaining 50%. Under § 752, A is treated as receiving a net cash distribution of $400.

If deemed distributions were treated as actual distributions under § 707(a)(2)B), the contribution of encumbered property would often result in a sale, even though one was not contemplated.

has again sold 25% of Blackacre, and will recognize the $175 gain on the sale in the year in which she receives the payment from the partnership. The difference of $25 between the stated principal amount and the imputed principal amount will be taxable interest income

to A, and an interest expense to the partnership.

24. If there has been a sale, A's amount realized is equal to the present value of $181.50 discounted by 10% for two years, or $150. §§ 453, 1274.

25. § 752, *Chapter Eight.*

In *Example #4,* A would undoubtedly be treated as receiving $400 in exchange for a portion of Blackacre, i.e., she would be treated as though she sold 40% of Blackacre for $400.[26] If such a rule were adopted, it would certainly have a chilling effect on the formation of partnerships. On the other hand, if there were a blanket exception for deemed § 752 distributions, the disguised sale rules could be easily circumvented by mortgaging property just prior to contribution. A taxpayer could "cash out" on her investment without recognizing any gain.

Addressing both concerns, Treasury determined that only liabilities which are incurred in anticipation of the transfer of the property to the partnership ("nonqualified liabilities") should be fully subject to the disguised sale rules. Therefore, if in *Example #4* the liability was *non-qualified*, A would be treated as if she received consideration of $400, the amount equal to the excess of the liability ($800) over her share of the liability ($400). That $400 represents 40% of the value of Blackacre. We would then divide the transaction into its separate components. Note, however, that we now have to take the liability into account. Because $400 of the liability was treated as consideration under the sale portion, only the remaining $400 remains to be attached to the contribution portion.[27]

	Sale Portion (40%)	**Contribution Portion** (60%)
Value	$400	$600
Basis	160	240
Liability	400	400

Analyzing each component:

The Sale. A has an amount realized for 40% of Blackacre of $400, and has a resulting gain from the sale of $240. ABC will take a cost basis of $400 and a new holding period in that portion of Blackacre.

The Contribution. A has contributed the remaining 60% of Blackacre to ABC. That portion of the property is worth $600, is subject to a liability of $400, and has a basis of $240. ABC will take a transferred basis in the contributed portion of Blackacre equal to $240.[28] A will receive credit in her capital account for the $200 net value of the contributed property.

26. This is a simultaneous transfer and the partnership's assumption of the liability would never have occurred but for the transfer of Blackacre.

27. Note that we do *not* divide the liability based on the percentage sold and contributed, the division is based upon the amount of the liability that is treated as consideration (that gets allocated to the sale portion) and the balance is treated as a liability encumbering the contribution portion.

28. § 723.

The balance sheet immediately after formation would be as follows:

	Assets		**Liabilities & Capital**
	Basis	*Book*	Mortgage $800
Cash	$200	$200	
Blackacre	640	1000	
	$840	$1200	

	Capital Accounts	
	Tax	*Book*
A	$(160)	$200
B	200	200
	$40	$400

The question remaining is what is A's outside basis? It will be the sum of (i) the basis of the contributed property ($240), less (ii) A's deemed distribution under § 752(b) ($400), plus (iii) A's deemed contribution under § 752(a) (50% of $800).[29] A's basis will therefore be $240.[30]

In contrast with the above result, which requires immediate recognition by A of gain of $240, if the mortgage was a qualified liability, then the disguised sales rules would not apply to the transaction.[31] The distinction between qualified and non-qualified liabilities is therefore extremely important.

Qualified Liabilities

The rules for identifying qualified liabilities are found at § 1.707–5(a)(6). The two most important factors in determining whether a particular liability is qualified are: (i) when it was incurred, and (ii) for what were the proceeds used. The regulations *conclusively* presume that a liability is qualified if it was incurred more than two years prior to the transfer of the property to the partnership and encumbered the property throughout that period.[32] Therefore, if a liability is "old and cold," it does not matter why it was incurred, or to what use its proceeds were put. In all cases it is qualified.

On the other hand, if a liability is incurred within two years of the transfer, it is qualified if:

(1) the liability is allocable to capital expenditures with respect to the contributed property (i.e., the proceeds were used to either acquire or improve the contributed property), or

---

29. Note this latter number is arrived at by taking into account the entire $800 mortgage, because it is indeed a partnership liability for which A has 50% liability.

30. This, appropriately, equals her tax capital account plus her share of liabilities.

31. Note the fact that a liability is qualified does not necessarily mean it won't be treated as consideration, as discussed below. If, however, A receives no actual consideration, as was the case in *Example #4,* the liability relief will not result in disguised sale treatment.

32. § 1.707–5(a)(6)(i)(A).

(2) the liability is incurred in the ordinary course of business and substantially all of the assets of the business are transferred.[33]

All other liabilities incurred within this two year time period are presumed to have been incurred in anticipation of the transfer (hence, nonqualified) unless the relevant facts and circumstances clearly establish the contrary.[34]

The reason that liabilities incurred for capital expenditures are qualified, even though incurred within the prohibited two year period, should be obvious: if the taxpayer does not pocket the loan proceeds but invests them in the underlying property, she has not in any way "cashed out" her investment. To the contrary, she has increased her investment.

The reason that liabilities incurred in the ordinary course of the contributor's business (e.g., accounts payable) are considered qualified *as long as* substantially all of the assets of the business are transferred to the partnership is less obvious. By their nature, these liabilities are present in practically all ongoing businesses. If their transfer resulted in adverse tax consequences, many proprietors would opt to remain proprietors rather than entering into partnerships. Furthermore, this type of liability does not lend itself to "cashing out" one's investment.

To illustrate the application of the qualified liability rule, reconsider **Example #4.** If the $800 mortgage had been incurred by A more than two years before transferring Blackacre to the partnership and had encumbered Blackacre ever since, the mortgage would be a qualified liability and A would recognize no gain on the contribution. This result would follow regardless of A's reason for incurring the liability or her use of the proceeds.

If, on the other hand, A incurred the $800 mortgage less than two years before transferring Blackacre to the partnership, we would need more facts to determine whether or not the mortgage is qualified. If the mortgage was incurred to acquire Blackacre, or if the proceeds of the mortgage were used for capital improvements to Blackacre, it is a qualified liability. On the other hand, if A invested the $800 loan proceeds in unrelated securities, the liability will be presumed to have been incurred in anticipation of transferring Blackacre to the partnership and therefore nonqualified. Although

---

33. There is a further requirement that the amount of the liability cannot exceed the value of the property that secures it.

34. This observation is based upon two regulations. First, § 1.707–5(a)(6)(i)(B) states that liabilities incurred within the two year period are still qualified as long as they were not incurred in anticipation of the contribution of the underlying property. The contributor, however, must clearly establish that this is the case to overcome the rebuttable presumption created in § 1.707–5(a)(7).

A can rebut this presumption by clearly establishing the contrary, absent additional facts, the mortgage will not be a qualified liability and A will be treated as having sold 40% of Blackacre to the partnership for $400, resulting in a gain of $240 as illustrated above.[35]

Special Rule for Nonqualified Nonrecourse Liabilities

In general, if a partner contributes property to a partnership that assumes or takes the property subject to a nonqualified liability, the partner is treated as having an amount realized equal to the excess of the amount of the liability over the contributing partner's share of that liability immediately after the contribution. In the case of a recourse liability, the normal rules under § 752 apply to determine that excess. For this reason, if the recourse liability in *Example #4* were nonqualified, A's amount realized from the sale would be $400, i.e., the excess of the amount of the liability ($800) over A's share of that liability immediately after the contribution ($400).

Nonrecourse nonqualified liabilities, however, involve a special rule. As you will recall from *Chapter Eight*, a partner's share of a nonrecourse liability is the sum of three amounts: 1) her share of the partnership's minimum gain, 2) her § 704(c) minimum gain, and 3) her share of "excess nonrecourse liabilities."[36] Excess nonrecourse liabilities generally are shared in the same way that the partners share profits. For purposes of determining a partner's share of a nonrecourse liability under § 707(a)(2)(B), the first two amounts are disregarded. A partner's share of a nonrecourse liability is determined by applying the same percentage used to determine that partner's share of excess nonrecourse liabilities.[37]

To illustrate, suppose the liability in *Example #4* were a nonqualified nonrecourse liability. Although A's share of the liability is $550[38] for purposes of § 752, her share of that liability for purposes of § 707 would be only $400, an amount determined solely on the basis of how the partners share profits. Therefore, A still would be treated as selling 40% of the property, not 25%.

35. Forty percent of A's basis, or $200 (40% x $500) must be allocated to the sale.

36. § 1.752–3(a)(3). See generally *Chapter Eight*.

37. § 1.707–5(a)(2)(ii). Treasury recently amended § 1.752–3 to permit excess nonrecourse liabilities to be allocated first to the contributor up to the amount of § 704(c) gain inherent in the property. This method does not apply for purposes of applying the disguised sale rules. § 1.752–3(a)(3).

38. A would first be allocated an amount of that liability equal to any § 704(c) minimum gain that would be allocated to her ($300); the balance would be allocated 50–50 between A and B in accordance with their profit shares, or $250 each.

Special Rule for Qualified Liabilities

There are circumstances in which even a qualified liability will be partially treated as consideration. So long as the transfer of property is not otherwise treated as a sale, no part of a qualified liability is treated as sale proceeds. If, however, the transfer is treated as a partial sale without regard to the qualified liability, a portion of the qualified liability will be treated as additional consideration. The amount of this additional consideration is equal to the lesser of:

(i) the amount of the liability that would have been treated as consideration if the liability had not been qualified; or

(ii) the product of the partner's "net equity percentage" times the amount of the liability.

The purpose of the first amount is to insure that a liability that is qualified will never be treated less favorably than one that is not. The purpose of the second amount is not immediately apparent and needs some explanation. "Net equity percentage" is the percentage of the partner's equity in the contributed property for which she received consideration (other than the qualified liability). It is determined by dividing the amount of that consideration by the partner's net equity in the property[39] before the transfer.[40] The thought is that if a contributing partner has cashed out a portion of her "equity" investment, then she will be deemed to have sold the corresponding portion of the property that is encumbered.

To illustrate, recall the facts of **Example #4**, where A transfers property with a value of $1000, subject to a mortgage of $800, but assume in this case that B contributed $150 cash to the partnership, and immediately after formation the partnership distributes $50 to A. Assume that the $800 liability was "old and cold," and hence qualified. If A receives no actual distribution from the partnership, either of cash or property, then none of the liability relief will be treated as a distribution of consideration under § 707(a)(2)(B). If, however, A does receive an *actual* distribution from the partnership, so that the transaction is treated as a partial sale without regard to the liability, then a portion of the $800 liability *will* be treated as *additional* consideration. Because, under our revised facts, the partnership actually distributed $50 in cash to A when she contributed the property subject to the liability, the regulations require that we treat a portion of the liability as additional consideration.[41] We determine that portion by focusing not on what portion of the *value* of the property is considered sold,

---

39. I.e., the fair market value less the qualified liability.

40. § 1.707–5(a)(5)(ii).

41. Note that if we did not, then A would be treated as selling just 5% of the property ($50/$1000).

but on the portion of A's *equity* that is sold. A's equity in the property was $200 ($1000 value less $800 liability), and the $50 cash consideration represents 25% of that equity. Therefore, 25% of the $800 liability ($200) is treated as additional consideration, bringing the total consideration received to $250. This represents 25% of the value of the property, and it is that portion of the property that A is deemed to sell. [42]

Analyzing the transaction as we did above:

	Sale Portion (25%)	Contribution Portion (75%)
Value	$250	$750
Basis	100	300
Liability	200	600

Analyzing each component:

The Sale. A has an amount realized for 25% of Blackacre of $250, and has a resulting gain from the sale of $150. ABC will take a cost basis of $250 in that portion of Blackacre.

The Contribution. A has contributed the remaining 75% of Blackacre to ABC. That portion of the property is worth $750, is subject to a liability of $600, and has a basis of $300. ABC will take a transferred basis in the contributed portion of Blackacre equal to $300.[43] A will receive credit in her capital account for the $150 net value of the contributed property.

The balance sheet immediately after formation would be as follows:

	Assets		Liabilities & Capital
	Basis	*Book*	Mortgage $800
Cash	$100	$100	
Blackacre	550	1000	
	$650	$1100	

Capital Accounts

	Tax	*Book*
A	$(300)	$150
B	150	150
	$(150)	$300

A's outside basis will be the sum of (i) the basis of the contributed property ($300), less (ii) A's deemed distribution under § 752(b) ($600), plus (iii) A's deemed contribution under § 752(a) (50% of $800). A's basis will therefore be $100.

---

42. Note that if we focused instead on the percentage of value of the property sold, only 5% would be treated as sold ($50/$1000), and only 5% of the liability or $40, would be treated as additional consideration. This would substantially reduce the gain to A, and the regulations take the position that it is more appropriate to focus on the extent to which A has cashed out her equity rather than value.

43. § 723.

Distribution of Loan Proceeds

Suppose, immediately after a partner contributes unencumbered property to a partnership, the partnership incurs a liability and distributes all or a portion of the proceeds to the contributing partner. How should that distribution be treated for tax purposes?[44] Suppose in **Example #4**, that A had transferred Blackacre to the partnership unencumbered, and that the partnership immediately incurred an $800 recourse mortgage, distributing the entire $800 to A. Absent a special rule, the entire $800 would be treated as consideration for the sale of the property. But if A had borrowed the $800 the day before she contributed the property encumbered by the mortgage to the partnership, only $400 of the liability would have been treated as consideration. Recognizing that the economic consequences of these two transactions are identical, Treasury promulgated a special rule: If a partner transfers unencumbered property to a partnership, and if the partnership incurs a liability and distributes all or a portion of the proceeds to the partner within 90 days of incurring the liability (determined under § 1.163–8T), then the distribution to the partner is taken into account only to the extent that it exceeds the partner's "allocable share" of that liability.

A partner's "allocable share" of a liability is determined by multiplying the partner's share of the liability by the following fraction:

$$\frac{\text{Amount distributed traceable to the liability}}{\text{Total amount of the liability}}$$

Applying this rule to our facts, A's share of the liability is $400. Assuming the entire $800 is traceable to the $800 liability, then only $400 of the $800 distribution is treated as sale proceeds. This puts A in precisely the same position that she would have been in if she had taken out the mortgage just before the contribution.[45]

Sections 704(c)(1)(B) and 737

In spite of § 707(a)(2)(B), taxpayers continued to engage in transactions involving contributions and related distributions that were not recharacterized as sales or exchanges under that rule.

---

44. These are essentially the facts of *Otey v. Comm'r*, one of the cases that was cited in the committee reports accompanying the enactment of § 707(a)(2)(A).

45. In *Otey*, the taxpayer contributed unencumbered land with a value of $65,000 and a basis of $18,000 in exchange for a 50% interest in a partnership. Shortly thereafter, the partnership took out a loan for $870,000 to develop the property and distributed $65,000 to the taxpayer. Under this rule, the taxpayer would have been deemed to have sold ½ of the property for $32,500 resulting in a gain of $23,500.

These "mixing bowl" transactions, which essentially permitted taxpayers to exchange property without recognition of gain, took two forms. The first was a contribution of § 704(c) property[46] to a partnership, followed by a distribution of that property to another partner.[47] After the distribution, the contributor had essentially exchanged all of her interest in the § 704(c) property for an undivided interest in the partnership's other assets. The second was a contribution of § 704(c) property, followed (more than two years later) by a distribution (often a liquidating distribution) of other property to the contributor.[48] Again, to the extent of the distribution, the contributor had exchanged the § 704(c) property for the distributed property. In both cases, Congress thought nonrecognition was inappropriate and enacted § 704(c)(1)(B) and § 737 to reverse the results. These provisions, which only apply to property distributions[49] not recharacterized by § 707(a)(2)(B), are discussed below.

Section 704(c)(1)(B)

Under § 704(c)(1)(B), if § 704(c) property is distributed to any partner, other than the contributing partner, within seven years of the original contribution, the contributing partner must recognize gain or loss in the amount and character that would have been allocated to her under § 704(c)(1)(A) had the property been sold to the distributee at its fair market value on the date of the distribution.[50] Both the contributing partner's outside basis and the partnership's basis in the § 704(c) property must be adjusted to reflect the recognition of gain or loss;[51] both are increased (immediately before the distribution) by any gain, or decreased by any loss, recognized by the contributor.[52]

To illustrate, consider:

Example #5: On January 1, 2010, A, B and C form an equal partnership to which A contributes Blackacre with a value of $100 and a basis of $40; B contributes nonmarketable stock in

46. This term is defined in § 1.704–3(a)(3) as contributed property with a book value different from the contributor's basis.

47. § 707(a)(2)(B) was inapplicable because the distribution was not made to the contributor, but to a different partner.

48. Prior to the enactment of § 731(c), typically the other property was marketable securities. As long as the distributions were separated by more than two years, § 707(a)(2)(B) was normally not applicable.

49. Neither provision applies to distributions of cash alone.

50. §§ 704(c)(1)(B)(i) and (ii), and §§ 1.704–4(a)(1) and (b)(1). The regulations provide that the deemed distributions which result from terminations under § 708(b)(1)(B) are not subject to this rule.

51. § 704(c)(1)(B)(iii).

52. § 1.704–4(e)(1) & (2). Consequently, the adjustments are reflected under § 732 in the basis results to the distributee partner.

X Corp. with a value of $100 and a basis of $60, and C contributes cash of $100 which the partnership uses to purchase Whiteacre. Assume that all three assets are capital assets in the hands of the partnership. On January 1, 2013, C receives Blackacre as a liquidating distribution from the partnership. At the time of the distribution, the partnership's balance sheet (expanded to show fair market values) is as follows:

	Assets				*Liabilities & Capital*		

	Basis	*Book*	*FMV*
Blackacre	$ 40	$100	$150
Whiteacre	100	100	150
X Stock	60	100	150
	$200	$300	$450

		Capital Accounts		
		Tax	*Book*	*FMV*
	A	$ 40	$100	$150
	B	60	100	150
	C	100	100	150
		$200	$300	$450

Section 704(c)(1)(B) requires A to report the amount of § 704(c) gain that would have been allocated to her if the partnership had sold Blackacre to C on the date of the distribution for its then value. Had the partnership sold Blackacre to C for $150 on January 1, 2013, the first $60 of gain would have been allocated to A; therefore, A must recognize $60 of capital gain as a result of the distribution to C. Immediately prior to the distribution, A's outside basis (and the balance in her tax capital account) is increased by $60 and the partnership's basis in Blackacre is also increased by $60 to $100. This latter adjustment is important for purposes of determining both the distributee's basis under § 732 and the partnership's basis adjustment under § 734(b) when a § 754 election is in effect.

Example #6: Same facts as ***Example #5***, except that the value of Blackacre is only $70 on January 1, 2013.

On these facts, if the partnership had sold Blackacre to C on January 1, 2013 for $70, the partnership would have $30 of capital gain, all of which would have been allocated to A under § 704(c); therefore, A recognizes only $30 in capital gain on the distribution to C. A's outside basis and the balance in her tax capital account are both increased by $30 and the partnership's basis in Blackacre just before the distribution is also increased by $30 to $70.

As an exception to § 704(c)(1)(B), if within a specified time following the distribution of the § 704(c) property, the partnership also distributes property which is of like kind[53] to the contributing

53. See § 1031.

partner, she is essentially treated as though she engaged in a like kind exchange.[54] In such a case, the amount of gain or loss that the contributing partner would otherwise have to recognize under § 704(c)(1)(B) is reduced by the amount of built-in gain or loss in the distributed like kind property immediately after the distribution.[55] To illustrate, consider the following:

> *Example #7:* Same as *Example #5*, except that when C receives Blackacre with value of $150, A receives a distribution of Whiteacre, also with a value of $150. Blackacre and Whiteacre are like kind properties. Under § 732, A properly takes a $40 basis in Whiteacre.

As we saw in *Example #5*, under § 704(c)(1)(B), A normally would be required to recognize a $60 gain as a result of the distribution of Blackacre to C. Since A received a distribution of like kind property, however, the amount of gain she must recognize is reduced by her $110 built-in gain in Whiteacre immediately after the distribution. Because the built-in gain in Whiteacre exceeds $60, A recognizes no gain as a result of the distribution of Blackacre to C.

Section 737

Section 737 also may trigger gain (but not loss) to a contributing partner if, within seven years of a contribution, the contributing partner receives a distribution of property, other than the property the partner contributed. If this occurs, the contributing partner must recognize gain equal to the lesser of:

> (i) the excess distribution (i.e., the excess of the property's value over the partner's outside basis (reduced by any money distributed)),[56] or

> (ii) the partner's net precontribution gain.

For this purpose, net precontribution gain means the net gain that would have been recognized under § 704(c)(1)(B) by that partner if all property that she had contributed within seven years of the distribution and still held by the partnership were distributed to another partner. In other words, taking into account only contributions that have been made over the last seven years, net precontribution gain is the amount of net § 704(c) gain that the partner still has not recognized on the date of the distribution. The character of

---

54. § 704(c)(2). The distribution to the contributor must occur before the earlier of 180 days after the distribution of the contributed property, or the due date for the contributing partner's tax return that would reflect the tax consequences of the earlier distribution.

55. § 1.704–4(d)(3). The built-in gain from the § 704(c) property is thus carried over into the like kind property, and will be recognized when it is sold or exchanged.

56. § 1.737–1(b)(1).

this gain is the same as it would have been had the partnership sold all the § 704(c) property to an unrelated party on the date of the distribution.[57] Immediately prior to the distribution (but after determining the amount of the excess distribution), the contributor's outside basis is increased by the gain recognized.[58] The basis of the § 704(c) property still in the hands of the partnership also is increased by the gain recognized.[59]

To illustrate this rule, consider:

> *Example #8:* Same facts as *Example #5*, except that B receives Whiteacre as a liquidating distribution on January 1, 2013 when Whiteacre's fair market is $150 and B's outside basis is $60.

B received a property distribution within 7 years after contributing the appreciated X Corp. stock to the partnership. Assuming that § 707(a)(2)(B) does not apply, § 737 requires B to recognize gain of $40, namely the lesser of:

> (i) the excess distribution of $90 ($150–$60),[60] or

> (ii) B's net precontribution gain of $40.[61]

Therefore, B must recognize $40 of capital gain on the distribution. For purposes of determining her basis in Whiteacre, immediately before the distribution B's outside basis is increased by $40 to $100 which, under § 732(b) and (c), becomes her basis in Whiteacre. The partnership's basis in the X stock is also increased by $40 to $100 to reflect the recognized gain.

It should be pointed out that §§ 704(c)(1)(B) and 737 can both be triggered by a single distribution. To illustrate, consider the tax consequences of a distribution of Blackacre to B. Since A contributed Blackacre and it is distributed to another partner within seven years of that contribution, under § 704(c)(1)(B) A must recognize $60 in gain. Note, however, that B has $40 of precontribution gain that B must recognize under § 737 upon receipt of Blackacre.

---

57. § 1.737–1(d). If more than one type of property is involved, the character of gain is determined by, and is proportionate to, the character of the partner's net precontribution gain.

58. §§ 737(c)(1) & 1.737–3(a).

59. § 737(c)(2). If more than one § 704(c) property is involved, the increase in basis is allocated among all eligible properties in accordance with § 1.737–3(c).

60. I.e., fair market value of the property distributed over the partner's outside basis (reduced by any money distributed).

61. The net precontribution gain of any partner is the amount of net gain that she would have recognized under § 704(c)(1)(B) if all property contributed by that partner within the last seven years and still held by the partnership at the time of the distribution had been distributed to another partner.

Disguised Sales of Partnership Interests

The 1984 legislation enacting § 707(a)(2)(B) not only targeted disguised sales of property, but also directed Treasury to identify when a liquidating distribution to one partner and a contribution to the partnership by another partner should be recharacterized as a disguised sale by the exiting partner of her partnership interest to the contributing partner. This was not an easy task. As an economic matter the two transactions (i.e., a sale vs. a contribution coupled with a liquidation) are very similar, but the tax consequences, especially to the exiting partner, can be substantially different.[62] Prior to 1984, the courts had offered partners and partnerships a great deal of flexibility in characterizing these transactions.[63] This was widely viewed as tax planning, not tax abuse, but the mandate of § 707(a)(2)(B) gave the tax bar pause.

Regulations addressing the issue were proposed in 2004. They were modeled fairly closely after the disguised sale of property rules discussed above. They were not, however, well-received and were characterized as "seriously flawed,"[64] a criticism with which we agreed. Treasury withdrew the proposed regulations in January of 2009, stating it wanted to rethink how to better distinguish the transactions. No revisions have yet been issued, nor do they seem to be on the horizon.

---

62. For example, § 736 has no application to sales of partnership interests.

63. See generally McKee et al. at ¶ 16.02.

64. For an excellent critique of the proposed regulations, see Blake D.

Rubin and Andrea Macintosh Whiteway, *Disguised Sales of Partnership Interests: An Analysis of the Proposed Regulations,* 107 Tax Notes 1149 (2005).

Chapter Sixteen

THE PARTNERSHIP ANTI–
ABUSE RULES

Background

Having reached this point in your study of partnership tax, you have hopefully developed an appreciation for the fascinating combination of complexity and flexibility that pervades Subchapter K. Because of these characteristics, sophisticated tax planners have increasingly used the partnership vehicle as a device for achieving tax savings never contemplated by Congress or by the Treasury. These transactions began with the tax shelter industry of the 1970's, which typically utilized highly leveraged investments to structure noneconomic tax losses for individuals, and evolved during the 1980's into sophisticated partnership structures intended to effect large-scale corporate tax avoidance. In May 1994, the Treasury fought back by proposing a partnership anti-abuse regulation under § 701 that authorized the Commissioner to recast any partnership transaction a principal purpose of which was to substantially reduce the federal taxes of its partners in a manner inconsistent with "the intent of subchapter K." The proposed regulation defined the "intent of subchapter K" as allowing taxpayers to conduct joint business activities through a flexible economic arrangement without incurring an entity level tax. More importantly, the proposed regulation took the position that Subchapter K was not intended

> to permit taxpayers either to structure transactions using partnerships to achieve tax results that are inconsistent with the underlying economic arrangements of the parties or the substance of the transactions, or use the existence of partnerships to avoid the purposes of other provisions of the Internal Revenue Code.[1]

1. Prop. Reg. § 1.701–2(a)(1994).

When proposed, the regulation created a fire storm. It was loosely drafted and very general, resulting in a scattershot rather than sniper approach; if read literally, a whole host of transactions that most members of the tax bar believed to be bona fide transactions could be viewed as inconsistent with the intent of Subchapter K. The proposed regulation was also, to some extent, inconsistent with many long standing statutory and regulatory rules which, in the name of administrative convenience, mandated tax results inconsistent with the underlying economic arrangements. From the date of its release, Treasury officials were compelled to reassure the public that the regulation was only intended to apply to the most aggressive transactions.[2] Although many members of the bar were sympathetic with Treasury's attempt to stem abusive transactions, most felt that the proposed regulation was poorly crafted. Indeed, many commentators believed that the proposed regulation was so broad and vague that, if finalized in its proposed form, it would not be sustained by the courts.[3]

In January of 1995 Treasury issued the regulation in final, and significantly altered, form. The final regulation creates two anti-abuse rules, the "general anti-abuse rule" and the "abuse of entity rule." Like the proposed version, the final regulation requires that partnership transactions be judged against a broad standard: whether the transaction is consistent with the "intent of subchapter K." The "intent of subchapter K," however, is defined in a much more restrictive and meaningful way. In addition, the final regulation added a description of the most important factors in determining when the general anti-abuse rule applies, and contains several examples illustrating its application. Finally, the final regulation added the abuse of entity rule which, under certain circumstances, permits the Commissioner to treat a partnership as an aggregate of its partners instead of as an entity. Both rules are discussed below.

The General Anti–Abuse Rule

The general anti-abuse rule states that:

... if a partnership is formed or availed of in connection with a transaction a principal purpose of which is to reduce substantially the present value of the partners' aggregate federal tax

2. See Reports of Assistant Secretary Leslie Samuels' Speech, *Highlights and Documents* Vol. 33 p. 2243, May 17, 1994.

3. The reaction of is well-captured in a quote in *Highlights and Documents*, July 26, 1994, at 1155: If the regulation is made final, "nuclear winter will descend on the productive joint venture partnership." cited in William F. Nelson, *The Limits of Literalism: The Effect of Substance Over Form, Clear Reflection and Business Purpose Considerations On the Proper Interpretation of Subchapter K*, Taxes 641 n.3, Dec. 1995.

liability in a manner which is inconsistent with the intent of subchapter K, the Commissioner can recast the transaction for federal tax purposes....[4]

The weapons available to the Commissioner to enforce this rule include disregarding the partnership (in whole or in part), adjusting the methods of accounting of the partnership and its partners, reallocating the partnership's items of income, or otherwise modifying the claimed tax treatment.

Intent of Subchapter K

Since tax lawyers generally attempt to structure transactions in a way that minimizes taxes, and a principal purpose for choosing a particular structure for a transaction is often to reduce (substantially, if possible) the aggregate federal tax liability of partners, the key to identifying if one is within the anti-abuse rule is in the definition of the phrase "intent of subchapter K." According to the regulation, the intent of Subchapter K is "to permit taxpayers to conduct joint business (including investment) activities through a flexible economic arrangement without incurring an entity level tax." The regulation takes the view that implicit in this definition are the following three requirements:

1.   The partnership must be bona fide and each transaction, or series of transactions, must be entered into for a substantial business purpose,

2.   The form of the transaction must be respected under substance over form principles, and

3.   The tax consequences to each partner and the partnership must accurately reflect their economic agreement and clearly reflect the partner's income. This third requirement is referred to as the "proper reflection of income" requirement.

Recognizing that certain provisions of Subchapter K and its regulations were adopted for administrative convenience or for other policy objectives, if the first two implicit requirements are met, the proper reflection of income requirement is also considered met as long as the manner in which the particular provision is applied to the transaction and the ultimate tax results are clearly contemplated by the provision, even though these results distort income.

Facts and Circumstances

Whether or not a particular transaction runs afoul of the general anti-abuse rule is ultimately a question of facts and circum-

---

4. § 1.701–2(b).

stances. The regulation lists several factors to consider,[5] the most important of which is a comparison of the purported business purpose for the transaction and the claimed tax benefits resulting therefrom. Under this factor, apparently even if one has a bona fide business purpose for planning a transaction in a certain way, if the claimed tax consequences are too favorable, the structure may not be respected. The other factors which may indicate abuse are:

1.   The present value of the partners' aggregate federal tax liability is substantially less than it would have been if the partners had owned the partnership's assets directly.

2.   The present value of the partners' aggregate federal tax liability is substantially less than it would have been if purportedly separate transactions are integrated into a single transaction.

3.   One or more partners who are necessary to achieve the desired tax results are substantially protected from loss and have little or no participation in the profits of the partnership.

4.   Substantially all partners are related to one another.

5.   Partnership items are allocated in compliance with the literal language of §§ 1.704–1 and 1.704–2 but with results that are inconsistent with the purpose of § 704(b) and those regulations. In this regard, particular scrutiny will be paid to special allocations to partners who are effectively in the zero bracket.

6.   The benefits and burdens of ownership of property nominally contributed to a partnership are substantially retained by the contributor.

7.   The benefits and burdens of ownership of partnership property are substantially shifted to the distributee partner before or after the property is actually distributed.

Scope

Although the general anti-abuse rule could potentially apply to all partnership transactions, the scope of the regulation is not entirely clear. Treasury certainly intended to limit the use of certain uneconomic rules found in Subchapter K and to backstop the partnership allocation rules of § 704(b). What is not clear is whether the anti-abuse rule also should be a backstop to existing anti-abuse rules. For example, if a transaction passes muster under the anti-abuse rule of § 704(c), should it also have to pass muster under the general anti-abuse rule? If a contribution of property to a

---

5.   § 1.701–2(c).

partnership is not recharacterized as a disguised sale under the § 707 regulations, is it possible that it would be recharacterized a sale under this rule? The final regulation implies that it could.[6] Indeed, the regulation makes it clear that the general anti-abuse rule is intended to be a new weapon in addition to all other "nonstatutory principles and other statutory and regulatory authorities to challenge transactions."[7]

If read broadly, this regulation could apply to many transactions for which it was not intended. For this reason, the Service announced that agents seeking to apply the anti-abuse rule must get approval from the National Office.[8]

Examples

It is impossible to identify all of the transactions to which the general anti-abuse rule may apply. Indeed, some of the transactions to which the rule may apply have not yet been designed. Nevertheless, the examples in the regulation are instructive in identifying several types of transactions with which Treasury was concerned. These include the choice of the partnership entity, the application of certain uneconomic rules that are only available in Subchapter K, and partnership allocations.[9]

Choice (or Use) of Entity

As a result of the uproar that followed the release of the proposed regulation, Treasury (apparently) wanted to assure the tax community that the anti-abuse rules were not intended to call into question every transaction where the use of a partnership structure results in a reduction of the partners' aggregate tax liability. In each of the first four examples of the final regulation, the taxpayers chose to operate in partnership form to avoid various legal restrictions. In the first example, a corporation and an individual chose limited partnership form because the individual wanted limited liability without an entity level tax; in the second, a nonresident alien and an S corporation chose partnership form because the nonresident alien was not eligible to be a shareholder of an S corporation; in the third, a domestic and foreign corporation chose partnership form to enable the domestic corporation to be eligible for the direct foreign tax credit (rather than the indirect); and in the fourth, a newly created REIT and two substantial real

---

6. § 1.701–2(d)Ex. 8(iii) (applying the general anti-abuse rule to a transaction that would also have been subject to the disguised sale rules).

7. § 1.701–2(i).

8. Ann. 94–87, 1994–27 IRB 124.

9. Originally there were two additional examples dealing with family partnerships which were withdrawn. The stated reason for the withdrawal is that these regulations apply only to the income tax, not the transfer taxes.

estate partnerships chose a limited partnership form to avoid §§ 351(e) and 357(c) because of the existence of excess liabilities. In each case, the form was respected under the general anti-abuse rule. Nevertheless, there are instances where the choice of partnership entity might be regarded as abusive as described below in the context of the abuse of entity rule.

Uneconomic Rules of Subchapter K

Four of the examples in the regulations focus on a type of aggressive tax planning that attempts to take advantage of certain uneconomic rules found in Subchapter K. This type of planning, referred to as "reverse engineering," was specifically targeted by Treasury. The key question in each example was whether the ultimate tax results were contemplated by the relevant provision. If they were, the transaction would be respected; if not, then the transaction would be recast. We are not going to explore these examples in depth because the relevant underlying provisions that Treasury utilized in the examples have been amended.[10] Nevertheless, since tax planners continue to structure their transactions to take advantage of various provisions within Subchapter K, we will examine the results in two of the examples to get a sense of the type of transaction that might be considered abusive.

Examples #8 and #9 both deal with liquidating distributions made by partnerships that had not made § 754 elections. In both examples, if the statute were applied literally, the results would have been uneconomic. In Example #8, the person who received the distribution had been a partner for several years and the tax consequences of the liquidation (although clearly uneconomic) were respected. The example holds that the partnership was bona fide and the ultimate tax results clearly contemplated by the statute. In Example #9, the partnership had been formed with the principal purpose of taking advantage of the elective nature of § 754—a clear case of reverse engineering. For this reason, the example holds that the transaction is inconsistent with the intent of Subchapter K and will not be respected.

Partnership Allocations

It is clear that Treasury intended the anti-abuse rule to back-stop the elaborate regulatory edifice created under §§ 1.704–1 and

---

10. Two of the examples (Examples #10 and #11) deal with the basis allocation rules under § 732(c) before they were amended in 1997. The other two examples (Examples #8 and #9) both deal with the elective nature of § 754 in the context of a distribution. As we have learned in *Chapter Twelve*, § 734 was amended in 2004 to provide that if there is a substantial basis reduction, the partnership must make the appropriate § 734(b) basis adjustments even in the absence of a § 754 election. Example #8 also deals with the contribution of property with a built-in loss to a partnership so that others might benefit from that loss. Under § 704(c)(1)(C) (also amended in 2004) this is no longer possible.

1.704–2 if a partnership allocation meets the literal requirements of those rules, but violates their underlying purpose. As you will recall from *Chapter Five*, the underlying purpose of the allocation regulations is to require allocations to be consistent with the economic arrangement of the partners: If an item of income or deduction is allocated to a partner, that partner must benefit from, or bear the burden of, that item.[11] For this purpose, the book allocations of a partnership are used as a surrogate for the economic arrangement, and the fundamental rule is that "tax must follow book." Nevertheless, there are instances where uneconomic results are clearly contemplated by the allocation regulations. The most stark example are nonrecourse deductions. As you learned in *Chapter Six*, no partner bears the economic burden of nonrecourse deductions. Another more subtle example is the value-equals-basis rule of § 1.704–1(b)(2)(iii)(c), under which an asset's value is conclusively presumed to be equal to its basis, even if that is demonstrably untrue. The anti-abuse regulation clarifies that allocations under these rules, even if they do not satisfy the proper reflection of income requirement, will be respected.[12]

The type of allocation that would be subject to the general anti-abuse rule is one whose results are *both* uneconomic *and* not contemplated by the § 704(b) regulations. Although the transactions involving such allocations are invariably complex, they are always based, at least in part, on a book accounting rule that is not based on sound economics. They also tend to involve a partner who is actually or effectively tax exempt. To illustrate, consider Example #7 of the regulations. Since this example is complex and may be hard to follow, it is useful to keep in mind what the parties are attempting to do: Under U.S. tax law, if a taxpayer sells a right to future income while retaining the underlying property, the taxpayer has income immediately without basis offset. This results in taxable income, but no economic income. In the partnership context, under the capital accounting rules which are governed by tax accounting principles, such a sale would result not only in taxable income but also book income, creating a disparity between book and economic income. In Example #7, the partnership has this type of income, most of which is allocated to a tax exempt partner who is promptly liquidated. This has the effect of creating a loss for the remaining partners.

The facts of this very complex example are as follows: A partnership, PRS, is formed by three persons, X (a foreign corporation), Y (a domestic corporation) and Z, a promoter. X contributes $9,000, Y contributes $990 and Z contributes $10. The partners agree to share all partnership items in proportion to their respec-

---

11. § 1.704–1(b)(2)(ii)(a).   **12.** § 1.701–2(d) Exs. 5 & 6.

tive contributions, i.e., 90%, 9.9%, and .1%. PRS immediately purchases offshore equipment for $10,000 and validly leases it under a long-term lease. Shortly thereafter, it sells its right to the lease payments for $9,000 cash, all of which is taxable income under current law. Under the partnership agreement, the $9,000 of income is allocated $8,100 to X, $891 to Y and $9 to Z. Immediately after the allocation, the PRS balance sheet is as follows:

Assets			Liabilities & Capital		

	Basis/Book	FMV
Cash	$ 9,000	$ 9,000
Equipment	10,000	1,000
	$19,000	$10,000

	Capital Accounts	
	Tax/Book	FMV
X	$17,100	$ 9,000
Y	1,881	990
Z	19	10
	$19,000	$10,000

At this point you should note two things: First, because X is a foreign corporation and the income from the lease is not U.S. source income, X is not taxed (in the U.S.) on its share. Second, although PRS is worth only $10,000, its book value and its aggregate inside basis is $19,000. The reason for this disparity is the fact that PRS must include the full $9,000 that it received for the lease in income even though none of it has been earned. This means that PRS has an inherent tax loss of $9,000.

Shortly after selling its right to income under the lease, PRS makes a liquidating distribution to X of $9,000. Just before the distribution, in accordance with the capital accounting rules,[13] PRS restates its capital, and "books down" its assets to their fair market value. The partners share the $9,000 loss for book (not tax) purposes in the same proportions that they shared the original $9,000 of income. Thus, the balance in each partner's book capital account is precisely equal to its original contribution. After the distribution, the balance sheet of PRS is as follows:

Assets			Liabilities & Capital		

	Basis	Book
Equipment	$10,000	$1,000

	Capital Accounts	
	Tax	Book
Y	$1,881	$990
Z	19	10
	$1,900	$1,000

13.   § 1.704–1(b)(2)(iv)(f).

Following this series of transactions, PRS has an inherent $9,000 tax loss in the equipment, $8,100 of which should be allocated to X. X, however, is no longer a partner. Therefore, if PRS sells the equipment, the loss will be allocated between Y and Z, even though they did not incur the related economic loss. At this point, however, neither Y nor Z has sufficient outside basis to permit them to deduct that loss (§ 704(d)). To avoid the limitations of § 704(d), PRS first borrows money on a recourse basis, which it uses to purchase real property, and then sells the equipment. As a result, Y and Z are able to deduct all of the $9,000 loss, including the portion ($8,100) properly allocable to X.

The regulation holds on these facts that PRS has been formed or availed of with a principal purpose of reducing substantially the present value of the partners' aggregate federal tax liability in a manner inconsistent with Subchapter K for several reasons: There was no substantial business reason for the transaction, it would not be respected under substance over form principles, the partnership was not bona fide, and the transaction does not properly reflect income.

Abuse of Entity Rule

As noted above, the general anti-abuse rule usually respects the partners' choice of entity. Nevertheless, § 1.701–2(e)(1) creates a special rule that states, if necessary to carry out the purpose of any provision of the Internal Revenue Code, the partnership will be treated as an aggregate of its partners, rather than as an entity.

A good example of a transaction subject to attack under the abuse of entity rule was involved in *Brown Group v. Commissioner*.[14] The law underlying this case is as follows: Certain income ("subpart F income") of a controlled foreign corporation ("CFC") is currently taxable to its U.S. parent. Subpart F income includes the income derived from buying personal property from a CFC's U.S. parent and reselling it to any party. The purpose behind the CFC rule is to prevent a U.S. parent from avoiding U.S. tax simply by using its foreign subsidiary as its agent for foreign sales. Foreign partnerships are not subject to the CFC rules. In *Brown Group*, a CFC was an 88% partner in a foreign partnership which had income which would have been subject to U.S. tax if it had been earned by the CFC. The Tax Court, viewing the partnership as an entity separate and apart from its partners, initially held that the CFC's distributive share of partnership income was not subpart F income, and therefore was not currently taxable to its U.S. parent.

14. 102 T.C. 616 (1994). After rehearing the Tax Court withdrew its original decision and found in favor of the government. 104 T.C. 105 (1995).

The court specifically rejected the aggregate theory of partnerships which would have led to the opposite conclusion. The *Brown Group* was highly criticized[15] and was reversed on rehearing shortly after the issuance of the final anti-abuse regulation. By incorporating the common law abuse of entity rule in the regulations, the IRS has not only made it easier to challenge transactions like that involved in *Brown Group*, but also has provided a deterrent to future similar transactions.

The abuse of entity rule is meant to clarify when a partnership should be viewed as an entity and when as an aggregate. If a particular Code or regulatory provision explicitly calls for the treatment of partnerships as entities, and the ultimate tax results are clearly contemplated by that provision, then the abuse rule does not apply. Nevertheless, even if the provision does explicitly provide for the entity treatment of a partnership, if entity treatment would undermine the very purpose of the provision, then the abuse of entity rule will require the partnership to be treated as an aggregate of its partners.

The new abuse of entity rule's purpose and application are well illustrated by the regulation in Example #1 of § 1.701–2(f). In this example, two domestic corporations are partners in a partnership which issues high yield debt. Under § 163(e)(5), if either of these domestic corporations issued this type of debt directly, its interest deduction would be limited; that provision makes no mention of partnerships. If the partnership entity were treated as the issuer of this debt, § 163(e)(5) would not apply, and its underlying purpose could easily be frustrated. Therefore, the regulation takes the position that with respect to this debt the partnership will be treated as an aggregate and each corporation will be treated as issuing its proportionate portion of the debt.

Is the Anti–Abuse Regulation Valid or Necessary?

Although the final version of the anti-abuse regulation is significantly clearer and more narrow than the proposed version, it has still generated significant controversy.[16] Some argue that the regulation merely makes it clear that the well-developed judicial doctrines of business purpose, substance over form, and clear reflection of income apply to partnerships. This was the position taken by the Assistant Secretary of the Treasury for Tax Policy at

---

15. See, e.g., David Shakow, *How Now Brown K?* 63 Tax Notes 1761 (1994).

16. For an excellent article critical of the regulations, see Alan Gunn, *The Use and Misuse of the Antiabuse Rules: Lessons from the Partnership Antiabuse Regulations*, 54 S.M.U. L. Rev. 159 (2001).

the time the regulation was issued, who stated that the regulation merely "confirms that these traditional doctrines apply in the partnership context."[17] Some commentators, however, have vigorously argued that the regulation goes well beyond simply restating current law, and that it not only imposes upon partnerships a stricter version of the common law business purpose and substance over form doctrines, but a proper reflection of income concept which has never been legislatively or judicially approved in the partnership context.[18] This calls into question whether the regulation is a valid exercise of Treasury's rule making authority.[19]

In recent years commentators have questioned whether the anti-abuse regulation serves any useful purpose. Although it has been in effect since 1995, not one court has relied on it in finding against a taxpayer. Courts tend to rely instead on traditional judicial doctrines, ignoring the anti-abuse regulation.[20] In the mind of at least one scholar, this has "rais[ed] doubt about both the need for and efficacy of the regulation."[21] According to one of the leading treatises on partnership taxation, "[i]t appears doubtful that the overall landscape of Subchapter K has changed meaningfully by reason of this Regulation."[22]

Although the anti-abuse rule may not have changed the law significantly, its presence significantly complicates the practice of partnership tax law, because it potentially applies to all transactions in addition to "nonstatutory principles and other statutory and regulatory authorities."[23] Since the recent enactment of § 7701(o), codifying the economic substance doctrine, the anti-abuse rule would seem to have become redundant. Indeed, one commentator has suggested "[t]he government would lose little from repeal of the antiabuse rule ... and that its repeal would

---

17. Letter from the Honorable Leslie B. Samuels, Assistant Secretary of the Treasury for Tax Policy, to the Honorable Robert Packwood, Chairman, Senate Finance Committee (December 29, 1994), reprinted in **Highlights and Documents**, January 3, 1995, at 75.

18. See William F. Nelson, *The Limits of Literalism: The Effect of Substance Over Form, Clear Reflection and Business Purpose Considerations On the Proper Interpretation of Subchapter K*, Taxes, December 1995, p. 641.

19. In one case, the taxpayer challenged the validity of the regulation as part of a motion for summary judgment, but the Court of Federal Claims found that the issue was not ripe for decision because the government could rely on

other theories. *Jade Trading LLC v. U.S.*, 60 Fed. Cl. 558 (2004). The government eventually won the case, but it dropped its argument based upon the anti-abuse regulation. *Jade Trading LLC v. U.S.*, 80 Fed. Cl. 11 (2007).

20. *Santa Monica Pictures v. Commissioner,* 89 TCM (CCH) 1157, 1191 (2005). In *Countryside Ltd. P'ship v. Commissioner,* 95 TCM (CCH) 1006 (2008) the Tax Court considered but rejected the application of the anti-abuse rule to the case before it.

21. Bittker & Lokken, Federal Taxation of Income, Estates and Gifts ¶ 86.4.

22. Willis & Postelwaite, Partnership Taxation at ¶ 1.03[6].

23. § 1.701–2(i).

greatly simplify the tax law.''[24] It would surely simplify the study of Subchapter K.

24. Monte A. Jackel, *Subchapter K and the Codified Economic Substalnce* *Doctrine*, 128 Tax Notes 321 (2010).

Index

References are to Pages

†